THE COMPLETE BOOK OF THE
CAT

THE COMPLETE BOOK OF THE
CAT

ANGELA SAYER

Octopus Books

First published 1984 by
Octopus Books Limited
59 Grosvenor Square
London W.1

© 1984
Octopus Books Limited

ISBN 0 7064 2036 5

Produced by
Mandarin Publishers Ltd,
22a Westlands Road
Quarry Bay,
Hong Kong

Printed in Spain

CONTENTS

INTRODUCTION
ANGELA SAYER

The enigmatic cat has fascinated and beguiled man for thousands of years, and continues to do so today. Indeed, interest in the cat and all things feline has never been greater, and the enthusiasm of cat-lovers for the animal is undiminished by whether the cat is a Persian show-stopper or a rescued, ragged-eared 'moggie'. Millions of homes in the civilized world have a pet cat or two, and many families in less affluent societies also count the cat as an essential attribute.

As we remove our pets ever farther from their natural environment, so we must replace their wild prey with a suitable diet, organize their breeding, and control the most unsocial of their habits. Yet it is quite amazing to reflect that the cat of today, often living a totally artificial life in a cosseted environment intended for humans, manages still to retain all the instincts and innate behaviour patterns of its wildest ancestor – even the most placid of pet cats, when provoked, is capable of becoming a snarling, spitting fury.

This book has been produced to help cat people to take better care of their pets as some form of recompense for having them live in their homes as comforters and companions, rather than following their natural pathways in the wild. It is the author's intention, through explanations of the cat's physical and psychological make-up, to help cat-lovers understand fully their pet's needs and to be able to cope with any problems which may occur during their cat's life from kittenhood through puberty to maturity, and during the processes of gestation and birth. An up-to-date review of the breeds and colour varieties available in pedigree cats is included to help potential buyers choose the most suitable cat, and for those tempted to start showing, full details are given explaining this aspect of cat ownership. It has been the author's intention to provide a full reference work for the cat-lover of today, and her aim to help gain better care, and therefore a better lot for all cats, and she is proud to have been chosen to produce what she genuinely feels to be *The Complete Book of the Cat*.

INTRODUCING THE CAT

That the cat has a special niche in human life is underlined by the fact that throughout history the domestic feline has been cherished, valued and protected. Ancient Egyptians from the mightiest ruler to the most humble farmer deified the cat, and most subsequent civilizations have held cats in high esteem. Poets have enthused over the beauty of the cat and writers have extolled all of its virtues and traits in a multitude of books published through the ages in many countries of the civilized world.

Throughout time, the cat has managed to remain virtually unchanged, self-possessed and totally independent. Though the cat tolerates its relationship with man and enjoys the comforts of a good home, the innate behaviour patterns of its wild ancestors are barely concealed beneath its domesticated appearance. The cat of today retains all the hunting skills and physical abilities of its forebears, and even the most pampered of pets will react to the thrill of the chase if given the opportunity.

Having a cat in the home is both rewarding and therapeutic. No other animal can provide such peaceful company, and no other pet is as fastidious in its habits or as easy to keep and care for. All cats are beautiful, but the individual tastes of cat-lovers are catered for in the wide range of colours and breeds available today. In the pages of this book we hope to show you what makes a cat a cat, how and why it behaves as it does, and how to choose the right cat for your life-style. We explore all the diverse and interesting feline varieties, explain the care of the cat in sickness and in health, and introduce you to the world of the show cat.

Today's cat has lost none of its natural agility and grace.

Despite its familiarity with humans and the fact that it is probably the most common of all domestic animals in many countries of the world, the cat has managed to retain its air of mysterious independence. Wherever there are concentrated populations of humans there are colonies of cats, kept either as pets or to kill pests or living as free-ranging ferals, minding their own business and existing in much the same way as cats have done for thousands of years.

No one knows how many domestic cats exist in the world today. Surveys conducted by pet-food manufacturers indicate that there may be up to 5.3 million cats in Britain, excluding the feral population, and that there are many more in the United States of America. The fecundity of cats is quite phenomenal. The female may reach sexual maturity at any time from three to nine months of age and the male from seven to twelve months, although feral cats may mature later, depending on the climate and the availability of food. After a gestation period averaging sixty-five days, the female cat produces a litter of two to six kittens, which are weaned and independent within twelve weeks. The female cat is capable of producing and rearing two to three litters every year, provided that she obtains sufficient nourishing food, and in favourable circumstances the survival rate of the kittens is high. It needs little imagination to see that in a cat's normal fertile lifespan she may be responsible for over one hundred offspring.

The enigmatic cat is both loving and ferocious, equally capable of living happily with humans or foraging boldly as a feral. It is cautious and courageous; languorous and lively; a carnivore with omnivorous tastes. Despite centuries of domestication, it retains, just below the surface, all the instinctive reactions and innate savagery of its successful little mammalian ancestor, *Miacis*, which first evolved during the age of the dinosaurs. Small in stature, the cat has always relied on its skill and speed to escape from predators and to hunt its own prey. Allied to its agility, it has an inbuilt caution, which has helped to ensure its survival, and specialized claws and dentition, which are perfectly suited to its carnivorous habits.

Even the ailurophobe, or cat hater, admires the highly developed maternal feelings in cats. Mother cats (queens) are totally absorbed in the care of their newborn young – suckling and washing them, purring and crooning over them, loath to leave the litter even to feed, drink or for physical relief. The

Right: Despite centuries of domestication, the cat still retains its basic innate behaviour patterns, and will happily hunt, despite being well cared for and fully fed.

Opposite left: More cat ways. A mother cat (top) will move her kittens at the merest hint of danger or disturbance, lifting each one carefully between partly closed jaws. The kitten held in this way immediately draws up its limbs and relaxes its neck, forming a perfect position in which to be carried. Free-ranging cats often catch prey with no intention of eating it (bottom). The shrew captured by this cat is bound to be discarded once dead, as it has a bitter taste, disliked by cats.

Opposite right: An Egyptian cat, the true feline form.

cat is perpetually on guard, and will growl and fluff out her coat at any unusual sound or at the approach of strangers. If danger threatens, she will bodily lift and move her kittens one by one to a place she considers to be of greater safety. It seems miraculous that the cat's canine teeth, designed for ripping and tearing flesh, do not damage the kitten in any way, and that despite the queen's journey, which may often involve jumps over windowsills and walls, the kitten never seems to be bruised or otherwise affected by the trauma.

As the kittens grow, the mother cat teaches them to play, to wash themselves and to eat solids. They are taught to defecate and urinate well away from their nest. If her kittens are threatened by a dog or a marauding tom cat, the mother will attack the aggressor quite fearlessly, fighting, if need be to her own death, in defence of her young. When she considers the time has come to wean her kittens, the mother cat will refuse to nurse them and will spend more time encouraging them to indulge in mock fighting and play-hunting, which build their muscles, develop their motor skills and sharpen their reactions. In this way she ensures that her kittens will grow up to be just like her – courageous, cautious, clean and very, very independent.

Feral cats often subsist quite happily in environments considered totally unsuitable by interfering humans. Though members of a feral colony may look a little battered, the majority fare well and are living very much as they would in their natural state. On many islands of the world feral cat colonies develop and maintain themselves at a naturally successful level. The limitations of the gene pools in such colonies often produce groups recognizable by colour and conformation. This patriarchal blue tom, dignified and bearing the scars of the battles fought to win his seniority, is more content than he would be if 'rescued' and neutered.

Male cats are by nature solitary, though in some environments they may develop a deep affection for others of their own species and, even more rarely, may live in a family group, helping to rear their own offspring. In the main, however, the tom thinks of little besides impregnating female cats and finding enough food to keep him fit for his task. In the wild state, the tom fights hard for his privileges and often bears many battle scars. The stud tom is usually kept in splendid isolation within his own accommodation, where he is allowed to entertain and service carefully selected queens of good lineage. Such male cats are often very affectionate and sometimes seem super-intelligent. They are rarely kept as pets because of their antisocial habit of marking their territory, including the house and its furnishings, with fine sprays of pungent urine. The neutered or altered male cat is dignified and socially acceptable, a paragon of virtue compared to his entire brother. He channels the efforts he would normally have spent in procreation into giving love and affection to his owners. He has no inclination to roam or to pick fights, and grows sleek and sturdy on small, regular meals.

Cats will not tolerate ridicule and resent any attempt at their mastery or domination, so it is rare to find a cat trained to enact set tricks. Some cats have a natural aptitude for clowning, however, and may turn somersaults, roll over or jump through outspread arms for a favourite reward. Many cats learn to retrieve small toys thrown for them and this aptitude may be hereditary, for a kitten of parents with this skill will retrieve even when it has gone to its new home, long before it has had the opportunity to learn the skill by watching its mother.

The language of cats is a subject in itself, and this, combined with the mystic purr, makes the cat family unique. The meaning of feline sounds will be explored later in this book, but it is possible that one of the main reasons for the relationship between humans and cats is their purr. Recent medical research has proved that by sitting and stroking a cat in time with its purr, a stressed human may gradually reduce his or her own blood pressure and pulse rate. Cats are being used increasingly for therapeutic purposes in homes for the aged and infirm, the mentally ill and the retarded. In some cases, the mere presence of a cat in a ward has produced startlingly constructive reactions in patients, many of whom had hitherto been thought to be deaf, dumb or severely impaired. The cat has been declared the perfect companion animal for such disabled persons. In the normal household, a cat provides comfort and calms nerves stretched taut by the tensions of today's world. It provides children with their first lessons in gentleness, tolerance and patience, teaches adults relaxation and unselfishness, and gives the lonely a focal point for each day.

Virtually unchanged in size and shape since the days of the Ancient Egyptians, and despite its fluctuating fortunes as it passed from a deity to a familiar and then to the often prestigious pet of today, the cat remains the enigmatic miniature tiger that endeared itself to the royal households of the Nile Valley. Today, however, the cat's genetic make-up has been so manipulated by humans that it sports coats of many colours, patterns and textures, and these have given rise to various breed groups within the species, which will be described in Chapter 5. Careful selective breeding has exaggerated certain characteristics of feline structure.

Above: Man's intervention in the natural scheme of things has resulted in the development to extremes of some feline features. In the Persian, for example, the heavy, long coat has been encouraged by selective breeding, as has the dramatic shortening of the face and nose.

Right: Cats' natural curiosity can never be quashed.

The nose of the Persian has been reduced, while that of the Siamese has been lengthened. Breeders have rigorously selected for heavy bones in the Shorthairs and the Persians, and for fine bones in the Siamese and Orientals. The basic structure of the cat has been undefiled by human manipulation of its genes, however, and the biology of the cat is the same whether it is a prize-winning pedigree Persian or a dockyard tabby.

Despite all the efforts to thwart nature, the great cat goddess Bastet has continued to watch over *Felis domesticus*, and all cats remain quite clearly identifiable as domestic cats – loving, loyal, fastidious felines, companions to, but never subservient or subordinate to, humans.

BIOLOGY OF THE CAT

Evolution appears to have been particularly kind in shaping the design of the domestic cat, working on such a well-ordered path of selection that the cat remains as intended – an efficient, perfect carnivore of convenient size, still well able to hunt and kill small animals. The cat's framework allows graceful, fluid and perfectly co-ordinated movement at all speeds. The sleekly muscled body and legs allow athletic, graceful leaps and bounds. Its retractable claws allow for swift running while sheathed, and for secure holding and gripping when extended. The cat's well-developed brain allows for swift assimilation of facts, and fast reactions. Its adaptable eyes can cope with extremes of light conditions, allowing perfect vision on the brightest of days as well as in the dimmest of twilights. Its flexible ears can manoeuvre to catch the faintest rustling sound, and its sensitive nose and the perceptive Jacobson's organ in its mouth can identify the most subtle of scents. Yes, the cat is a practically perfect product of its early environment and, luckily for us, has adapted to our modern life-style without changing unduly its physical make-up.

A relaxing cat displays the typical carnivorous teeth of its kind.

THE SKELETON

Although the domestic cat is so much smaller than a human, its skeleton contains 230 bones, compared with the 206 bones of a human skeleton. But, just like our skeleton, the feline skeleton is a bony framework supporting the body tissues. The bones of the limbs, spine, chest and pelvis provide a sophisticated system of levers manipulated by the cat's powerful muscles, while other bony structures protect the vital organs; for instance, the arched ribcage and pelvis protect the heart, lungs and reproductive system, and the rigid skull protects the delicate brain.

The cat's skeleton is made up from four distinct types of bones, known as long bones, short bones, irregular bones and flat bones. The long bones are approximately cylindrical in shape with hollow shafts containing bone marrow, in which the red blood corpuscles are manufactured. These bones include the limb bones such as the femur, the humerus, the tibia, the fibula, the radius and the ulna. The short bones consist of a core of spongy material surrounded by compact bone, and are to be found in the cat's toes and kneecaps. Irregular bones are similar to short bones in composition, and are the bones which form the spine. The flat bones consist of two layers of compact bone with a central layer of spongy bone, and they form the cat's skull, pelvis and shoulder-blades.

The skull is formed from interlocking sections of flat bone, and in very young kittens the edges are not fused, so great care should be taken to avoid head injuries. The flat pieces of bone forming the skull are pierced by hundreds of tiny holes, through which pass blood vessels and nerves.

One end of the spine, or vertebral column, is attached to the skull and the other end terminates in the tail tip. Some of the bones of the vertebral column are hollow and contain the spinal cord, while bony projections on each of the segments provide attachment points for the strong muscles of the back. Mobile, rather than rigid, connections from the spine to the pelvic girdle and the shoulder joints help to make the domestic cat one of the most agile and flexible of all mammals.

The arrangement of the cat's collarbone means that it has a high degree of free movement in the shoulder region. The shoulder-blade, or scapula, is almost triangular in shape and is attached to the first long bone of the foreleg, the humerus, which in turn is attached to the two long bones of the forearm – the thick radius, behind which lies the thinner ulna. The forearm of the cat is easily discerned since it is the part of the foreleg which stands free from the body, while the part formed by the humerus runs down from the high point of the shoulder, along the line of the ribs, to the elbow.

The forepaws correspond with the fingers of the human hand, being formed from sets of three small bones, each of which forms one digit. The final bones of each digit articulate, enabling the claws to be extended or retracted. The cat has no thumb, its position being taken by two small, apparently redundant bones forming the dew claw.

The pelvis provides an encircling structure to protect vital internal organs. A ball-and-socket joint connects the pelvis to the very long femur, or thigh bone, which connects at its lower end to another long bone, the tibia. Here is found the kneecap, or patella, which slides over the smooth end of the femur. From the kneecap down, the hind limb stands free from the cat's body. The tibia is reinforced by a slimmer long bone, the fibula, down to the cat's well-developed hock. The bones of the hindfoot are very similar to those of the forefoot, but the first toe is absent. The cat's silent, swift gait is aided by its flexible leg joints and the fact that it walks and runs on tiptoe.

The cat's ribcage is formed from elongated, flattened bones. Thirteen pairs of ribs are attached by strong muscles, which can vary the volume of the chest cavity, enabling the lungs to expand and contract. Although the rib bones are not hollow, they do contain substantial amounts of bone marrow and are therefore able to produce a proportion of the body's red blood cells.

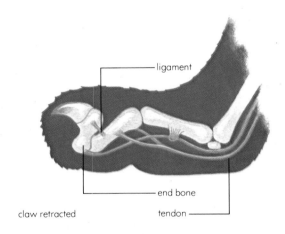

claw retracted

ligament — end bone — tendon —

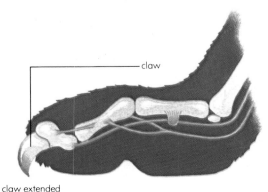

claw —

claw extended

Left: The cat's claws are normally kept hidden inside a leathery sheath at the end of each pad. During hunting, fighting, climbing and balancing, they are extended by the action of a series of tendons and ligaments. Leg muscles pull on a rigid tendon which runs along the base of the pad to each claw. This moves the bone attached to the claw forward, pushing the claw out from its sheath of skin. To pull the claws in again, the cat relaxes the connecting leg muscles and an elastic ligament attached to the top of the end bone retracts the claw.

Opposite: There are over 240 bones in a cat's skeleton. They provide a light yet strong framework on to which the muscles are attached. The stretching cat shows just how flexible the spine really is. The combination of flexible joints and powerful muscles enables the cat to move with great speed, precision and grace.

Skeletal problems Although excellent protection and support is provided by the skeleton of the cat under normal conditions, the animal may suffer fractures and dislocations as a result of road accidents or when jumping from too great a height. In such cases expert veterinary attention can often bring about permanent repairs to such injuries, leaving no serious after-effects. When a dislocation does occur the region swells severely, causing considerable pain. Some cats suffer regular kneecap dislocation, and this is thought to be a hereditary condition, known as luxation of the patellae. Such cats should be neutered to prevent the trait being passed on to another generation.

All breeds of domestic cat have retained the same basic size, shape and structure as their ancestors, unlike dogs, which have been selectively bred to produce a wide range of heights and shapes. Cats are therefore fortunately free from many of the skeletal abnormalities that can afflict dogs.

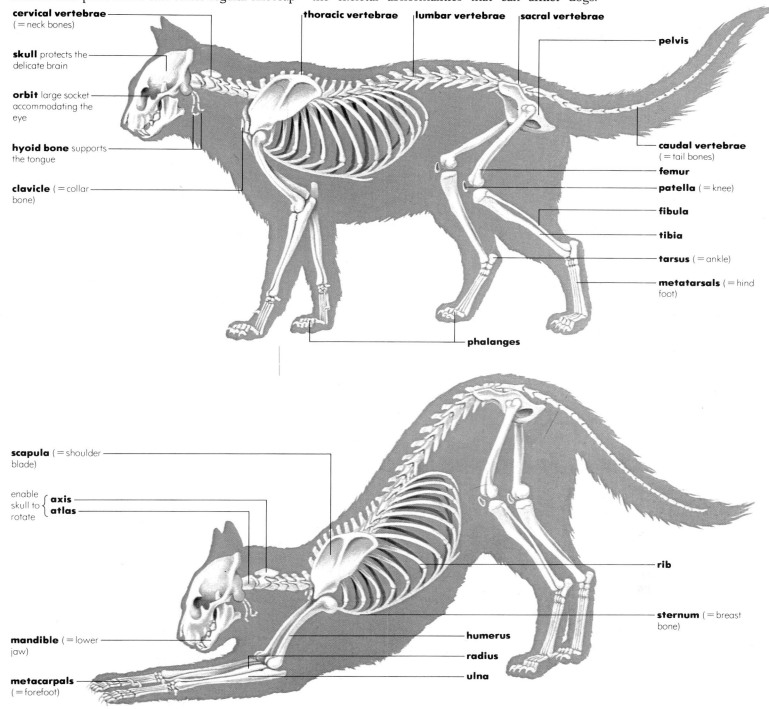

cervical vertebrae (= neck bones)

skull protects the delicate brain

orbit large socket accommodating the eye

hyoid bone supports the tongue

clavicle (= collar bone)

thoracic vertebrae

lumbar vertebrae

sacral vertebrae

pelvis

caudal vertebrae (= tail bones)

femur

patella (= knee)

fibula

tibia

tarsus (= ankle)

metatarsals (= hind foot)

phalanges

scapula (= shoulder blade)

enable skull to rotate { axis / atlas

mandible (= lower jaw)

metacarpals (= forefoot)

rib

sternum (= breast bone)

humerus

radius

ulna

Some of the defects which are occasionally encountered, however, include bent, kinked or shortened tails, cleft palates, flattened chests, polydactylism and split-foot. A cleft palate may be associated with a hare-lip, and both defects are caused by the failure of the two halves of the upper lip and hard palate to come together in the normal way in the embryonic kitten. Sometimes the condition is produced through recessive genes, and it is probable that the administration of certain drugs to the pregnant queen at a critical stage in gastrolactation can also prevent the correct closing of the two halves of the skull structure. Kittens born with such deformities are unable to suckle and should be put painlessly to sleep.

A deficiency of some essential vitamins is thought to cause the flattened chest effect seen in some kittens, although genetic factors may also be involved. The flattened ribcage does not allow the proper expansion and contraction of the lungs, so breathing problems increase as the kitten grows. Kittens with this deformity may live, however, depending on its severity.

The presence of extra toes on one or more of the feet is fairly common in the cat. This condition is known as polydactylism, and it rarely causes any problems unless there are so many extra toes that the cat appears to have double paws on each leg and is therefore very clumsy in its movements. This defect is a show fault in pedigree cats. In split-foot, a cleft is apparent in the centre of one or both front paws, while the remaining toes may be fused

together and often have double sets of claws. Cats with split-foot pass the trait on to their kittens through a dominant gene, and should be neutered.

Common tail faults such as kinks, where the tail is bent at a joint, are found more often in Foreign and Oriental cats than in the ordinary domestic pet. Some kinks are very minor, involving a joint near the tail tip, and may even be undetectable except by the most experienced and discerning cat fancier. Other kinks may be so severe that the tail is twisted and shortened. Extreme tail deformity is seen in the Japanese Bobtail, where the tail has multiple bends, producing the bobtail effect. Kinks occur at the tail root, too, and here they are considered a very serious defect, as other organs may be affected by the bone deformity.

THE MUSCULAR SYSTEM

A complex network of muscles overlays the feline skeleton and is responsible for the general outline shape of the animal as well as for providing the power for movement. The muscles which straighten and extend a joint are known as extensor muscles, while flexor muscles bend and flex the joint. Abductor muscles move the limbs away from the body, while adductors draw the limbs towards the body. All muscles consist of specialized fibrous tissue designed to contract in response to stimuli received from the nerves. Three types of muscles are found in the cat's body: striped, smooth and cardiac. Striped (or striated) muscle operates all the

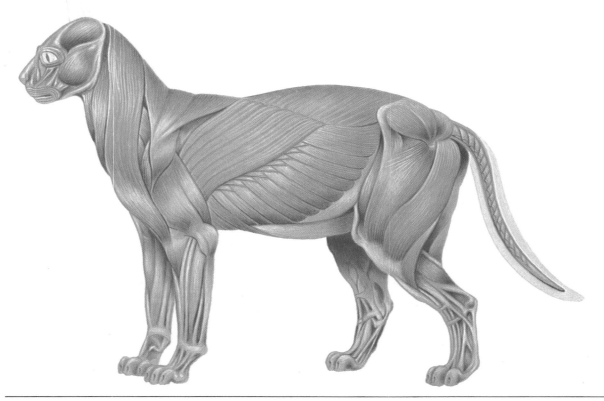

Left: The cat has a complex muscle system which gives it strength, speed and agility. The hindquarters are heavily muscled and the hindlegs provide powerful acceleration, enabling the animal to leap considerable distances. Strong jaw muscles, with well-developed anchorage points on the skull, are capable of inflicting a killer bite to the cat's prey.

Opposite: A cat leaping. The muscles in the hindlegs are fully extended as the cat leaves the ground. The spine is stretched out as the front legs are brought forward, ready to land or pounce on some unsuspecting bird or mouse. Balance in the air is provided by the tail, held stiffly upright.

Right: The knee and ankle joints provide a very powerful springing mechanism with which the cat can jump upwards to a great height. Here the cat measures up the height of the jump, then leaps up from a crouching position, landing on the wall with its hind legs and using its upright tail for balance. The cat jumps down carefully, and flexible joints in the legs absorb the shock of landing.

limbs and other parts of the animal's body that are under voluntary control. Smooth or unstriated muscle is connected to the parts of the body not under voluntary control, including the intestinal wall and the walls of the blood vessels. Cardiac muscle is unique in having the ability to contract and expand with rhythmic action without becoming fatigued, and is found only in the heart.

CIRCULATION AND RESPIRATION

All parts of the cat's body require oxygen, and this is carried by the circulatory system. The cat's heart beats at about 110 to 140 times each minute – about twice as fast as the human heart – and its pump-like action first pushes the blood around part of the circuit to the lungs, where it is oxygenated. The blood then passes back through the heart and around the rest of the circuit, which includes all the other organs of the body. Certain arteries carry the blood at high pressure from the heart, forcing it through fine capillaries into the tissues, where exchanges of gases, nutrients and hormones take place. Blood at low pressure is collected by the veins and returned to the heart for re-circulation. The lungs are a pair of spongy sacs providing the necessary link between the body's blood system and the oxygen in the outside atmosphere. The muscular action of the ribcage draws air into the lungs, where it eventually passes into the tiny alveoli — special air sacs encased by thin-walled blood vessels that allow oxygen to pass into the bloodstream and carbon dioxide to pass out. The blood thus 'picks up' oxygen for use in the body and returns carbon dioxide to the lungs for expulsion as the cat breathes out.

As well as conveying oxygen and carbon dioxide, among the blood's other functions are the transport of food to the body cells and the removal of waste products. Nutrients are collected from the digestive system (including the intestines, the liver and the pancreas) once the food eaten by the cat has been broken down by the body's digestive system into simpler chemical substances.

DIGESTION

Digestive processes start in the cat's mouth, where food is first mixed with saliva. Then, after swallowing, the food passes into the stomach, where digestive juices and the churning action of the stomach break the food down still further. From the stomach, the liquidized mixture passes a little at a time into the small intestine, where further digestive juices from the pancreas and the gut lining are added. Bile, manufactured by the liver and stored in the gall bladder, aids the digestive process, and nutrients from the liquid are absorbed by the blood through the intestinal wall. In the large intestine most of the water left in the liquid is removed, leaving semi-solid faeces to be passed through the anus.

EXCRETION

The kidneys are the principal waste-disposal organs of the body. They filter unwanted materials and excess water from the blood to form urine, which is stored in the bladder before being passed out of the body. The kidneys' most important role is in maintaining the body's critical water balance. In hot weather, or if the cat is deprived of drinking water, the urine becomes very concentrated as the kidneys greatly reduce water excretion.

GLANDS

The bodily functions of the cat are controlled on two levels: by the nervous system and by the endocrine system. The cat's nervous system is very precise. Its sensory perceptors are able to detect every event important to survival, while the brain initiates nerve messages to control the body's responses. The endocrine system consists of a set of glands which secrete hormones. Hormones are basically chemical 'messengers', designed to travel through the bloodstream and to cause certain organs to carry out specific functions. Each gland secretes specialized hormones: the thyroid hormone influences growth; the adrenal hormones influence kidney function, mobilize the cat's body for flight or fight and help it to counteract stress; and sex hormones influence reproductive processes. The pituitary gland produces several hormones: one helps to regulate the blood pressure and others act on particular glands, stimulating production of their own hormones. The pituitary, often termed the 'master' gland, is under the direct control of the hypothalamus, the control centre of the cat's brain.

SKIN AND FUR

To the cat lover, the fur of the cat is often judged by its appealing colour, pattern or texture. To the cat, the fur is important as a barrier between its body and the environment, maintaining its temperature and protecting against injury and excessive sunlight, wind and wet.

The skin of the cat is made up of two main layers. The outer layer is constantly being replaced as the surface cells die and are sloughed off. Its

The cat's fur acts as a protective barrier between its body and the environment. Its ability to control to a certain extent the direction of groups of hairs enables the cat to use the fur to regulate body temperature. The coat generally covers the body in smooth, loose-lying insulative layers, but when necessary, the hairs can be raised, causing the coat to open and allowing air to pass between the hairs, either to cool the skin or to gain extra heat. The fur is also fairly water-resistant, and the guard hair layer deflects rain, keeping the soft, warm undercoat dry. Below is shown the fur of a shorthaired cat and, at the bottom, that of a longhaired for comparison.

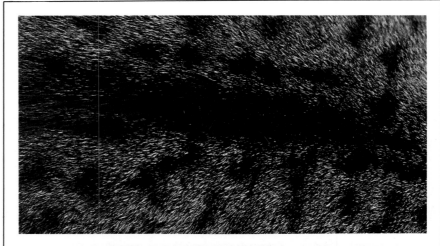

function is mainly one of protection. The inner layer contains important specialized structures such as glands and pigments.

The condition of the cat's skin can often give an indication of the animal's state of health. In a fit, healthy cat the skin is loose, elastic and pliable. If the skin at the scruff of the neck is taken in the hand, lifted and then released, it immediately resumes its normal position. In the sick cat, the skin becomes stiff and unyielding. When the scruff is lifted, it remains in the pinched position and must be massaged back into place. The colour of the skin, too, can be a barometer of the cat's condition. A pallid appearance often points to a severe infestation by parasites, or to stress, trauma, shock or a lack of some vital dietary requirement. A blue tone to the skin might denote respiratory disease, heart failure or leukaemia, while a reddish tone indicates an inflammatory condition of the skin itself or of the underlying tissues. A yellowing of the skin suggests jaundice: one symptom of several of the more serious of feline diseases.

Sweat glands are contained in the cat's skin, and these are found over the entire body with the exception of the nose. There are two types of sweat glands. Apocrine glands secrete a milky fluid which may be involved in attracting sexual partners. In some areas of the cat's body groups of apocrine glands, along with sebaceous glands, certainly do produce scented secretions important in territorial marking and for leaving recognition markings on humans and other animals. These groups of glands are situated on the chin, the lips, the temples and the base of the tail. The cat also has eccrine sweat glands. These are found in the pads of its feet, and produce secretions which cause sets of damp footprints whenever the cat is hot or apprehensive. Usually, however, the sweat glands seem to play little part in temperature control in the cat, which may be seen to actively lose body heat by panting and by the cooling effect produced by saliva applied to the coat during self-grooming, which then evaporates.

The hairless areas of the cat's body, such as the nose, footpads and nipples, have a distinctive skin structure. The nose leather is extremely sensitive to touch, and is kept damp by mucosal secretions from the nostrils. The skin of the footpads is thick and rough, and more sensitive to pressure than to touch. It provides a tough surface for walking and climbing, while allowing the distinctive, silent tread so characteristic of the cat family.

Right: The nose leather of the cat is an extremely sensitive area. Not only is it used to test by touch, it is also thought to be the cat's barometer, being receptive to subtle changes in temperature and humidity.

Far right: The skin of the pads found beneath the paws of the cat are sensitive to pressure rather than touch, and when a cat uses a paw to test by touching, it uses the fur-covered tip of the paw, not the hairless pad.

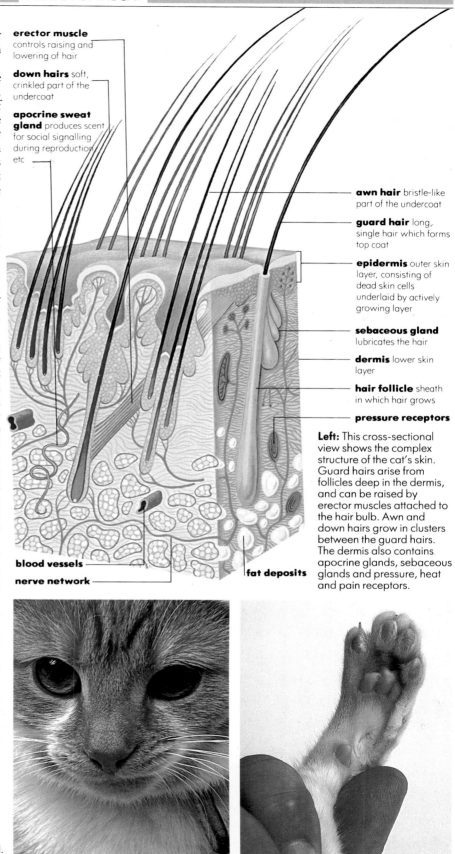

erector muscle controls raising and lowering of hair

down hairs soft, crinkled part of the undercoat

apocrine sweat gland produces scent for social signalling during reproduction etc

awn hair bristle-like part of the undercoat

guard hair long, single hair which forms top coat

epidermis outer skin layer, consisting of dead skin cells underlaid by actively growing layer

sebaceous gland lubricates the hair

dermis lower skin layer

hair follicle sheath in which hair grows

pressure receptors

blood vessels

nerve network

fat deposits

Left: This cross-sectional view shows the complex structure of the cat's skin. Guard hairs arise from follicles deep in the dermis, and can be raised by erector muscles attached to the hair bulb. Awn and down hairs grow in clusters between the guard hairs. The dermis also contains apocrine glands, sebaceous glands and pressure, heat and pain receptors.

The claws of the cat grow continuously from the base. They are formed of keratin, a horny protein that also forms the outer layer of the skin. The inner layer, or dermis, of the claw is known as the quick, and is covered by a hard cuticle. The dermis is attached to the terminal bone of the toe and can be retracted under a fold of skin lying over the tip of the toe.

Hair (fur) is derived from the outer layer of the skin and acts mainly as an insulating layer, keeping the cat warm in cold weather and cool in hot weather. The fur forms a complete pelt over the body, and is modified in some areas to form whiskers, eyelashes and the sensitive carpal hairs on the back of the forelegs. Normal cat fur is made up of three different types of hair – guard hairs, bristle or awn hairs, and wool or down hairs. The topcoat or overhair of a cat consists of guard hairs and awn hairs and acts as a protective covering, while the insulating undercoat is composed of the soft down hairs. Seen under a microscope, a guard hair is straight and tapers evenly to a fine point, while an awn hair is thinner than a guard hair and swells noticeably near its pointed tip. Awn hairs vary considerably and are graded into three main types, some being very similar to guard hairs in appearance, while others are almost as thin as down hairs. Shortest and slimmest of all the hairs in the cat's coat are the down hairs, which are of similar

diameter all along their length and often appear to be slightly crimped due to tiny undulations in their structure.

Most cats are endowed with all three types of hair, but the coats of the Rex breeds are markedly different (see page 103).

Each individual hair is a long, thin, cylindrical structure pointed at one end and terminating in a tiny bulb at the other which is embedded in the dermis. Each hair is formed separately in a hair follicle, and special pigment cells inject colour granules into the hair as it grows, helping to produce a coat of the cat's genetically determined

Above: A fine set of whiskers or vibrissae adorn an Abyssinian.

Left: Claws are formed of keratin – the same protein that forms the outer skin layer of the cat. When the outer layer of claw becomes worn, scales form which the cat removes at regular intervals by the action known as 'stropping'. This is seen as regular scratching with alternate forepaws on a tree.

colour and pattern. Special muscles attached to large follicles enable the hairs to stand upright and erect whenever the cat is startled, angry or feeling cold.

Moulting, or the shedding of dead hairs, generally takes place during certain seasons of the year. Hair loss also follows some debilitating illnesses, as well as infectious skin diseases such as eczema, mange and ringworm. Poisoning can induce hair loss, and a hormone imbalance of the type sometimes experienced by neutered cats can also produce a form of eczema, leaving bare areas along the cat's spine and flanks.

Whiskers Vibrissae, or whiskers, are specialized hairs which grow in neat rows on either side of the cat's upper lip. They are extremely sensitive and the slightest touch causes a message to be transmitted directly to the brain. Cat's whiskers are used for touching and testing objects and obstacles, for sensing environmental changes and in registering certain emotions. Cats with poor vision may be seen to actively use their whiskers for testing their environment, walking cautiously and turning their head from side to side. Cats with normal vision also use their whiskers in dim light conditions to help feel their way about.

Whiskers are used by the cat to test and touch objects and obstacles, and for sensing changes in the environment. An alert cat examining a sight, smell or sound for possible danger opens the eyes wide, points the ears towards the source and also puffs out the whisker pads, causing the vibrissae to extend forwards. A relaxed cat holds its whiskers sideways and back.

VISION

Although humans have better overall daylight vision than cats, it is in the twilight that the feline really comes into its own. While it obviously cannot see in total darkness, it has very good vision in the dimmest of lights. It is the ability of the cat's pupil to expand and contract in response to the amount of light available that explains the variable appearance of the cat's eye. In dim light the iris relaxes and the pupil dilates. Light passes through the curved cornea and lens to strike the retina at the back of the eye. The light is then reflected by a special layer of iridescent cells called the tapetum lucidium, and this causes the strange glowing effect often seen when cats' eyes are seen at night in the headlights of a car or in photographs taken with on-camera flashlights. It is probable that the tapetum, or even the retina itself, may have a photo-multiplying effect on received light. The delicate mechanism of the feline eye must be protected from the effects of very strong light, however, and during such conditions the iris is able to contract, closing down to a mere slit.

The eyes of the cat face forward, and the fields of vision overlap, producing stereoscopic vision, enabling the cat to accurately judge distances when searching out and attacking its prey and when jumping. Cats' eyes are comparatively large and are set in deep sockets. They do not move freely, and so the cat often has to turn its head, and sometimes its whole body, in order to keep objects in sharp focus. Cats are said to be colour blind, but while they might not see colours as we do, they certainly have sophisticated methods of distinguishing between colours, for, as any cat owner will testify, many cats show preferences for certain colours of equipment, bedding and dishes.

In addition to the upper and lower eyelids, the cat has a third eyelid known as the nictitating membrane, or haw. This is a sheet of pale tissue normally tucked out of sight at the inner corner of each eye. As the eye moves within the socket, this membrane moves diagonally upwards and over the front of the eyeball, removing dust and dirt and keeping the eye lubricated and moist. Whenever a cat is incubating an illness, out of condition or perhaps harbouring internal parasites, the tiny pad of fat normally found behind the eyeball is inclined to shrink, causing the eyeball to retract slightly into its socket. This in turn causes the haw to partially extend across the eye. The cat is then said to 'have its haws up', and this condition is often taken as an early warning of illness.

Apart from the raised haws, the eyes of the cat can be used in other ways to diagnose illness, for a change in their general appearance is often the first sign that something is affecting the cat's health. Weeping or discharging eyes point to the onset of diseases such as pneumonitis, rhino-

peripheral vision of
right eye

main vision

tracheitis or cat 'flu, while a distinct change in the colour of the iris indicates jaundice. The eyes are also sensitive to foreign bodies such as grass seeds and awns which may lodge in the eyelids, and they may be injured during fights and scuffles. Any change in the appearance of your cat's eyes should be investigated without delay by a veterinary surgeon. Drops or ointments should never be used in the eyes unless these have been professionally prescribed.

HEARING

Sounds consist of vibrations, and reach the cat's ears as pressure waves. The vibrations of the waves trigger nerve signals to the cat's brain. The cat has

Above: Like many predatory animals (and humans) the visual field of the cat's left eye overlaps with the visual field of the right, a condition known as binocular vision. Some of the optic nerve fibres cross over from one side of the brain to the other and so images from both eyes can be compared in the visual cortex. This enables the cat to accurately judge the mouse's distance. Cats also have an extensive peripheral visual field, which can pick up movement to the side of the head.

Right: Cats can detect higher frequency wavelengths than man, including ultrasonic sounds. The cone-shaped ear flap or pinna funnels sound waves into the cat's inner ear, and muscles at the base of the ear enable it to twist forwards and sideways, homing in on the high-pitched squeak of a mouse or a rustle in the grasss.

peripheral vision of left eye

main vision of left eye

binocular vision

ear. Here the sound waves are analysed and converted into nerve impulses to be sent along the auditory nerve to the brain. Being of relatively high intelligence, and with a sophisticated mammalian brain, the cat is capable of learning a wide range of special sounds, including its own name and a series of simple command words.

The cat's ear is able to register frequencies approximately two octaves higher than the human ear, but is less sensitive to the lower frequencies. Hearing acuity may diminish with the onset of old age, and indeed some elderly cats become totally deaf. Deafness can also result from ear disease, or it may be hereditary, when it is sometimes linked with white coat colour in cats – particularly when the white cat also has blue eye colour. In such cats the genetic factors giving rise to the coat and eye colour affect the cochlea, producing changes severe enough to inhibit the passage of sound waves. Cats with normal hearing are able to accurately locate the source of the slightest sounds, a trait which has ensured the survival of the species, and a boon for the animal which prefers to hunt at dawn and dusk.

Ear movements are expressive of the cat's many moods, and the ear flaps are particularly vulnerable to injury, especially during cat fights. Although the pinna may bleed profusely when torn, it usually heals quite quickly unless the underlying cartilage has also been damaged. Severe irritation such as that caused by infestation with ear mites can also cause damage, as the cat uses its strong hind claws to scratch in an attempt to relieve the itching. This ruptures the blood vessels under the thin skin of the pinna and may result in the formation of a large haematoma or blood blister. Unless veterinary treatment is available for this condition, the ear flap crumples as the swelling is naturally reabsorbed, leaving the cat with a collapsed and deformed ear. Having large, open ears causes other problems, too, for the ear canal is easily infested by tiny mites.

highly sensitive hearing: it is able to differentiate between a much wider range of sounds than a human, including ultrasonic sounds, to which we are totally oblivious.

The ear of the cat consists of three sections. Outwardly we see the mobile, cone-shaped pinna, or ear flap, naturally erect and forward-facing, but equipped with more than a dozen muscles, which enable it to move and accurately collect the slightest of sound vibrations, thus determining their source. The pinna acts as a funnel down which sound travels to the eardrum, stretched across the ear canal. The middle ear is made up of three small bones which act like a system of levers and convert the large, weak vibrations of the eardrum into small, strong vibrations of the cochlea of the inner

SMELLING AND TASTING

Like most carnivores, the cat has a highly developed sense of smell. Very sensitive nerve endings in the form of fine olfactory hairs line the nasal cavities, and these are linked with nerve cells connected to the brain. Here the olfactory region is much larger than would normally be expected in an animal as small as the domestic cat, and this indicates just how vital to its survival is the sense of smell.

As well as performing a vital function in the hunt for food, this sense is important to the cat in its sexual life. A small pouch lined with receptor cells exists in the roof of the cat's mouth; this is known as the vomeronasal sac, or Jacobson's organ, after its discoverer. When the cat receives an unusual or subtle scent, the minute particles of the scent are caught by the tongue and pressed against the roof of the mouth. The cat grimaces with a distinctive facial gesture called the flehmen reaction as the scent is transferred to the Jacobson's organ for identification. The reaction can be stimulated when a tom cat smells another cat's urine, or scents a female in heat, and many cats exhibit this strange expression when given catnip.

The catnip plant (*Nepeta cataria*) exudes a fragrance found highly intoxicating by many cats, and diluted oil of the plant has been used to successfully trap wild cats such as the puma and the lynx. The essential oil of the catnip plant is called nepetalactone, and it has been extracted and chemically structured to make it available for application to cat toys, scratching posts and beds. The reaction of cats to catnip varies, and of the entire feline population only about 50 per cent will show a response to the scent, and this capacity to detect nepetalactone appears to be inherited. Those cats that do respond often appear to enter a trance-like state which lasts for about ten minutes.

The tongue The cat's tongue is very specialized, with a rough surface caused by the presence of large papillae. These are used for rasping and softening food, licking the meat from bones and grooming the fur. The papillae along the centre of the tongue do not carry taste receptors, but special mushroom-shaped papillae along the front and side edges of the tongue, and several cup-shaped papillae at the back, do carry taste buds. The cat shows no response to sweet tastes. It is remarkable, too, in its strong sensitivity to water tastes, and its receptors for tasting water far outnumber the few sweet taste buds present in the animal's mouth.

The tongue is long, strong and flexible, and its edge is capable of curling like the bowl of a spoon, enabling the cat to lap liquids. It generally laps three, four or five times to fill the mouth before swallowing. When eating prey, the cat may lick the carcass to soften it before starting to eat.

Above: Covered with projections called papillae, the cat's tongue is used for removing meat from bones, softening food, and for the effective grooming of its coat.

Left: This young ginger tom cat has detected a subtle scent, probably left by another cat, and in order to thoroughly analyse this, presses minute particles of the scent with its tongue against the roof of the mouth. Here, Jacobson's organ enables identification of the odour. This typical grimace is called the flehmen reaction.

TEETH AND DIET

The cat's dentition is highly specialized, as befits a small, successful carnivorous animal. In the adult the mouth has twelve incisors, four canines, ten premolars and four molars, giving a full set of thirty teeth. Kittens are born with tiny teeth just visible in the pale gums, and by six weeks of age these have erupted and are needle-sharp. Young kittens aid their own teething process by chewing on any hard material available and should be given long, thin strips of raw meat at this stage of their development. The baby teeth are generally shed quite painlessly as the permanent teeth come through, but very occasionally double dentition occurs and the kitten stops eating. A veterinary surgeon will soon remove the stubborn teeth – usually the canines – and the soreness of the mouth is alleviated.

Cats' teeth are designed not for chewing but for tearing and biting. When prey is caught the cat first tears a piece from the carcass and swallows it whole. The salivary juices therefore have very little time to go into action while the food is in the cat's mouth. Added to this is the fact that the salivary glands produce little or no ptyalin, the powerful enzyme produced in humans that starts the breakdown of starches into blood sugars. This means that starches present in the cat's diet remain virtually unchanged by the time they reach the small intestine, and therefore there is very little point in feeding starchy foods to your cat. Conversely, the stomach of the cat contains much stronger digestive juices than that of a human's, and it is able to reduce quite hard bone to soft matter. Small rodents and birds may be swallowed in chunks, and any parts not quickly broken down, such as feather and fur, may be regurgitated and either discarded or re-eaten by the animal.

The eating habits of cats are not always sensible or hygienic, and as they also use their tongues for regular self-grooming sessions they inevitably ingest large amounts of dirt, dust, grease and hair. Despite this it is the consumption of stale or tainted food that causes most of the gastric upsets seen in the animal. Cats like to drink almost stagnant water, given the opportunity, and often drink from fish ponds and bird baths treated with chemicals. Very often, serious bouts of sickness and diarrhoea in feline pets can be traced to this propensity for drinking unsuitable water.

Other causes of severe gastric upset in the cat can be ascribed to infestations of intestinal worms, and to the provision of quite unsuitable diets. Too much milk often causes diarrhoea, since the cat may not be able to deal with the lactose in cow's milk. Too much fish can result in the regurgitation of a great white 'rope' of undigested food. Whole minced poultry also causes problems, for tiny shards of bone can pierce or damage the lining of

the bowel, and the cat passes blood-stained stools. Self-grooming by the Longhaired cat might result in the formation of furballs, when ingested hair becomes impacted into a solid mass in the stomach. A furball is indigestible and impossible to pass in the normal way, and the cat may become lethargic and ill unless it is able to vomit it up.

Confined cats, denied a full natural diet and an outdoor life, must be compensated. They need well-balanced meals with plenty of different textures, ensuring that their mouths and gums are sufficiently exercised and that their digestive systems are well maintained. Regular grooming is necessary, even in the Shorthaired varieties, to ensure that cats do not form furballs and to keep the skin in good condition.

Above: Even when provided with ample drinking water, the cat often prefers to drink from puddles or even stagnant garden pools.

Below left: Eating grass is a natural feline habit, and cats confined to the home or a cattery should be provided with either pot-grown grass or regular bunches of coarse grasses gathered from untreated and unpolluted areas. Grass is thought to provide the cat with necessary traces of folic acid, and to aid its digestive processes.

COMMUNICATION

The cat's calls and purrs are very varied, and no animal expresses itself as well as the domestic feline. Although the full function of the cat's vocal cords is not understood, it has been discovered that there are superior or false vocal cords as well as inferior or true vocal cords. It is thought that the true vocal cords produce the cat's various cries and mews, while the false cords are responsible for its purr. Cats purr with contentment, with anticipation and with affection, and many cats purr as they approach death, even when in considerable pain. Some cats purr loudly, and some so softly that no sound is heard, the purr being detected only by feeling the unmistakable vibrations in the animal's throat. Purring may start in the young kitten as early as one week of age, while it contentedly nurses from its mother. It cannot be induced in such young kittens by stroking or petting, however, as it can in many older cats. Such young cats purr only in a monotone; older cats are able to purr using two or more notes.

Cats communicate with one another and with humans by using body language, but have also evolved a whole language of distinctive cries, where different sounds express different emotions. Growls are varied and very meaningful, and cats are also able to hiss, spit and scream.

REPRODUCTION

The cat has a typically mammalian reproductive system, although with some feline modifications. The male cat has paired testes which produce sperms and the male hormone called testosterone. The testes descend from the abdominal cavity into the sacs of the scrotum when the kitten is still within the queen's uterus or, more rarely, shortly after birth. Very occasionally one or both testes fail to descend and may result in a sterile or partially sterile cat. A male cat with only one testicle is called a monorchid and a cat without descended testicles is called a cryptorchid. If such cats are fertile, they may pass their condition on to their offspring.

Monorchidism and cryptorchidism is a nuisance to breeder and pet owner alike, for while it is advocated that such cats should be neutered, it is often difficult for the veterinary surgeon to locate the hidden testes, and the normally simple operation becomes complicated and may be lengthy and laborious. If sterile, and therefore left un-neutered, the monorchid or cryptorchid male cat can become a menace, for he has all the characteristics of the entire tom, including strong-smelling urine and the inclination to liberally spray-mark all his territorial boundaries at regular intervals. Male cats become sexually mature before they reach one year of age, and it is at this time that wandering, fighting and spraying might begin, and the subtle change is noticed in the cat's general aroma as his urine develops its tom cat smell.

In the female cat, paired ovaries lie on either side of the spine, just behind the kidneys. The ovaries produce the female hormone called oestrogen and, following the stimulus of mating, will shed several eggs. The eggs pass down the Fallopian tubes to be fertilized by sperm from the male cat. Fertilization can occur up to three full days after mating; then the eggs spend another five days in the Fallopian tubes before passing into the uterus. At this period another hormone, called progesterone, is secreted by the ovaries, and this substance enables the fertilized eggs to implant in the lining of the uterine wall. This is a critical stage in successful reproduction, and if any adverse events occur, such as illness in the female cat, shock or trauma, then implantation is prevented.

The female cat may have her first heat in kittenhood, but puberty most commonly occurs between nine and ten months of age. The first heat is often triggered by favourable weather conditions, particularly in free-ranging cats. Producing kittens too early in life may seriously deplete a young cat's calcium reserves at a critical stage in her own development and, whenever possible, the young cat should be prevented from having an unwanted early pregnancy. The gestation period in the cat averages sixty-five days, and kittens born before the fifty-seventh day are unlikely to survive. Queens may go well over term, possibly due to delayed conception after mating, and live kittens have been successfully produced after a seventy-two-day gestation period. The average litter consists of about four kittens, which are born with fur, but are deaf, blind and quite helpless. The litter feeds from the

Above: The cat runs in a series of bounding leaps. Pushing off with its back feet, it reaches forward, stretching the spine as it does so. On landing, the front feet touch the ground first, followed by the back feet. The cat then takes off again with the back legs in a smooth, flowing movement. The flexible spine allows the cat to cover a considerable distance, stretching itself forward in each leap.

mother cat for about eight weeks, although solid food will be taken from about the fourth week of age. As the kittens become more and more independent, the queen spends less time with them and her hormones curtail her lactation and prepare her body for another breeding cycle, and her life returns to normal.

LOCOMOTION

Feline movement is generally sinuous, graceful, elegant and effective. Except in play, cats rarely move without purpose. The propulsion comes from the animal's hindlegs, which are long and strongly muscled, while the forelegs are supportive, and designed for grasping and holding prey. A high degree of muscle control produces the characteristic stealthy approach that a cat uses in hunting, when the animal appears to flow forward in slow motion, and is able to stop in mid-stride – freezing the pose for seemingly interminable seconds – before gliding forward once more. The sequence during a normal walk is: right foreleg – left hindleg – left foreleg – right hindleg. When the cat is purposefully going to a decided destination, the walk becomes a brisk lope, still in the same limb sequence, but covering the ground at twice the pace.

The cat is also capable of producing short, sharp bursts of high speed, though attempting to maintain this for any length of time produces exhaustion. The gallop, used in rapid escape from danger, or in the final rush to secure prey, consists of a series of long, low leaps. In hunting, this final explosive burst of power follows a build-up of power in the hindquarters, when the cat is seen to wriggle its tail end rapidly from side to side before propelling its body forward.

Above: The cat walks in four time: right foreleg, followed by left hindleg, then left foreleg, followed by right hindleg. The movement is graceful and even, producing a flowing gait.

Below: The sequence of events during the hunting and capture of prey. The cat locates the prey and freezes (1), crouching low to the ground with eyes wide, ears well forward and quivering tail (2). It may stalk its prey or, if within range, pounce (3). Cats will often play with their newly caught prey for a time (4) before finally killing it with a swift bite to the back of the neck.

JUMPING

The cat is a superb jumper, and is generally able to clear four or five times its own height from a crouching, stationary position. It first measures the height by eye, then tenses the hindquarters before propelling itself forwards and upwards to land a little above its objective, allowing room for accurate landing with the hindlegs; the forelegs are used only to correct the balance and to gain a safe foothold if necessary. Descending is a more difficult operation for the cat, as the landing must be taken on the weaker forelimbs. The animal tends to check and recheck the depth of the descent and to find all possible ways of reducing the distance of the drop, edging the body downwards head first as far as possible before pushing off with the hindlegs. Whenever possible, the cat converts a steep descent into a split descent by making an intermediate jump, attempting to finish with a less angled jump to put less stress on the forepaws on landing. When a cat does make an enforced vertical jump down from a great height, this sometimes stings and shocks the forepaws, causing the cat to sit and shake its limbs and lick its pads.

Cats are also able to jump straight up in the air, landing to either side or behind their take-off point; this is a defence tactic, used automatically when they are surprised.

Climbing upwards is simple for the cat, and it may often climb for what seems like pure enjoyment. The climbing sequence usually starts with a jump, either from a short, sharp running start or from a stationary crouch. The hindquarters propel

the cat upwards and, using unsheathed claws to grasp and grip, the cat climbs in a series of short, sharp moves, the joints flexed and the spine arched. Reversing the process results in the same problems as posed by jumping down. The cat's claws, hooked and ideal for climbing up, point in the wrong direction to provide security for the descent, so this is generally made tail end first, the cat lowering itself in short drops until it is near enough to the ground to make a turning jump and land on its feet.

Fit, playful cats often become overexcited in play, especially after playing with crisp, wind-blown autumn leaves, and may climb rapidly up a tree or high pole, going higher and higher until they find themselves unable or unwilling to get down. If left long enough, most will eventually attempt the descent, but a few may have to be rescued by ladder, possibly by the fire brigade!

SELF-RIGHTING REFLEX

An automatic sequence of events has been evolved in the cat which enables it to land on all four feet when falling from a height, no matter what position its body was in at the start of the fall. High-speed photography has enabled careful study of this almost unique ability in the cat, which follows a precise sequence. First the head is levelled until it is horizontal and upright; then a reflex action brings the forepaws up to the head; next the spinal column twists; finally the hindlegs flex to bring the cat completely upright, with arched back and tensed limbs, the moment before it reaches the ground. The tail is used as a counterbalance and the impact is cushioned throughout the body. Cats do injure themselves in falling from very great heights despite this remarkable reflex action, however, and often suffer fractures of the limbs and pelvis. It is also quite common for a cat to suffer an injury by splitting the hard palate in the mouth as a result of hitting its chin on the ground.

BALANCE

The cat's powers of co-ordination are acutely developed, as befits an animal designed for hunting and killing prey. The cat's brain receives incoming information both from its eyes and from the specialized organ within the inner ear, known as the vestibular apparatus, which detects both acceleration and the direction of the animal's head movements. This data combines with information from the cat's muscles and joints to enable the brain to give the cat a perfect sense of self-orientation – it has exact knowledge of its position in space at all times. Any sudden change in a cat's orientation produces an immediate reflex response designed to restore balance. For instance, pushing a cat suddenly will result in an instantaneous extension of the limbs on that side, preventing a fall.

Left: Though climbing upwards is a simple manoeuvre for the cat, descending often causes problems. A cat may go down head first from a moderate height, but will generally let itself down slowly in reverse from an extreme elevation.

Below: All cats have an in-built ability to balance perfectly on very narrow ledges and branches, even when these are rocking and bending. The cat uses its extended claws for grip.

Opposite left: When jumping down, one of the cat's front feet reaches the ground in advance of the other, and partially absorbs the force of impact. Then the second front leg takes the force of the remaining body weight, equalizing the load.

Opposite right: The cat's claws and natural agility make it an adept climber.

Left: Any cat that is not overweight can balance successfully on an area the same size as a man's open palm.

FELINE BEHAVIOUR

Learning about cat behaviour can help to enhance any cat-owner's enjoyment of his or her pet, while an understanding of the animal's basic psychology can assist in simple training and lead to expert husbandry. The cat's highly evolved brain allows for sophisticated patterns of behaviour, some of which are typically mammalian, and others of which are unique to the domestic cat. In this chapter we explore all aspects of feline behaviour, from the cat's normal predatory habits of stalking, hunting and killing, through washing, sleeping and dreaming, to the cat's own effective form of body-language. Since the cat's brain is so similar to that of man, the animal provides an ideal model for psychological experimentation, and though many of us find such use of animals to be unacceptable, it is true to say that during the past few years the cat has been of immense value in research into human behavioural problems.

Cats are often considered to be less intelligent than dogs, mainly because they refuse to perform tricks and often fail to respond to commands. I am not convinced that the performance of unnatural antics necessarily equates with high intelligence, and am more inclined to believe that the cat merely channels its brain power into different avenues of behaviour, enabling it – for instance – to survive if necessary in a strange environment. It could be argued that the cat is in fact more intelligent than the dog.

Cats communicate by a highly developed system of vocalisation and body language.

Although it has a physical component, the nervous system of the cat is of paramount importance in the control of its behaviour, and a brief discussion of its biology is therefore included here.

THE CENTRAL NERVOUS SYSTEM

The central nervous system consists of the brain and the spinal cord, and it controls and co-ordinates all the activities of the cat. Incoming information from the various senses is constantly monitored and analysed for its degree of importance before being further processed. Highly urgent signals receive an immediate response, insignificant signals are discarded, while some signals are accepted and stored away in the memory for future use. Its highly developed mammalian brain and nervous system make the cat among the most perceptive and alert of all animals. Millions of years of evolution have resulted in a carnivore which is both efficient and powerful.

The modern cat's brain still shows some characteristics found in primitive brains. There are three distinct areas, each of which has a separate function. The forebrain is concerned mainly with the sense of smell – an important function in a predator which hunts mainly at dawn and dusk, feasting on small, elusive animals. It also contains the thalamus, which receives impulses from the spinal cord, and the hypothalamus, which controls all the internal regulation processes of the body. The midbrain is the seat of the optic lobes and is concerned mainly with signals received from the eyes. The hindbrain consists of the cerebellum, which is responsible for controlling balance, and the enlarged end of the spinal cord, called the medulla oblongata, which controls the cat's circulatory and respiratory systems.

Though the areas of the brain are clearly defined, all parts are interdependent. In the core, the same functions are performed as in the cat's ancestors, which scurried about long before humans set foot on Earth. This central structure regulates the endocrine glands and controls the animal's respiration and metabolic rate, ensuring that the body keeps all its functions running normally and

Though it may appear to be otherwise, the cat on the right of this picture is the aggressor—ears flattened sideways, chin tucked in, whiskers forwards, tail up, hips well under the body ready to spring, and the head turned for a sideways attacking bite. The cat that is striking is doing so in self-defence, and its body and head postures are all defensive.

provides a constant internal environment. It is the key to life, for it controls and monitors such functions as body temperature, heartbeat and respiration, the balance being regulated by special chemical processes called feedback mechanisms found in the hypothalamus.

Digestion is controlled by a primitive structure called the limbic system, which also monitors and processes any activities requiring sequential responses. This is vital both for the survival of the individual cat and for the species as a whole, for these activities include hunting, eating, mating and escaping, all of which involve steps that must be carried out in the correct sequence for the activity to be totally effective.

The most recently evolved brain area in the cat, as in humans, is the cerebral cortex. This is the region of the brain which controls the 'higher' activities such as vision, perception and memory. It forms the surface layer of the cerebral hemispheres, which resemble a giant shelled walnut, being deeply wrinkled and convoluted thus giving the brain a greater surface area without increasing the size of the animal's skull. The two hemispheres are divided by a deep groove running from the front to the back of the brain. The left hemisphere controls most of the functions of the right side of the body, while the right hemisphere controls the functions of the left side, and a network of neurons (nerve cells) connects both hemispheres in order to correlate all incoming information. The front portion of the cortex controls the function of the legs, the body is controlled by the central regions, and the rear areas control the processing of all visual stimuli. The similarity of the brain of the cat to that of humans has been a prime factor in the animal's extensive use in experiments designed to increase the knowledge and skill of neurosurgeons, and many brain-damaged humans owe their lives and recovery to research carried out on cats, despite the strong feelings this work often evokes when sensationalized in the press.

THE PERIPHERAL NERVOUS SYSTEM

Peripheral or somatic nerves lie outside the spinal cord and act upon the striated muscles attached to the cat's skeleton. These nerves consist of mixed fibres: afferent fibres, which convey incoming information from the skin, whiskers, muscles and joints to the spinal cord, and then on to the brain; and efferent fibres, which carry messages sent by the brain down the spinal cord to the muscles, causing them to react. Each portion of the cat's body has a particular section of the spinal cord that acts as a centre for receiving and sending its own nerve messages.

Circulation and digestion are two examples of activities which continue whether the cat is awake or asleep, and such actions are controlled by the autonomic nervous system. This system has two distinct parts, the nerve fibres which form them being known as sympathetic and parasympathetic nerves. The sympathetic nerves become activated whenever the cat is emotionally aroused, causing increased heartbeat, dilation of the arteries of the heart and muscles and contraction of the arteries of the skin and internal organs. These fibres also cause secretion of hormones into the cat's bloodstream. When this rapid sequence of events takes place, the cat is immediately prepared for any sudden action, for example attack or defence.

The parasympathetic system works in a different manner and affects only one organ at a time, controlling and protecting the body's resources. Both these systems may work simultaneously or may function naturally in a set sequence. A good example of the co-operation of the systems is seen in the complete sex act of the tom cat. First the parasympathetic causes excitement and allows erection of the penis and stimulates mounting behaviour, then the sympathetic system must be employed to enable ejaculation to take place.

A descending cat. Notice the care it takes to ensure each foothold as it negotiates this unnatural ledge.

Above: A young cat exploring the smells and sounds emitted from the fledglings inside a rather vulnerably sited nest box.

Above right: Having located her prey, the lilac tabby has approached as close as possible behind low cover and now crouches, hips and tail swinging rapidly from side to side, building up the necessary momentum for her attacking, leaping run.

Opposite: In play, the kitten learns and develops the motor skills that it will require in subsequent hunting forays.

Domestication has done very little to modify the basic make-up of the cat, and it remains a naturally solitary creature, designed to rely entirely upon its own skills, perception and rapid reactions in order to survive. The high development of their autonomic nervous system enables domestic cats to survive as ferals and strays, even under hostile and dangerous conditions.

PREDATORY BEHAVIOUR

Young kittens begin to exhibit predatory behaviour from the age of about six weeks. In the home, the mother cat may be seen bringing small pieces of meat to the nest box and making a special encouraging sound to attract the youngsters' attention. The cat may pat the meat towards the kittens or even throw it into the air, pouncing on it as it lands and generally acting as though it were a small mouse or bird. The kittens may be attracted to the game and join in, or may appear rather alarmed at the whole procedure. Occasionally, one will pounce on the meat and, making threatening growls, gobble it down. Quite often the mother cat will start to play with the kittens, then quickly eat the meat herself. At this stage of development, the kittens start to practise hunting movements for themselves, crouching in ambush, pouncing on one another and making mock attacking runs from behind the furniture. The mother cat also encour-

ages pouncing and grasping behaviour in her family by sitting quietly beside the nest box and waving her tail from side to side to provide an irresistible target for the kittens' teeth and claws.

Cats normally prefer to hunt alone, and within the confines of their own territory they will have favourite ambush and stalking points. Some cats roam long distances from home to visit particular hunting grounds. Very occasionally cats from the same family learn to hunt together, each seeming to sense the others' intentions as they work out strategic positions and co-operate in carefully timed and judged attacks.

Having excellent vision even in rather poor light conditions means that the cat can hunt successfully in the twilight periods of dusk and dawn. The acute hearing enables the location of prey, and the whiskers, or vibrissae, and sensitive hairs at the ear tips allow the cat to feel its way through dense and entangled undergrowth. The soft paw pads and retracted claws assist silent, speedy movement, while the powerful hindquarters provide propulsion whenever an attacking run or spring is required. The cat attacks in a swift bounding leap, grasping its victim with extended claws and holding it until a disabling bite is delivered. Hungry cats generally dispatch their prey quite quickly, usually with the efficient neck bite practised during kitten playtimes. The well-fed cat, excited by the stalk, hunt and capture, may play

with the prey for some time before the kill is made.

Even the most gentle of pet cats will hunt if given the chance, for despite centuries of domestication, the cat still has a great drive to seek out and catch other small mammals and birds.

If the cat decides to eat large prey, such as rabbits or hares, the entrails are devoured first. After a rest, the cat may then eat the entire carcass, even though it weighs almost as much as its own body, in which case it will probably fast for two or three days before hunting again. With smaller prey, the cat may eat the head first and then devour the rest of the body, including all fur or feathers and bone, regurgitating any undigested parts an hour or two later. Cats eating fresh prey regularly rarely drink because of the high fluid content of the carcasses. Pet cats fed only on processed foods must always have access to fresh drinking water. Eating fresh prey also keeps the cat's teeth and gums in good condition and the jaw muscles well exercised.

The sporting aspect of predatory behaviour may be most easily observed in a cat hunting prey across open ground, when every ounce of its skill is required for even a chance of success. The cat first approaches as near to the prey as it can, using every conceivable means of cover. When it is within reasonable striking distance, the cat flattens its body to the ground and continues on a forward course, gliding fluidly over the ground with belly pressed to the earth, head outstretched on the fully extended neck and ears turned forward to catch every sound. The hips and shoulder-blades provide the highest points of its stalking outline, and these are kept level and low. When the cat senses that the time is right, it builds up momentum by swinging its hips and tail, and then, with a sudden burst of pent-up energy, the body shoots forward in a fast attack.

Playing with disabled or dead prey allows the cat to practise its pouncing and trapping techniques. Highly aroused by such games, the cat may continue to toss the body around for an hour or so, diving and leaping upon it, patting it under objects and hooking it out again with extended claws, passing it under its own body to rake at it with the hindlegs, ignoring the prey and then, as if seeing it for the first time, diving on it again with enormous enthusiasm.

Cats kept entirely indoors should be compensated for their loss of hunting opportunities by providing them with suitable toys and by joining them in hunting games. Catnip-filled mice and other similarly shaped toys are easy to toss, pat and spring upon, while large feathers and furry pipe-cleaners tied to bits of string can be pulled along to encourage pouncing. The stimulation of such interest is important, for it discourages obesity and ensures the survival of the animal should it become lost and a stray. Trying to repress its instincts can only alter the very essence of the creature we like to term 'the tiger in the hearth'.

SLEEPING AND DREAMING

The cat has two quite distinct types of sleep – the light variety taken as a series of catnaps during the day, and deep sleep. During light sleep its blood pressure remains the same as in the waking state, its body temperature drops very slightly and the muscles are in a mildly tensed condition. In deep or paradoxical sleep the blood pressure falls and the temperature rises, while the muscles completely relax. Electroencephalograph recordings, known as EEGs, taken during the light-sleep periods show characteristic slow wave patterns, while similar recordings made during deep sleep show short, jagged patterns. During periods of deep sleep the cat's hearing remains extremely acute and any sharp or sudden noise produces instant arousal.

Cats seem able to sleep at any time of the day or night, in any temperature and in most surroundings, however uncomfortable. A cat obviously prefers a warm, draught-free spot, but the hardness or softness of the surface does not seem to be important, and cats may be seen completely relaxed and dozing contentedly on such unlikely surfaces as corrugated iron, narrow ledges and wire netting. In the home, a cat may choose to sleep on the arm of a chair or with its head hanging downwards over the side, stretched out on its side or on its back. Some cats seem to sleep most of the time while others are content with occasional naps. Small kittens sleep a great deal, and this is important to their development. If the weather is warm, kittens prefer to sleep singly, but if it is cold they will form into a furry pyramid, gently moving in time with their regular breathing. Newborn kittens spend most of their first week of life in deep sleep, and during the next three weeks they have increasing periods of wakefulness. After four weeks, kittens begin to experience light sleep sessions, and this coincides with completion of the formation of the synaptic junctions in their brains.

Dreaming takes place during the periods of deep sleep, and the cat may be seen to twitch, stretch, growl or purr. Its legs may move as though walking or running, the tail may twitch, and the mouth may make sucking-like movements. We cannot know just what the cat dreams about, but it is probably sifting and sorting through its recent experiences, while the brain sorts out and discards irrelevant information and stores useful data in the long-term memory. At least one-third of the cat's sleeping time is spent in deep sleep and this appears to be essential for its full health and well-being. Cats need peace and security in order to enter into this deep phase, and many cats are deprived of sufficient periods of deep sleep while being boarded during the holidays, and so become stressed and ill. In experiments, cats deprived of deep sleep for several weeks experienced a significant speeding up of the heart-beat rate. After the experimental period ended and the cats were able to sleep as and when they chose, they spent very long sessions in deep sleep as though trying to regain the lost periods. It took some time for the cats to regain their normal pattern of alternating periods of light and deep sleep, and it was only then that the heart-beat rates also returned to their normal level.

WASHING

When a cat awakens, it generally stretches and flexes its entire body, yawns and is instantly ready for action. If it has been in the sunlight or under a heat lamp it may well start self-grooming, for it appears that the action of light and warmth on its

coat stimulates the washing action, through which the cat absorbs its nutritional requirement of Vitamin D. To wash itself, the cat uses its tongue and paws. The tongue is particularly well designed for grooming, being covered with tiny projections, called papillae, which enable it to function as a brush and a comb. The cat sits up and licks around its lips and then, licking its preferred paw until it becomes damp, it passes this paw over its face and head, over and into the ear, across the eyes and down the cheek to the chin. The other forepaw is then licked and used in the same manner on the opposite side of the head. Each shoulder and foreleg is licked and groomed in turn, then the flanks, the genital region, the hindlegs and finally the tail from root to tip. When the cat encounters a tangle, a patch of rough skin or a burr, its teeth are brought into action to tease out the problem, and the cat may bite at any patches of dirt it discovers between the toes and on the pads of the paws as part of the grooming programme.

Some cats wash frequently, while others allow their coats to get quite grubby before attempting to clean up. Family cats often indulge in mutual grooming sessions, and may purr and play with one another at the same time. Mother cats spend long periods washing their kittens and this helps to form the necessary bond between them in preparation for the kittens leaving the nest – a vulnerable time in the wild. Many cats wash meticulously after being touched or stroked by humans, obviously trying to erase all traces of the alien scent from their coats. Sick cats may stop washing themselves, and this function must be carried out for them, otherwise they often lose the will to live. A cat is naturally clean and fastidious, and the mere fact that it has been washed and gently groomed often helps towards recovery.

Opposite left: Cats are notorious for adopting seemingly impossible or uncomfortable attitudes for resting and sleeping.

Oposite right: A hindpaw makes an excellent tool for scratching behind the neck and ears.

Above left: Though each cat apparently finds its own favourite self-grooming routine, certain characteristics are common to most felines. The flexible spine allows the rough tongue's application to even the most inaccessible spots.

Above: A well-licked paw is used to wash the face and ears.

Left: Mutual grooming is carried out between friendly cats, but is a social gesture rather than a hygienic one.

TERRITORIAL MARKING

Cats have various methods of identifying property and places. They have scent glands on the head – the temporal glands, above the eyes on either side of the forehead, and the perioral glands along the lips. Both these sets of glands are used for marking by rubbing the head against the chosen object or friend, and there are other marking glands near the root of the tail. When rubbing with the forehead the cat seems to feel pleasurable sensations and often purrs, and when marking with the lips and chin, it becomes almost ecstatic, particularly if another cat has previously marked the same spot. In some cases the cat drools, rubbing its lips firmly against the chosen object, and may even rear up on its hindlegs in order to press the lips or chin even more firmly. The tail glands are used as a sort of period sign after the signature left by the action of the temporal glands. The full sequential action is best observed as a cat insinuates itself into its owner's space by weaving its body around his or her legs, perhaps as a meal is being prepared. The cat winds its body around the legs, leaning inwards and allowing its forehead and lips to rub, followed by the contact of the entire length of its body, and finally the tail is wound round and wiped along the area to be marked.

Territorial marking is also performed by head and tail rubbing, and some cats strop markers at the edge of their boundaries, depositing sweat from the paw pads into the roughened wood. Cats also defecate at their boundaries, and male cats spray urine on their chosen markers. Urine spraying by the entire male cat is the strongest method of feline marking. A very dominant male approaches his markers, turns his back and sprays a few drops of his very distinctive and odorous urine at the object. He may then back up and rub his tail and hindquarters on the spray, or he may turn and vigorously strop the area. Some female cats spray from time to time, particularly those which have been given contraceptive pills to prevent oestrus. They adopt the typical male posture, tail raised and quivering, and direct small amounts of urine backwards at their chosen site. Though their urine does not have the strong scent of the male's spray, it is nevertheless sticky and difficult to clean from wallpaper and household furnishings.

Some neutered cats spray, too, and this behaviour can be particularly annoying if the cat performs indoors and is not noticed until the habit has formed. Spraying often starts due to a change such as the introduction of a new pet or a human baby to the home. Pets may start to spray when their owners are suffering from extreme stress, which is transmitted to the cat. When a veterinarian is presented with a cat that has started this unsociable habit, it is usually traced back to some trauma – death, divorce, even new furnishings!

Free-ranging cats have quite distinct territories which they defend and may try to increase. This is almost always achieved by psychological rather than physical warfare. Most cat fights are more noise than actual battle, though cat fights and skirmishes do occur and are generally brief, bitter and very bloody. Cats usually mark out their own territorial boundaries, and respect those of others. When cats use a communal pathway, they tend to avoid confrontation with other cats and will wait until the pathway is clear before proceeding. Quite often two cats will stare each other out before circling to avoid the necessity to fight. Areas unmarked and, therefore, unclaimed by particular cats are considered neutral ground and provide suitable meeting places for cats to get to know one another, again cutting down unnecessary fights. The defence of territory is too consuming of time and energy to be an ideal pastime for the entire feral male cat. These patterns of avoidance, combined with marking and a set of definite pathways, with routes taken at defined times, ensure that most of his energies can be spent as nature intended, on seeking mates and procreation.

Opposite: A cat may become very possessive over its own scent-marked area. This cat resents the intrusion of its friend, and defends its sleeping basket.

Below left: A male cat scent marking his territory by 'spraying' urine.

Below: A territorial dispute. The resident tabby tom proclaims his territory by patrolling his boundary (1), and spray marking at a scent post (2). A second tom arrives and the tabby erects his fur and arches his back in aggression (3). At this point the intruder could avoid a confrontation by taking up a submissive posture, but instead challenges and a fight ensues (4). The fight ends in victory for the resident tabby, which sees off the intruder (5).

CAT COLONIES

Wild or feral cats live in family groups, some of which have a mature tom cat in attendance, while others are all-female, usually consisting of sisters and their female offspring. Males may lead solitary lives on the outskirts of such groups. Quite a complex hierarchical organization can develop within cat colonies and once the 'pecking' order is established, all cats within the group appear content with the level at which they are accepted by the others.

In a large cat colony each tom is ranked according to his importance and this is decided by confrontations and fights. Once the order is established few fights break out unless a tom decides to attempt to elevate his status, or a newcomer enters the colony.

In feral colonies, where cats may be captured, neutered and then returned to the colony, chaos rules as the hierarchical structure is altered overnight. Status is closely connected with sexuality and neuters lose the feline right, and possibly the will, to remain in exalted positions.

FELINE COMMUNICATION

Cats recognize each other basically by smell, and when two friendly cats meet they normally touch noses and may rub their foreheads together. They sometimes also rub their bodies together and sniff at each other's anal regions. The body language is very expressive indeed, for the cat has a whole range of facial expressions, and also uses its body and tail to convey its feelings and intentions.

An alert cat has an open, direct gaze, and points its whiskers and ears forward. If it is also rather nervous, the nostrils may twitch as it attempts to identify the scent and relate it to the other signals being received from eyes and ears. When a person or animal has been recognized as a friend, the cat's tail goes straight up in a gesture of greeting and it will make an approach.

When a normal, non-aggressive cat receives a threat from another cat or a dog, it first freezes, engaging the intruder with a direct, wide stare, and then the tail starts to flick slowly from side to side, and the ears and whiskers point forward seeking identification. If the intruder approaches more closely, the cat draws in its chin, flattens the ears and gradually turns its body sideways. Simultaneously, the body hairs begin to erect and the tail bushes up. This display is intensified as the intruder gets even nearer and the cat emits fierce snarls. In its most menacing defence position it is completely sideways on to its antagonist and the fur is totally erect over the entire body and tail, presenting the largest possible body area to view. The chin is drawn in to protect the throat, and the eyes are narrowed and focused firmly on the intruder. The ears are laid flat on the head, and the lips are drawn back to reveal the teeth as the cat snarls its warning. The muscles of the cat's back and hindquarters are tensed for fight or flight, and the weight of the front of the body is taken on one leg, while the other leg, with claws unsheathed, is poised to strike. If the antagonist withdraws, as well it might when faced with such opposition, the cat may move forward, grumbling, lip-smacking and salivating, then sniff the ground where the would-be assailant has been, and perhaps strop at the area with the forepaws and spray or defecate before resuming its normal composure.

Extreme agitation in the nervous cat is quite unmistakable. Its eyes open wide and move rapidly from side to side as if seeking an escape route, while its body is crouched down, chin tucked in and ears held sideways. Such a cat is dangerous to touch, for it may react violently as if it is receiving an electric shock. It should be coaxed and 'talked-down' until it resumes a normal appearance.

The expressive tail of the cat speaks volumes to anyone who cares to study the meaning of its many gestures. Carried erect, the tail signals contentment, and stiffly upright conveys a welcome 'hello'. An

erect tail with a slightly waving tip means a contented cat, but one who is not going to stand any nonsense, while a tail lashing from side to side indicates anger and may even warn of an impending attack. A really angry cat holds its tail straight out behind, with all the hairs erect, and just before launching into battle bends the tail over and perhaps also slightly to one side.

Although the structure of the cat's vocal cords is not perfectly understood, it is known to possess superior, or false, cords as well as the inferior, or true, cords. It is believed that the cat's many expressive sounds are produced by the true cords while the false cords may be responsible for the purr. However, zoologists differ in their theories on the purring mechanism, and one school of thought attributes purring to turbulence in the bloodstream of the vena cava, which is the main vein returning blood from the body to the heart. According to this explanation, where the vein constricts to pass by the liver, diaphragm vibrations are set up in the thorax and are passed through the windpipe to echo in the skull's sinuses.

This very frightened little tabby kitten has backed up as far as possible from the source of possible danger, and in order to ward off its attacker assumes a defensive posture. Erecting the coat to look as large as possible it turns sideways on, tucks in its chin to protect its throat and hisses furiously.

Although some cats purr softly and only rarely, most cats regularly purr with contentment and to show affection to those they love. Tiny kittens purr as they nurse from their mother, though they do not purr in response to human strokes until several weeks later. Young cats purr in monotone while older cats purr with two or three regular, resonant tones. Cats may purr in response to a look from their owners, a friendly voice or when groomed, and some purr even in pain, such as labour, or during a terminal illness.

Other feline sounds are more varied than purrs, and most cats have a whole range of vocalizations. The language of the cat can be broken down into three general sound categories. The quietest may be likened to the human murmur, and feline murmuring includes soft purring and the gentle sounds used in acknowledgement or to answer a greeting. Murmuring sounds are made with the mouth closed and can usually be invoked by a high-pitched human 'Mmmmmm?', also made with the mouth shut and with a questioning lift after a duration of a couple of seconds.

The second category of feline sounds may be thought of as vowel sounds, and are all variations of the 'miaow', each being used to express a different need or emotion. They range from the plaintive 'mew' to be let in or out, through the differently pitched 'mee-owww' of complaint, to the amusing 'mr-ow-ow-ow-ow' made by kittens talking over their food. A cat's individual voice is caused by the way in which it produces its vowel sounds, and some cats, mainly the Oriental varieties, often develop very distinctive voices easily recognized by their owners.

The third type of feline sounds includes the high-intensity noises made in communication between cats, often in anger or as a warning. It also includes the scream emitted by the female cat on mating, the shrieking cry of the attacking male and the curious 'judddddrr' made by cats observing birds outside a closed window.

Perhaps the most interesting range of feline sounds is that made by a mother cat as she communicates with her kittens at the critical period when they leave the nest. She encourages them to follow her or to come to her with a soft 'prrrrp?', scolds them with mews and gentle growls, and teaches them to come for food by making a cry very similar to that she gives in oestrus, though softer and often muffled, as she emits it while holding the food in her mouth.

Kittens are able to purr, spit and growl, and have a distinctive urgent distress call which is quite impossible to ignore. As they grow, further sounds are added to the repertoire and the voice is fully developed at about three months, though extra sounds and intonations are added for many months, depending upon the animal's environment and learning opportunities.

Above: A contented cat has upright ears and relaxed whiskers (left). When angry (right) they are brought forward with ears pressed back. When striking out (centre) the eyes narrow, and the cat spits and bares its teeth. **Below:** A cat may turn its head when listening intently, in order to pick up and analyse the slightest sound.

Cats have very strong maternal instincts and make excellent mothers, protecting their litters fiercely when necessary, even at risk to their own lives.

SEXUAL BEHAVIOUR

After reaching sexual maturity, male and female cats may continue to breed throughout life, though the prime years for fertility seem to be from two to eight years in the female cat and from two to seven years in the male. Older females may continue to breed every year, but the number of live kittens diminishes with age. Older entire males continue to seek queens in, season, but take pains to avoid possible confrontations with younger, stronger males. Pet cats fare better than ferals because they do not have to work for their rations and are kept free from cold, danger and parasites.

Most cats prefer to breed in the spring, but, unlike the bitch, the queen does not follow set patterns of oestrus. Some breeds of pedigree cat, notably the Siamese and similar varieties, would have three or four litters each year if allowed their freedom, while other breeds would probably produce two litters each year. The weather plays an important part in the sexual cycle of female cats allowed a fairly natural life with access to a garden or a large outdoor run. Those in artificial environments, kept indoors at all times with carefully monitored central heating and long hours of white light, will breed at any season of the year. Farm and feral cats keep to the normal pattern of reproduction for the species, and usually produce a litter in early spring and another around midsummer. If the weather is very mild, then a third litter may be produced in the early autumn.

Unless constant and very regular periods of oestrus cause a queen to lose weight and general condition, a young pedigree female should be restrained from mating until she reaches ten months of age. This ensures that she will be just over one year old by the time the kittens are born, and so be physically and mentally mature enough to cope with the pressures of lactation and motherhood. Such young queens must be carefully fed throughout their pregnancy, for the development of the kittens in the uterus drains the cat's calcium reserves, which may still be needed for building her own skeleton. Queens seriously lacking in calcium at the time the kittens are born may attack the kittens, and even kill and devour them. This cannibalistic behaviour is brought about by the lack of calcium affecting synaptic junctions in the brain, preventing the transmission of the messages necessary for the release of hormones which simultaneously stimulate the milk flow and trigger the mothering instinct. The long period of lactation also depletes the calcium reserves of the queen and these must continue to be replenished in the diet. In the wild, cats receive all the calcium they require by eating the entire carcasses of their prey. Calcium is abundant in the skeletons of birds and small rodents, and is present in an easily assimilated form. Many pet cats are fed only on high-quality muscle meat which is deficient in this important mineral. Breeders often supplement the diet with cow's milk in order to provide the required calcium, but many cats are unable to digest this properly and so it leads to diarrhoea. When a queen is allowed to breed too frequently her calcium level gradually drops and eventually she may suffer from lactational tetany while feeding the latest litter. This illness is sudden in its onset and the queen may go rapidly into shock; without emergency treatment death quickly follows.

Oestrus in the female cat is quite easy to recognize and consists of four stages. First there is pro-oestrus, in which the reproductive organs undergo changes in preparation for mating, fertilization and pregnancy. During this time the queen is restless, may seem extra-affectionate when stroked, and paces around the house, perhaps going frequently to the door or looking out of the windows. An observant owner may notice a very slight change in the appearance of the vulva at this time.

Some five days after the onset of pro-oestrus, the true oestrus begins and lasts about seven days. This is the receptive period during which the queen is ready and willing to mate. She may become very agitated and roll about on the floor, possibly crying and wailing and trying to get out of the house. As this period reaches a peak, her cries become more and more intense and take on a deeper note, and her rolling becomes more violent. If she is stroked down her spine, the queen takes up the mating position, crouched down, head extended with the chin near the ground, and hindquarters raised with the tail stiffly bent to one side. If mating does not take place, metoestrus begins and the reproductive system relaxes until the resting stage, called anoestrus, is reached. During this the queen remains calm and contented until the next cycle begins.

Top to bottom: In a controlled mating situation, the male cat has no other males to distract or attack him. Once the female shows that she is receptive, the male runs towards her from behind and, straddling her crouched body, grasps the scruff of her neck before mating takes place.

The male cat can mate at any time once he has reached sexual maturity and is not subject to periods of heat, though he is inclined to search out queens more vigorously in the spring and summer than in the autumn and winter months of the year. The male is attracted to the female by her distinctive and evocative odour, and her inviting calls. The scent and cry of a receptive queen is said to carry for some kilometres and is immediately recognized and responded to by the male. Once in close proximity to the calling queen, her posturing and rolling excites the male and he will mount and mate her as quickly as he can.

In controlled breeding, male cats are given their own accommodation, and female cats are brought 'to stud' for mating on the second or third day of oestrus. After a suitable period of acclimatization, with a wire partition or screen keeping them apart, the cats are allowed together and mating

should take place. Pedigree stud cats and feral toms employ exactly the same mating techniques. The receptive female adopts the classic mating position described above and the male, having circled her and possibly attempted to sniff at her tail end, runs to her from behind and to one side and quickly takes the loose skin at the scruff of her neck in his jaws. He waits a moment to test the queen's reaction and then places one foreleg on either side of her shoulders and treads alternately with his hindpaws at her haunches, encouraging her to lift her rump. A receptive queen starts to tread with her own hindlegs at this stage, while an unreceptive queen will wriggle and squirm out of the male's grip and run away. As soon as the queen is settled in the correct position, the male curves his back around into an arc and effects penetration, upon which the queen starts to cry with a low growling note gradually rising in intensity. A few rapid rhythmic thrusts of the male's hips produce ejaculation, after which the male releases the queen and jumps well away. The queen snarls, hisses and growls and may pursue the male, striking out with unsheathed claws, before rolling vigorously about on the floor and pushing herself along with outstretched limbs. After a moment or two both cats sit quietly and begin to clean their genital areas, and very soon after both cats will be willing and able to mate again.

Compatible cats mate frequently throughout the queen's oestrus. In the wild, several cats may be attracted to one female and she will hold court as her suitors square up to one another. Much caterwauling occurs as the males decide their order of priority and dominance, and a few short and bitter battles may break out between equally dominant toms. Sometimes an inferior male takes the opportunity to mate with the female while his superiors are engaged in the power struggle, but it is normally the most dominant male in the neighbourhood that mounts and mates with the female. She may mate with the same male several times or with several different males.

The entire male cat, allowed to come and go as he pleases, treats his home merely as a shelter and a place to draw his daily rations. He is motivated at all times by his powerful sexual drive, and spends his days in patrolling and spray-marking his territory, seeking and mating queens, and fighting to underline his dominance whenever necessary. These activities are punctuated by long periods of rest and recuperation. When toms fight, their long canine teeth can inflict deep puncture wounds which will quickly seal on the surface but trap bacteria beneath the skin, leading to the formation of painful abscesses.

On meeting, two toms confront each other in a threat display, puffing out their cheeks and huffing,

Though cats make a great deal of noise during fights, in many cases they inflict little serious damage to one another.

The mother cat teaches skills to her kittens from the moment they start to toddle out of the nest.

and sometimes salivating as they emit low growls. Hunching up the hips and shoulders and drawing in the chin, both cats try to look as large and as powerful as possible. If no female is nearby to aggravate the situation, the cats often circle, avoid direct contact and eventually pass on their respective ways, but otherwise the threat may develop into a full-scale fight.

A fight commences with stiff-legged circling and then each cat lunges at the other's throat and bites as hard as possible. The cats lock together in a rolling ball of flying fur as they rake each other with the claws of their back legs. When they break apart, one may attempt to run away and will sometimes receive a deep bite at the root of the tail or testes – the final insult delivered by the victorious tom. On subsequent meetings, a male who has asserted his dominance in this way may underline his position in the neighbourhood by approaching a submissive male, biting his neck and mounting him briefly before letting go and walking away on stiff legs. A submissive male usually takes steps to avoid such confrontations, or crouches and presents his scruff to his superior. Cats very rarely indulge in homosexual behaviour, and the mounting by the dominant male is merely to show superiority. Male cats seldom fight with females, but females may fight through jealousy – over the attentions of a human, perhaps – or over food.

MATERNAL BEHAVIOUR

From puberty, the behaviour patterns of the female cat are tuned to pregnancy and motherhood, and she will be persistent in her desire to mate in order to fulfil her destiny. Cats are spontaneous ovulators – that is, they shed ripe ova only after the act of mating – and if mating is regularly denied a queen may become sterile or go through periods of false pregnancy.

The female cat makes a model mother, secreting her young from predators and any other dangers, and keeping them spotlessly clean and well fed from the moment of birth. She cares for her kittens in a totally selfless, dedicated manner until they are able to feed themselves and face the world alone. The males take no part in the rearing of kittens, though in some feral colonies males have been observed playing with weanlings.

Once the queen has mated and the fertilized ova have implanted in the uterine wall, hormones secreted by her glands give rise to certain patterns of behaviour. She becomes more sensitive to dangers, her appetite increases and she grooms herself more meticulously than ever. If she is a free-ranging cat, she will hunt with more purpose and eat her prey, and she will also browse on a range of selected grasses and herbs. As her pregnancy progresses she takes extra care in selecting safe, dark, sleeping sites. Her grooming sessions increase and she pays extra attention to her enlarging breasts. Her increasing girth may make her toilet of the anal area rather difficult, and the thoughtful owner can help to keep her clean with a dampened tissue.

As the gestation period of about nine weeks reaches its end, the queen explores every possible nesting site for the impending birth. Cats do not always display good judgement in their final selection, and so it is a sensible precaution to confine a heavily pregnant cat to one room, with several suitable boxes, until the kittens are safely born. The room should be one in which the cat feels secure and comfortable, well away from young children, dogs, noisy teenagers and general hustle and bustle. The box or boxes provided should be dark and contain plenty of paper for the queen to rip up for her nest.

When the birth is imminent, the queen paces restlessly and may go frequently to her toilet tray. First-stage labour can be very long and drawn out, and the cat rarely accepts food during this time. When second-stage labour commences the queen will, with a little encouragement, go into her box. With a first litter, the birth of the first kitten may take a long time, and the queen's contractions become stronger and more frequent. Kittens may be born head first or tail first, both presentations being equally common. Prior to the expulsion of the first kitten, a sac of fluid may be passed, which is quite normal and prepares the way for the birth. The sac may be licked away by the labouring queen before being observed by her owner.

The membranes of the sac are licked away from the body of the newborn kitten by the mother's rough tongue, which also helps to encourage the infant's regular breathing to expand its tiny lungs. The placenta is passed, still attached to the kitten by the umbilical cord. The queen usually eats

the placenta, and then chews the cord to within a couple of centimetres of the kitten's body. This stump dries within a few hours and drops off to leave a neat navel within ten days.

After the birth of the first kitten, the rest of the litter follow at regular or irregular intervals and the queen usually deals with them all in the same determined, businesslike manner. When the last kitten has been born, the cat washes her own legs and genital region. She then gathers all the kittens together and, lying on one side, encircles them with her body, encouraging them to nurse. Purring contentedly and kneading with her forepaws, she relaxes and may not leave the nest for about ten or twelve hours. Eating the rich placentas provides enough nourishment for the queen for at least a full day after her kittens' birth.

It would appear that the normal instincts for hunting and eating prey are hormonally suppressed

Above: A proud and protective mother and her young kitten.

Left: The newborn kitten is licked quite vigorously to clean away the foetal membranes and to stimulate respiration.

during the time the queen is giving birth. This is probably to ensure that the newborn kittens are not eaten, and explains why a newly confined mother cat will accept virtually any young animal for fostering at this time. Even baby rats, squirrels and hedgehogs, normally prey, are accepted and fostered by cats.

Young kittens only urinate and defecate when stimulated to do so by the licking action of the mother's rough tongue. After nursing the youngsters, the queen washes and grooms each one in turn, and swallows all the excreted material, keeping the nest spotlessly clean. Once the kittens start eating solids, at four to five weeks of age, the excreted material changes dramatically in its constitution and the queen ceases this cleaning routine, the kittens being encouraged to empty themselves well away from the nest.

Three to four weeks after the kittens' birth, the queen may decide to move the litter to a new nest. This behaviour is logical in the wild, for the nest may be starting to get stale and attract predators, and even after centuries of domestication some queens still get an uncontrollable urge to move home. Having found another, often quite unsuitable, nest the queen takes each kitten in turn and moves it. She grasps a kitten right around the neck, holding it in her jaws yet somehow managing to avoid marking it with her teeth, and then, lifting her head, carries it between her straddled forelegs to its new bed. The kitten's normal response to being held in this way is to draw its legs up into the foetal position and let its body go completely limp. The kittens rarely suffer any harm through being moved, but it is as well to check that they are warm, out of draughts and not on some high ledge or shelf from which they could fall and injure themselves.

As the kittens grow and eat solids, the mother gradually weans them and her milk supply dries up. She encourages play-hunting and mock fighting, and, in the wild, would keep the kittens with her until almost full grown and totally independent.

For the first few weeks, the queen is kept very busy feeding her kittens and keeping them spotlessly clean.

CHOOSING A CAT

When people first decide that a cat would make an ideal pet, they often give little thought to the diversity of types, breeds and colours which are available in the wide world of domestic felines. Though most cats are of basically the same size, they do vary slightly in character depending on the breed or basic type, and certain varieties need more upkeep and coat care than others. Therefore, it is important to choose the cat which will best fit in with your own temperament, life-style and leisure time.

Two cats are always better than one, for the feline has a mysterious mathematical formula all its own in which two cats together seem able to provide more than double the happiness afforded its owner by one cat. In human terms this means that two cats play more and give more love and affection, so that having two cats will more than doubly repay the extra cost of owning the second one. Two cats eat better, relax better and will keep each other company while you are working or on vacation.

The important point when choosing a cat is to select the breed with the right character and temperament, the right type of coat and, least important perhaps, the right colour. Ensure your kitten is in good health, properly reared and weaned, free from parasites and has a sweet nature, and then you can expect to have a loving pet around the house for many years to come.

Farm kittens can be as appealing as those from a pedigree litter.

Various factors must be taken into account before deciding which cat to take into your home. First you need to consider whether you would prefer a pedigree or a non-pedigree cat, whether it should be male or female, whether you want to breed or show your pet, and whether you want to start with a young kitten or, perhaps, give a home to a needy adult. Of course, one or other of these factors may be decided for you, for cats often seen able to make decisions for humans – many cats and kittens in need of new owners have been lucky enough to find the perfect homes quite by chance.

Cats are great company and are not as demanding as dogs. They are clean, need very little exercise and can be kept in places where a dog would be a disaster. Today's heavy traffic and dire dangers for cats – including theft for their fur or for vivisection – have caused many owners to keep their pets carefully confined indoors, and cats live quite happily under such conditions so long as they are given lots to do, plenty of companionship and a good, balanced diet. Changing a litter tray soon becomes routine, and a log or carpet-covered cat tree takes care of the animal's need to strop its claws.

Your own life-style and temperament should be taken into account when deciding on the right cat or kitten. Some breeds are naturally quiet and self-effacing, some are complete extroverts, while many are middle-of-the-road types, enjoying a good romp but being generally undemanding.

Taking a fully grown cat into the home needs careful planning. The transition must be made as calm as possible, for the cat will be disturbed by its change of environment. You must make sure that all possible escape routes are blocked and that everything is done for the animal's peace, comfort and safety during its acclimatization. Taking in a kitten is less troublesome and traumatic, but bear in mind that it may need five small meals a day at first, and should not be left alone for long at such a critical stage in its life.

MALE OR FEMALE?

The sex of your cat is important. If you want to breed cats, you should buy the best female that you can afford, in the breed you have carefully selected as being just right for you. If possible, buy two females of the same age and preferably from the same background, but of different bloodlines. These will form a good foundation for your own strain in generations to come. Never buy a 'breeding pair' of cats – there is simply no such thing. Granted, you need a male and a female in order to produce kittens, but your specially selected females can, when mature, be taken to an equally carefully selected stud male, and you can use different males for each subsequent litter while you attempt to produce the kitten of your dreams. Keeping a stud male is a job for the very experienced, not the novice, and cannot be undertaken lightly.

In males (top), the anal opening is separated from the opening concealing the penis by the testicles. In females (above), the anus and vaginal slit are closer.

Foreign Shorthair

Longhair or Persian

British Shorthair

ONE CAT OR TWO?

For people who primarily want pets, the ideal choice is two cats, preferably from the same background and of similar or complementary type, either of the same or opposite sex, and both neutered as they reach puberty. In this way the cats have the chance to develop their true characteristics, but will give no problems, such as unwanted kittens or unsocial behaviour patterns. You will have pets which you may show if you wish, in special neuter-cat classes, and which should live good, long, healthy lives. You will also find that two neutered cats reared and raised together will love one another and play together well into old age.

Some cats, particularly those of Oriental descent, loathe being left alone for any length of time. If this is the type that appeals strongly to you, why not consider having two? The two cats, brought up together, will become inseparable friends, keeping each other company whenever they have to be left at home or in the boarding cattery.

NON-PEDIGREE OR PEDIGREE?

Non-pedigree cats come in all types, shapes and colours, and may be acquired from the local cat sanctuary, pet shop, through advertisements in the press or you may hear of a neighbour or a farmer with kittens needing homes just at the opportune moment. Whatever the source, you must make

absolutely certain that the cat or kitten you choose is healthy and strong.

Pedigree kittens should be bought from a breeder, never through a pet shop or agency. All good breeders insist on meeting the prospective owners of their carefully bred youngsters, and want to be assured that the kittens are going to knowledgeable, caring homes. You can see most of the available breeds and their colours and varieties by visiting cat shows. There are many such events held in major towns every year, and these are advertised in the cat press and sometimes on radio and television. At a cat show you are able to wander around the pens until you see a breed that really appeals to you, then you can find the owner and

Left: An Oriental Lilac or Lavender. This breed is lively, intelligent and easy to groom, like all the Oriental varieties.

Below and opposite below: Built on the same basic body plan, the major types of pedigree cat nevertheless show quite distinct differences in coat and body build.

Siamese   Rex (Devon)   Semi-longhair (Birman)

talk about your fancy. Every breeder will regale you with the attributes of his or her favourite breed, and it will be up to you to analyse its true characteristics. Many kittens may be on sale, and usually look very appealing. However, you should resist the temptation to buy at the show, for the stress of a long day out, allied with the teething period, and following soon after an intensive weaning and vaccination programme, may cause some kittens to be a little off-colour for a few days. Back in their usual environment they will quickly bounce back to health, but being taken by a new, well-meaning owner to an unknown home may prove a little too much and the kitten could be set back severely in its development. If you decide you want a particular kitten at a show, pay a deposit and agree to collect it ten days later. This gives it time to get over the show, and gives you time to prepare your home for the arrival of the new member of the family. While at the show, however, you could take the opportunity to purchase equipment for your litter.

WHAT TO LOOK FOR

Whether you decide on a pedigree or a non-pedigree cat, you will need to look for the same basic factors when actually selecting your kitten. First and foremost the kitten must have been properly weaned, and this does not mean merely that it is capable of eating some solids while still receiving some of its mother's milk. It should have been on solids for several weeks and totally removed from its mother's milk for at least a fortnight before going to a new home. Many people believe erroneously that a kitten which is seen eating four small meals a day must be weaned. In fact, it probably still consumes a surprising amount of its mother's milk, and its digestion may still be tuned to such specialized food. The sudden withdrawal of the queen's milk, allied to the stress of entering a new environment, can cause gastritis.

The kitten you choose as your new pet and companion should look clean and smell wholesome. Its body should be firm and slender with no sign of a potbelly, which could indicate an infestation of internal parasites, and the ribs and hips should be well covered. Underneath the tail, the genital area should look clean, for any staining points to loose stools or diarrhoea. Next, examine the head carefully. The kitten should have clear, bright eyes, with no sign of discharge, and the third eyelid should not be visible at the inner corners of the eye. The inside of the ears should look clean and slightly moist; any dark flecks could be the result of ear mites, parasites which are quite difficult to eradicate. The mouth should look healthy with pink gums and sharp white teeth, and the tongue should be pink with no sign of any ulceration. The nostrils should be clean with no discharge, and the breath should be sweet.

ASSESSING A KITTEN

Whether you buy your kitten from a dealer, or from an acquaintance whose queen has just produced a litter, you will want to be sure that the kitten is in good condition and not carrying any diseases or other ailments which will cause you problems at a later date. Having made your initial choice from a litter, use the visual checklist here to help you determine the health of your prospective purchase.

First of all, check the body for firmness and lack of lumps, etc., and look to see that the rear end is clean.

The kitten's eyes will tell you a great deal about its general health, and should be clear and bright.

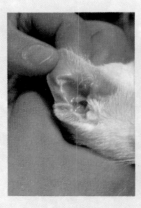

Inside, the ears should look fresh, slightly moist and spotlessly clean – dark grits indicate mites.

The mouth should be clean and pink and the teeth bright and sharp. Look for soreness or ulceration.

The coat should be clean and soft. Look for signs of fleas behind the ears and along base of spine.

The kitten should wear its skin like a very loose overcoat. If you lift the skin gently between thumb and forefinger at the scruff of the neck, it should spring back into place when released; if the skin remains pinched up for a while, the kitten is suffering from dehydration. The coat should be soft and smell fresh, and you should part it at the base of the tail and behind the ears. Any dark gritty specks here are likely to be flea-dirt – the excreta of the cat flea, left behind when the flea feeds on the animal's blood. Fleas carry cat diseases, so never buy a kitten which has been infested with these pests.

Once you have satisfied yourself that the kitten seems healthy, ask for pedigree papers if it is a purebred kitten and discuss details of any vaccinations that it has had or that it will require. With pedigree kittens, it is advisable also to ask to see copies of its parents' certificates of testing against feline leukaemia, and to find out whether or not your kitten has been registered and with which bodies, and to obtain the relevant papers with which to transfer ownership to your own name.

Before taking your kitten away, remember to ask for details of its diet. If you are at all confused, the breeder will issue you with a written diet sheet to help you through the transition stage.

When making your choice of cat you will be faced with an enormous variety: the coat may be longhaired, semi-longhaired or shorthaired; and you may have a cat of the snub-nosed, chunky type, the long, svelte and elegant type, or of intermediate type. Most non-pedigree cats fall into the intermediate category, though some do have profuse coats, and these can be a problem to groom unless they are carefully trained from early kittenhood. In the pedigree cat world you will find every combination of coat length, colour and pattern you could imagine and, therefore, there has to be a cat that is exactly right to suit anyone's taste.

In Chapter 5, the breeds are divided into six main groups, and the colours and patterns discussed are common to most of the cats within these groups. First, there are the Persians or Longhairs – chunky, heavyweight cats with round faces, huge round eyes, small ears and long, profuse, flowing coats. The Shorthairs are similar to the Longhairs in conformation, being round and cobby, but have dense short fur. Both the Longhairs and the Shorthairs have quiet, gentle natures and are very undemanding except, of course, that the Longhairs require daily grooming to keep the coat from matting.

Opposite top: It is often difficult to choose a kitten, especially when faced with a wide choice, as presented by this Seal Point Siamese queen with her own and foster kittens.

Above left and left: When choosing a kitten, Persians, such as these, are very appealing, but it should be remembered that the long coats need extra regular care and grooming.

Unlike the Persian, the Birman has a fine, silky coat which is less likely to form mats and tangles. Nevertheless, it needs regular grooming to maintain it in the good condition shown by this beautiful Blue Point.

The Orientals include the distinctive Siamese cats and all the varieties bred from Siamese ancestry. All have long, fine bodies, wedge-shaped heads, almond eyes and large pointed ears. The coat is very short, fine and silky. The Semi-longhairs are similar to the Orientals in bone structure but have long, silky fur. This group contains the Balinese, the Somali, the Turkish, the Birman, the Ragdoll, the Angora, the Turkish Angora and the Maine Coon. The Orientals and Semi-longhairs are very outward-going cats, interested in everything going on around them and wanting to be part of the activities within the family. The Oriental coat is easy to keep in good condition with a minimum of hand grooming, while the Semi-longhairs do need brushing regularly, but the coat does not mat like the softer coat of the Persian.

The Foreign group contains some diverse breeds of cat, not so extreme in structure as the Orientals. The Burmese is a cousin of the Siamese but is heavier in bone, and is unlike any other cat in character, being inquisitive and rather mischievous. The Abyssinian, with its unique, ticked coat, rather like a wild rabbit's, is inclined to be rather reserved but fiercely loyal to its owner. The Korat, perhaps the most ancient of all breeds, has a silver-blue, shorthaired coat and beautiful, lustrous eyes, and is, perhaps, the cat for the connoisseur. Finally, the Russian is a green-eyed cat with a dense blue coat, which makes a wonderfully loving, quiet-voiced but amusing pet. All the Foreigns are easy to keep, though they do not do well as single pets. They are easy to train and groom, and respond well to lots of love and plenty of play.

The last group contains the cornish Rex and the Devon Rex, two curly coated breeds which are available in every known cat colour.

COAT COLOURS AND PATTERNS

Tabby cats Tabby is the most common coat pattern of domestic cats throughout the world and includes diverse markings and colours. The tabby pattern varies from the ticked type, as seen in the Abyssinian cat, where each hair has bands of colour, through the mackerel-striped and the closely related spotted design to the very precise whorls of the blotched or classic tabby coat. However, all are the result of one gene, known as agouti, which alone determines whether a cat's coat pattern is tabby or non-tabby.

The ticked tabby may not be the most common coat pattern found in domestics today, but it closely approximates to the wild-type coat, and may still be seen in species such as the jungle cat, and several small wild felines which inhabit arid regions of the world. In the wild, the agouti gene produces excellent coat patterns for camouflage, enabling species so clothed to merge into their natural

environment, ensuring their success in ambush and in hiding from larger predators. The agouti gene is dominant to the non-agouti gene, which allows a cat to have a plain black, blue or any other non-tabby coat. This means that a kitten needs only one tabby parent in order to be born a tabby, and also ensures that two non-tabby parents are unable to produce tabby kittens.

Non-pedigree cats come in a very wide range of tabby patterns, but the blotched variety is probably the most common. The majority of these tabbies are shorthaired, though quite a lot of semi-longhaired tabbies are also seen, especially in feral colonies. Some non-pedigree tabbies have a strong tawny shading underlying the tabby pattern, and many have white markings, particularly on the legs and throat.

Pedigree tabbies must conform to very precise standards of points drawn up by the various registering bodies, following the desires of breeders. Different countries of the world recognize slightly different colour ranges for tabby Longhairs and Shorthairs, but here only the basic patterns and colours will be discussed. Whether the tabby pattern is ticked, striped, spotted or blotched, it is likely to be made up of the basic cat coat colours, except in the Abyssinian and its derived breeds, where the colours are modified.

Tabby is the natural coat pattern of the domestic cat, and it is easy to see why. This non-pedigree grey tabby is very well camouflaged even in a modern garden setting. Imagine how he would look in a totally natural, wild environment.

The black form of tabby is misleadingly called the brown tabby, and this colouring is found in the Longhairs, Shorthairs, Orientals and Rex cats. A brown tabby has a ground colour of a rich light brown, with jet black tabby markings overlaying it. The dilute form of the brown tabby, the blue tabby, is much rarer and has a ground colour of a light warm grey, with tabby markings of slate blue. The chocolate tabby is only commonly found in the Oriental group, and then generally in spotted and blotched patterns. Its warm fawn coat bears bright bronze markings. An elusive 'light' gene affects some chocolate cats, producing a lighter, brighter chocolate tabby known as the cinnamon tabby. When the 'dilute' gene is present with chocolate, the lilac tabby may occur. This has a light mushroom-coloured coat with an often faintly etched pattern of a deeper lilac-grey.

Red tabby cats are found in several breeds and, unlike their non-pedigree counterparts, which are usually a light, bright ginger, pedigrees must have markings in deep rich red on a lighter ground colour. The dilute form, known as the cream tabby, is rarely seen on the show bench. Silver tabby cats are very beautiful, and pedigree versions are found in the Longhairs, Shorthairs, Orientals and Rex cats. The base coat colour is virtually white, and in the black-silver, the black tabby markings, whether ticked, striped, spotted or blotched, give the undercoat a silver appearance. Other colours may overlay the silver, though these are rarely seen except in the Orientals and the Rex cats, and include the blue-silver tabby, the chocolate-silver tabby, the cinnamon-silver tabby and the lilac-silver tabby.

When tortoiseshell colouring accompanies the agouti, tabby-tortoiseshell cats, which are almost without exception females, may occur in all colour combinations and patterns. In Britain, these are called tortie-tabbies, but in the United States they are generally referred to as torbies.

Black and blue cats From the original wild-type agouti cats, the first variant to appear was almost certainly the pure black or melanistic form, caused by a simple spontaneous mutation which effectively blots out the tabby banding on the animal's coat. Melanistic animals often appear in wild populations of feline species. In the leopard, for example, the jet-black panther is commonly born to the normally spotted mother.

Right: Lilac or lavender is the dilute form of chocolate, and is further modified in appearance by the coat pattern in which it appears. In the Oriental or Foreign Lilac (shown here), the coat colour should be pinkish-grey.

Far right: There are several self blue breeds. This is a Russian Blue kitten.

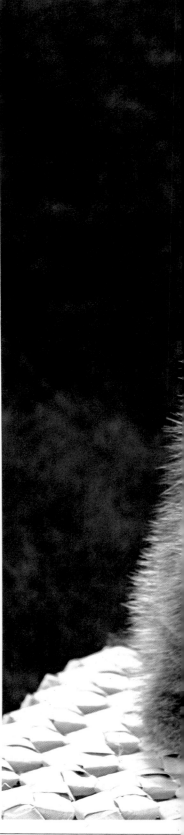

To meet pedigree standards, black cats are required to be just that – pure jet black without any white hairs or shadowy tabby markings. Black is an accepted colour right through the Longhair, Shorthair, Oriental and Rex groups, accompanied by its dilute form, the blue. Blue colouring has always been greatly favoured by cat fanciers, and has been selected for in virtually every known breed. There are even some recognized breeds which are only accepted in their blue form, notably the Korat, the lucky cat of Thailand.

Chocolate and lilac cats Though rarely seen in non-pedigree cats, chocolate and its dilute form lilac are popular colours for the more exotic pedigree breeds. Chocolate, like blue, is a modified form of the black pigment melanin. When the cat's genetic make-up causes the melanin to break down and form into certain clumps the cat's coat appears blue, and a different gene can cause the clumping to occur in a different pattern, making the coat look chocolate-coloured. These effects are caused by the action of quite separate genes, but they can work together, when the cat's coat will appear lilac. The genes for blue and chocolate are recessive to the dominant gene for black colour. While blue cats appeared spontaneously in cat families, the first record of the chocolate colouring is attributed to Chocolate Point Siamese cats imported to Britain from the East at the turn of this century. Most of today's chocolate-coloured varieties obtained their preliminary doses of the appropriate gene from outcrossings to suitable Siamese, followed by several generations of backcrossing to cats of the required conformation, thus retaining the new colouring while regaining the desired type.

Chocolate is a very variable colour in cats, ranging from a light bland shade resembling a milk-chocolate bar to a rich dark shade similar to plain cooking chocolate. When the 'light' gene is also present, the chocolate colouring is further lightened and brightened – for example, in the Abyssinian cat, this gene changes the normal colouring to a light rufous tone; in the tabby, it produces a bright coppery tone; and it transforms the Havana or Oriental Chestnut into an Oriental Cinnamon, a light reddish chestnut in colour.

Lilac in the cat has been well described as a sort of pinkish grey colour and, like chocolate, it is very variable, often depending for its intensity on hair length and density. It is also grossly affected by the agouti gene, and the lilac colour of a Lilac Tabby Oriental is quite different to that of a Lilac Oriental. The 'light' gene also functions in combination with lilac to produce cats known as fawn in some countries of the world and caramel in others. 'Light' lilac is, as might be expected, a paler, more ethereal version of standard lilac colouring, but it is often difficult to identify except by the most experienced of fanciers or judges.

Red, cream and tortoiseshell cats Red is really the pedigree term for ginger and is caused by the action of a semi-sex-linked gene. Cream is the simple dilute version of red and obeys the same genetic rules when mixed with other colours and patterns. Red and cream varieties are found in all breeds, and even in non-pedigree populations whole colonies of gingers and tortoiseshells abound. A problem encountered by breeders of pedigree reds and creams is that these colours often let the ghost tabby pattern, normally invisible in cats of other colours, show through. This means that many genetically self-coloured red and cream cats look like red tabbies or cream tabbies. One breed that has overcome this problem by careful selection is the Burmese, where the red and cream varieties are often virtually unmarked.

Tortoiseshell is the term used for cats with coats consisting of a mixture of red and black hairs, usually clumped together to form random patches and sometimes intermingled. Just as the dilute gene affects red to produce cream, so it affects the tortoiseshell to give blue-cream. When the chocolate gene is added to red, chocolate-tortoiseshell is produced with chocolate and light red patches. The addition of chocolate and dilute genes to red gives the lilac-cream variety, a very pretty coloration with palest lilac and pastel beige patches. White-spotting

Opposite top: This bright, alert kitten is a Red Spotted British Shorthair.

Opposite bottom: Tortoiseshell is the term given to female cats in which the coat is an admixture of black and red patches. This is a well-marked British Shorthair.

Left: The inhibitor gene acts on the cat's coat colour and causes the silver effect. When present in conjunction with the gene for agouti, or the wild type coat, a silver tabby cat will result, and may be Classic, Spotted, Mackerel or Ticked, the patterns distinctly marked on a silver basecoat.

genes added to tortoiseshell produce tortie-and-white or calico cats. Almost all tortoiseshell cats are female due to the semi-sex-linked nature of the red gene, and any males produced generally prove sterile.

White cats White cats appear in the Longhair, Shorthair, Oriental and Rex groups; there are White Turkish in the Semi-longhair group, and in the Foreign group breeders are working on the development and recognition of the Russian White. White is an absence of colour produced by a dominant gene, and this means that kittens may be produced when only one parent is white and that white kittens cannot be born unless one parent, at least, is white.

Most white cats of pedigree breeds occur in three sub-varieties named according to eye colour. In Longhair and Shorthair varieties, they may be orange- or copper-eyed, blue-eyed or odd-eyed, where one eye is orange or copper and the other eye is blue. In the Oriental White true Siamese blue eye colour is required, while in the Russian White the eyes must be clear green.

The white gene sometimes causes deafness, particularly in the blue-eyed Longhairs and Shorthairs. The gene affects the cochlea shortly after the kitten's birth, causing loss of hearing. In some odd-eyed white cats, deafness is only apparent in the ear adjacent to the blue eye.

Bi-colour cats This term is usually applied to cats of normal feline colours with the addition of large areas of white caused by the action of the white-spotting gene, which has the effect of masking off patches of the coat's normal colour. Selective breeding has resulted in very evenly marked bicolour cats, which may be of any standard cat colour with white. There are bicolour Longhairs and Shorthairs, and the pattern is also found in the Cornish Rex. More extensive areas of white spotting produce harlequin or calico cats. Harlequin cats are white, with patches of one other colour, while Calico cats are white with markings of two other colours, such as red and black or blue and cream.

Silver cats A gene called an inhibitor is responsible for silver colouring in the cat, and it works by suppressing the development of pigment in areas of the coat. As mentioned earlier, when allied to the tabby pattern the inhibitor gene produces a striking effect with black markings showing bold and clear against the near-white base coat. When the inhibitor acts in the presence of the non-agouti gene, a whole range of rare and beautiful feline coat colours may be produced.

Perhaps the best known of all silver breeds is the Chinchilla, renowned for its great beauty and photogenic appeal. It is a Longhair with a pure white coat lightly tipped with black at the end of each hair to produce the silvered effect. Heavier tipping or shading produces colours known as shaded silver or pewter, and cats with such heavy tipping that they appear almost self-coloured are known as smoke cats. Short-coated versions of the Chinchilla are found in the Shorthair, Oriental and Rex groups, and are called silver-tipped cats. These groups also contain shaded silver and smoke varieties. The red gene allied to the inhibitor produces a whole range of varieties called cameos. Red- or cream-tipped silvers are known as Shell Cameos, heavier tipping results in Shaded Cameos and the very heavily tipped varieties are called Cameo Smokes. In some American associations, the red cameo Longhairs are known as the Red Chinchilla, the Red Shaded and the Cameo Red. Cameo varieties exist in most of the groups, and there are also occasional tortoiseshell variations, where black and red or blue and cream overlay the silver-white undercoat.

Himalayan cats This colouring is produced by a gene known as the Himalayan factor, which has the effect of reducing the colouring of the coat so that it only appears in its full intensity at the cat's extremities, correctly termed its points. Allied to the distinctive colouring produced by the Himalayan factor is eye colour, which in these colourpointed cats is always a definite blue. The points of Himalayan-patterned cats can be of any known feline colour and, traditionally, cats with black extremities are called seal points, while the others are more logically known as blue points, chocolate points, lilac points, red points and so on.

This factor produces several breeds of cat, including the Colourpoint Persian (known as the Himalayan in the United States), the Siamese in the Oriental group, Shorthaired Colourpoint or Himalayan, Balinese, Birman and Ragdoll cats in the Semi-longhairs, and Si-rex.

Burmese cats The effect of the Burmese gene is to produce a cat showing very slight points of greater intensity than the body colour, although this effect has been almost eliminated by selective breeding. The Burmese range of colours is interesting to observe, especially when each is compared with its Oriental equivalent, for each Burmese colour is several tones or shades lighter. The Brown Burmese, for example, though genetically black, appears to be a dark chocolate brown, while the Blue Burmese is only slightly darker and colder in tone than the Oriental Lilac. Red and Cream Burmese may show ghost head markings.

Though it is genetically a black cat, the Brown Burmese, as its name suggests, appears to be a dark brown cat to the human eye.

Rex cats There are two Rex breeds, called the Cornish Rex and the Devon Rex after the counties of England in which they were discovered. Both have distinctively curled coats, but each is caused by a quite different gene, and so the cats are never crossed.

In the Cornish Rex, only a few guard hairs, often looking more like awn hairs, usually occur, and in some cats the awn hairs, too, are missing. This leaves a short, fine, silky undercoat, which ripples into tight waves and feels like soft velvet. The Devon Rex coat feels more like suede than silk, for the guard hairs are modified instead of being missing, and resemble awn hairs, with uneven length and split, broken ends. Devon Rex often have sparsely furred bodies, with longer hair forming ringlets on the abdomen and curls on the tail, limbs and behind the ears.

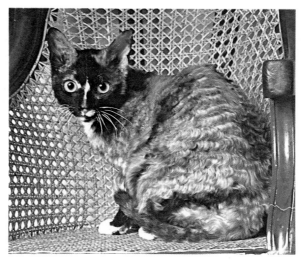

This Tortie-and-white Cornish Rex (left) has a superbly waved coat, as has the white Devon Rex, pictured taking the Spring sunshine (below).

PEDIGREES OF THE WORLD

Though there appears to be a very large range of cat breeds, pedigree cats may be simply divided into six groups. First there are the Persians: these are longhaired cats of stocky build, with a round head, round eyes, round paws and a short, thick tail. Their shortcoated counterparts, the British, American and European Shorthairs, are all very similar, as are the Exotics, bred from a Persian crossed with a Shorthair. A long, svelte and elegant body, with fine bone, a long head, oriental eyes, tiny oval paws and a long, tapered tail are the hallmark of the Orientals, the Siamese and the Siamese-derived varieties. The semi-longhaired group consists of cats with Oriental conformation but long silky coats, or with conformation halfway between that of the Oriental and the Shorthair, but still with long, flowing coats and brush-like tails.

The Foreign Shorthairs are all distinctive breeds, each with its own standard for conformation, coat type, colour and pattern. This group includes the Abyssinian, the Burmese, the Korat, the Russian Blue and others. Rex cats are curly coated and are of different genetic origin. Less extreme than the Orientals, the Cornish Rex has fine bones, while the Devon Rex is distinguished by its pixie-like face and huge bat ears. Though different countries of the world have slightly different breed standards for their pedigree cats, the feline varieties remain remarkably constant.

A superb Seal Point Birman, a Semi-longhaired variety.

LONGHAIRS OR PERSIANS

Today's wonderful range and variety of Longhairs are the descendants of two quite distinct types of long-coated cats brought to Europe during the sixteenth century. The first was brought from Ankara (also known as Angora) in Turkey to the shores of France in the custody of naturalist Nicholas-Claude Fabri de Peiresc. These Angora cats were described as 'ash-coloured, dun and speckled cats, beautiful to behold'. They had long, silky fur, long noses and fairly large ears, and while the ash colouring would indicate a blue and dun colouring a cream it is interesting to guess what was meant by the description 'speckled'. Some of the Angora cats and their offspring were sent to England, where, for a while, they were known as French cats. Later, stockier long-coated cats were brought from Iran and mated with the lighter-framed Angoras. By the end of the eighteenth century this indiscriminate breeding had caused the demise of the Angora in favour of the Persian, a cat with a more substantial-looking appearance.

To the amusement of his friends, in 1868 Charles H. Ross produced a book all about cats. This preceded the first cat shows, and among the anecdotes he mentioned the different varieties of cats favoured at the time and took pains to describe them accurately. Of the cat of Angora he wrote 'a very beautiful variety, with silvery hair of fine silken texture, generally longest on the neck, but also long on the tail. Some are yellowish, and others olive approaching the colour of the lion; but they are all delicate creatures, and of gentle dispositions.' Describing the Persian cat he wrote 'a variety with hair very long and very silky. Perhaps more so than the cat of Angora; it is however differently coloured, being of a fine uniform grey on the upper part with the texture of the fur as soft as silk, and the lustre glossy; the colour fades off on the lower parts of the sides and fades, or nearly so, on the belly.' In 1876, Dr Gordon Stables published one of the first cat books detailing all the different varieties. Called *The Domestic Cat*, it referred to Longhairs as Asiatic cats, with markings and colours similar to the European or Western cats. The author wrote 'the heads of the white, blue and black ought to be

Below left: The Red Persian is comparatively rare at cat shows, probably due to the fact that it is difficult to produce a specimen totally free from ghost tabby markings.

Bottom left: The Tortoiseshell is an all-female variety, whether it is coloured all over – when it is known as the Tortoiseshell Persian – or pointed, as in the Colourpoint.

Below: A Black Persian, groomed to perfection for the show bench, is an inspiring sight. The long, dense coat must be jet-black to the roots with no rusty tinges or odd white hairs. Black Persians have been popular show cats for over a century, despite the fact that they are difficult to breed true to the standard.

small, round and sweet, the expression of the countenance to be singularly loving'. Regarding eye colour he said 'a blue eye in a white Persian, a hazel in a black and a lovely sea-green in a tabby'. He also gave instructions for fellow judges in the assessment of the Asiatic cats: 'First scan your cats, remembering the difference in size you are to expect in tabbies from the other. Next see to the length and texture of the pelage, its glossiness, and its freedom from cinder holes or the reverse. Then note the colour, and the evenness or unevenness of the markings. The head must be carefully noted, as to its size and shape, the colour of the eyes and nose, ditto the whiskers; mark too the lay of the ears and its aural tuft. Lastly take a glance at the expression of the face.'

Another early judge of cats, John Jennings, writing in 1893 described French, Russian, Chinese and Indian Longhairs, which he said 'partake a great deal of the Persian'. He remarked that the French cats were chiefly blue and bred by the Chartreuse monks. He also decried the fact that Persians were getting shorter in the face and tending to become wiry.

Harrison Weir ran the first cat show in 1871, and in 1889 set out the first 'points of excellence' for the Longhair varieties of that time. Type was constant for all, but mention was made of the different fur texture and tails required for the Persians, the Angoras and the Russians. The Persian was required to have a fine, silky, very soft coat, the tail covered with long and silky hair throughout; the Angora coat was to be woollier than that of the Persian and the tail like a fox's brush; and the Russian needed to be even woollier than the Angora and the tail shorter, fuller and with a blunt, tassel-like end. The colours accepted in the show ring for the Longhairs at that time were white, black, blue, grey, red and any other self-colour, while the tabbies could be brown, blue, silver or light grey with white.

The Cat Fancy took off, and in the United States the first show was held in 1895 at Madison Square Gardens in New York. Organized by an Englishman, Mr J. Hyde, it was to be the forerunner of successful shows in Boston and Chicago. Back in Britain, the National Cat Club had formed in 1887 and started registering cats. It suffered setbacks at first, but after a reorganization in 1898 settled down to business without further problems until 1910. Queen Victoria owned two Blue Persian cats and attended cat shows, as well as offering special prizes and awards.

By the time the Governing Council of the Cat Fancy was established in 1910, there were several specialist clubs for Longhairs, including the blue Persian Cat Society, the Black and White Cat Club, the Chinchilla Cat Club, the Silver and Smoke Cat Society, and the Orange, Cream, Fawn and Tortoiseshell Society. All drew up breed standards and nominated people to be their approved judges.

From these early beginnings, today's wide range of varieties of Persians or Longhairs has evolved. This section will examine the breed standards for these varieties as required on the modern show bench. Persian cats are all very similar in build, though subtle differences do occur between specific varieties. The following tables show the basic requirements for conformation of Persians or Longhairs in the United States of America and the United Kingdom, and the colour requirements, which are the same for both countries unless otherwise stated.

CONFORMATION

Head
USA Round; massive; great breadth of skull; round face with rounded bone structure; short snub nose with break; full cheeks; broad, powerful jaws; full, well-developed chin; small, round-tipped ears, tilted forward, not unduly open at the base, set far apart on the head, and fitting into its rounded contour.

UK Broad and round; short, broad nose; full, round cheeks; broad muzzle; good width between the ears, which should be small, neat and well covered with fur; firm chin; level bite.

Eyes
USA Large, round and full; set far apart, brilliant, giving sweet expression.

UK Large, round and wide open, with a pleasing expression.

Body
USA Cobby type, low on the short, thick legs; deep chest; equally strong across shoulders and rump with short, well-rounded middle piece; medium to large in size; level back; large, round paws, toes carried close, five in front, four behind.

UK Cobby and solid, massive but not coarse; short, thick legs; round paws.

Tail
USA Short in proportion to body, carried without a curve, slightly lower than the back.

UK Short and full, not tapered; a kink considered a defect.

Coat
USA Long, thick, standing away from body; fine texture, glossy; long all over body including the shoulders; immense ruff which continues as a deep frill between the front legs; long tufts on ears and between toes; very full brush-like tail.

UK Dense, long, thick and soft, never woolly in texture; flows over the body; extra long at ruff and frill; long on tail giving a full brush-like appearance; tufts on ears and toes.

Faults
USA Incorrect colour or markings; white spotting; overshot or undershot jaw; light bone; tail abnormality.

UK Incorrect colour or markings; white spotting; kinked or abnormal tail; incorrect number of toes.

FULL-COLOUR LONGHAIRS

The full-colour Longhairs may be either self-coloured (known as solid-colored in the USA), or non-self, sometimes called broken colour. The self-coloured cats are white, black, blue, chocolate, lilac, red and cream, while all the remaining colour varieties fall into the non-self category for show purposes.

WHITE
Pure, glistening white; pink nose leather and paw pads. Eyes: deep blue [Blue-eyed White]; deep orange or copper [Orange or Copper-eyed White]; one deep blue, one deep orange or copper, both of equal intensity [Odd-eyed White].

BLACK
Dense coal-black, sound to the roots, free from lighter undercoat and rusty coloured tinges; black nose leather; black or dark brown paw pads; eyes brilliant copper or deep orange.

Above: This exquisite Blue Persian has a fine full ruff of fur around his neck, enhancing his round head.

Above right: The Lilac Longhair or Persian is a comparatively new colour variety in which perfect type has still to be achieved.

Right: A superb Cream Persian with a full, well-groomed coat, excellent head and the correct eye colour.

BLUE
Level tone of colour from nose to tail; lighter shades of blue preferred though all shades allowed; blue nose leather and paw pads; eyes brilliant copper or deep orange.

CHOCOLATE
Medium to dark chocolate-brown, sound to roots, free from lighter undercoat, markings or shading; nose leather and paw pads brown with a rosy tone; eyes brilliant copper or deep orange.

LILAC
Pinkish dove-grey, sound to roots, free from lighter undercoat, markings or shading; nose leather and paw pads lavender-pink; eyes orange.

RED
Deep rich and clear red, sound to roots, free from markings or shading; lips and chin same as coat colour; nose leather and paw pads brick-red; eyes brilliant copper or deep orange.

CREAM
Level shade of pale buff-cream preferred, sound to roots, free from markings or shading; nose leather and paw pads pink; eyes brilliant copper.

TORTOISESHELL
Brightly and clearly patched in black with light and dark red; a light or dark red blaze on the face is desirable; Nose leather and paw pads may be mottled; eyes brilliant copper or deep orange.

TORTOISESHELL-AND-WHITE
As for Tortoiseshell with the addition of white.

CALICO
White with bright clear patches of black, light red and dark red; eyes brilliant copper or deep orange.

In the Odd-eyed White, one of the full, round eyes must be deep blue, and one must be deep orange or copper. Both eyes should be of equal intensity.

BLUE-CREAM (USA)
Blue with patches of solid cream, clearly defined and well broken on body and extremities; eyes brilliant copper.

BLUE-CREAM (UK)
Intermingled in pastel shades of blue and cream; eyes copper or orange.

DILUTE CALICO
White with clearly defined patches of solid blue and cream; eyes brilliant copper.

CHOCOLATE-TORTOISESHELL
Brightly and clearly patched in chocolate and light red; a red blaze on the face is desirable; eyes brilliant copper or deep orange.

LILAC-CREAM
Intermingled in pastel shades of lilac and cream; eyes copper or orange.

BI-COLOR (USA)
Black, blue, red or cream; all with white on feet, legs, underside, chest and muzzle; inverted 'V' blaze on face desirable; white under tail and white collar allowed; eyes brilliant copper.

BI-COLOUR (UK)
Any solid colour with white; patches of colour to be clear and evenly distributed; not more than two-thirds of the coat to be coloured and not more than a half to be white; face patched with colour and white; eyes brilliant copper or deep orange.

VAN BI-COLOR (USA)
Predominantly white cat with markings of black, blue, red or cream confined to the head, tail and legs; one or two small coloured patches allowed on body; eyes brilliant copper.

CHINCHILLA
Undercoat pure white sufficiently tipped with black to give a sparkling effect; legs may be shaded; ear tufts, chin, chest and stomach pure white; eyes and lips outlined with black; nose leather brick-red; paw pads black; eyes emerald or aquamarine.

CHINCHILLA GOLDEN
Undercoat rich cream sufficiently tipped with seal-brown to give golden effect; legs may be shaded; ear tufts, chins, chest and stomach rich cream; eyes and lips outlined with seal-brown; nose leather deep rose; paw pads seal-brown; eyes emerald or aquamarine.

PEWTER (UK)
As for Shaded Silver except eyes should be orange or copper.

Opposite top: The Dilute Calico is evenly marked in blue and cream, with large areas of white.

Opposite bottom: With their black-tipped white coats and black-rimmed emerald eyes, Chinchilla cats make perfect models.

Right: This Cream Bi-colour has a superb head. The white areas, as required by the standard, cover less than half of the coat.

Below: The Blue-cream Persian has patched colouring in the US, and intermingled colouring in the UK.

Below right: Though bi-colours look attractive with symmetrical markings, those like this Black Bi-colour with offset markings also have great appeal.

SHADED SILVER
Undercoat pure white with a mantle of black shading; legs shaded; ear tufts, chin, chest and stomach pure white; eyes and lips outlined in black; nose leather brick-red; paw pads black; eyes emerald or aquamarine. (In the UK, a Shaded Silver with orange eyes is known as Pewter.)

SHELL CAMEO OR RED CHINCHILLA
Undercoat white sufficiently tipped with red to give a sparkling appearance; face and legs slightly shaded; ear tufts, chin, chest and stomach white; eyes outlined rose-pink; nose leather and paw pads rose-pink; eyes brilliant copper or deep orange.

SHADED GOLDEN

Undercoat rich cream with a mantle of seal-brown shading; legs shaded; ear tufts, chin, chest and stomach rich cream; eyes and lips outlined in seal-brown; nose leather rose-pink; paw pads seal-brown; eyes emerald or aquamarine.

SHADED CAMEO OR RED SHADED

Undercoat white with a mantle of red shading; legs and face shaded; ear tufts, chin, chest and stomach white; eyes outlined rose-pink; nose leather and paw pads rose-pink; eyes copper or deep orange.

CHOCOLATE SMOKE

White undercoat heavily tipped with chocolate so that in repose cat appears chocolate but in motion the white undercoat is clearly visible; mask and points chocolate with hairs white at base; white frill and ear tufts; nose leather and paw pads brown with rosy tone; eyes copper or orange.

LILAC SMOKE

White undercoat heavily tipped with lilac so that in repose cat appears lilac but in motion the white undercoat is clearly visible; mask and points lilac with hairs white at base; white frill and ear tufts; nose leather and paw pads lavender-pink; eyes brilliant copper or orange.

RED SMOKE OR CAMEO RED

White undercoat heavily tipped with red so that in repose cat appears red but in motion the white undercoat is clearly visible; mask and points red with hairs white at base; white frill and ear tufts; nose leather and paw pads rose-pink; eyes brilliant copper or orange.

TORTOISESHELL SMOKE

White undercoat heavily tipped with clearly patched black and red, as in the pattern of the Tortoiseshell, so that in repose cat appears tortoiseshell but in motion the white undercoat is clearly visible; mask and points tortoiseshell with hairs white at base; blaze of red tipping desirable on face; white frill and ear tufts; nose leather and paw pads may be mottled; eyes brilliant copper or orange.

SHELL TORTOISESHELL

Undercoat white delicately tipped with black and red in patches, as in the pattern of the Tortoiseshell; face and legs tipped; ear tufts, chin, chest and stomach white or very slightly tipped; blaze of red tipping on face desirable; eyes outlined rose-pink; nose leather and paw pads rose-pink; eyes brilliant copper.

SHADED TORTOISESHELL

Undercoat white with a mantle of clearly patched black and red tipping, as in the pattern of the Tortoiseshell; face and legs shaded; ear tufts, chin, chest and stomach white or slightly shaded; blaze of red shading on face desirable; eyes outlined rose-pink; nose leather and paw pads rose-pink; eyes copper.

BLACK SMOKE

White undercoat heavily tipped with black so that in repose cat appears black but in motion the white undercoat is clearly visible; mask and points black with hairs white at base; white frill and ear tufts which appear silver; nose leather and paw pads black; eyes brilliant copper or orange.

BLUE SMOKE

White undercoat heavily tipped with blue so that in repose cat appears blue but in motion the white undercoat is clearly visible; mask and points blue with hairs white at base; white frill and ear tufts; nose leather and paw pads blue; eyes copper or orange.

BLUE-CREAM SMOKE

White undercoat heavily tipped with patched blue and cream so that in repose cat appears blue-cream but in motion the white undercoat is clearly visible; mask and points blue-cream with hairs white at base; blaze of cream tipping desirable on face; white frill and ear tufts; nose leather and paw pads may be mottled; eyes brilliant copper or orange.

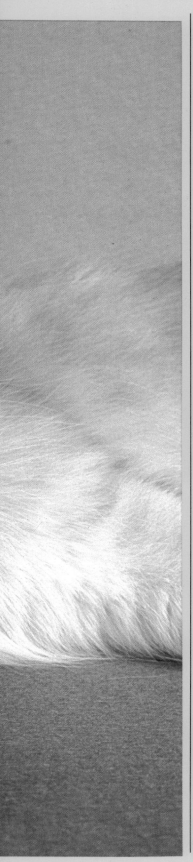

CHOCOLATE-TORTOISESHELL SMOKE

White undercoat heavily tipped with chocolate and light red so that in repose cat appears chocolate-tortoiseshell but in motion the white undercoat is clearly visible; mask and points chocolate-tortoiseshell with hairs white at base; blaze of light red tipping desirable on face; white frill and ear tufts; nose leather and paw pads may be mottled; eyes brilliant copper or orange.

LILAC-CREAM SMOKE

White undercoat heavily tipped with lilac and light cream so that in repose cat appears lilac-cream but in motion the white undercoat is clearly visible; mask and points lilac-cream with hairs white at base; blaze of light cream desirable on face; white frill and ear tufts; nose leather and paw pads may be mottled; eyes brilliant copper or orange.

Left: The Shaded Cameo has a pure white undercoat, each hair of which is tipped with red, giving the characteristic shaded effect to the cat's coat.

Top: In the Black Smoke, the cat appears basically black, but with white undercoat. The ruff and the ear tips are also white, and enhance the cat's beauty.

Above: The Shaded Golden is a feline rarity and is very arresting in its appearance, having gold-brown shading overlying the rich cream undercoat.

TABBY LONGHAIRS

Despite the fact that the long coat of the Persian tends to diffuse the full effect of tabby patterns, show standards nevertheless set out various definitive patterns, and judges look for these when assessing a cat's potential and quality for top awards.

THE BLOTCHED, MARBLED OR CLASSIC TABBY PATTERN

The markings are dense and clearly defined on a base coat of a different, paler colour. The legs are evenly marked with bracelets extending from the ankles to meet the body markings, and the tail is evenly ringed. There are several unbroken necklaces on the chest and neck; frown marks on the forehead form the letter 'M'; an unbroken line runs back from the corner of each eye and a line extends back across each cheek. Vertical lines extend over the head to the shoulder markings, which resemble a butterfly's wings laid over the cat's shoulders. Both upper and lower pairs of the 'wings' are defined and should have dots inside each outline. Markings down the back consist of three well-separated stripes down the spine to the root of the tail and a large blotch on either side of the body is encircled by one or more unbroken rings. The body markings should be identical on either side of the cat with a double row of spots on the chest and stomach.

THE MACKEREL TABBY PATTERN

The markings are dense and clearly defined on a base coat of a different, paler colour. All markings resemble narrow sketch-lines. The legs are evenly marked with bracelets extending from the ankles to meet the body markings and the tail is evenly ringed. There are several unbroken necklaces on the chest and neck; frown marks on the forehead form the letter 'M'; unbroken lines run back from the frown mark, over the head to the shoulders; unbroken lines run outwards from the eyes to the ear base. Spine lines run together at the saddle and narrow vertical stripes run down the body. The body markings should be identical on either side of the cat with a double row of spots on the chest and stomach.

THE PATCHED TABBY PATTERN

The markings are similar to a classic tabby with the addition of clear patches of red, light red or cream. Cats of this pattern, which produce a Tortie-tabby Persian, ae invariably female, and are generally referred to as Torbie cats. There are Brown Torbies, Blue Torbies and Silver Torbies.

Above: The Blue Tabby Persian, a fairly rare variety, is very attractive with its deep blue markings etched on a base coat of pale blue-ivory.

Left: Hummingbird Remus is a fine example of the Silver Tabby Persian. Though his coat is full and flowing, the correct classic pattern is clearly defined in jet-black on silver.

Opposite top: The Brown Tabby has black markings on a rich tawny background. Though this is perhaps the most strikingly marked of all the tabbies, the 'Brownie' appears in only small numbers at cat shows.

Opposite bottom: This handsome Red Tabby with its strong markings in rich red on a deep red ground is of a specialized breed known as the Peke-faced Persian.

BROWN TABBY
Ground colour rich tawny brown; markings dense black; lips and chin same shade as rings around eyes; heels black; nose leather brick-red; paw pads black; eyes copper or hazel.

BLUE TABBY
Ground colour including lips and chin pale blue-ivory; markings deep blue; heels blue; nose leather old-rose; paw pads rose-pink; eyes copper or orange.

RED TABBY
Ground colour including lips and chin rich red; markings very deep rich red; heels deep red; nose leather brick-red; paw pads pink; eyes brilliant copper.

CREAM TABBY
Ground colour including lips and chin very pale cream; markings of buff-cream giving good contrast but remaining in dilute range; heels deep buff-cream; nose leather and paw pads pink; eyes copper or orange.

BROWN PATCHED TABBY
Ground colour rich tawny brown with markings of dense black and red clearly defined; red blaze on the face desirable; nose leather and paw pads may be mottled; eyes brilliant copper or orange.

BLUE PATCHED TABBY
Ground colour pale blue-ivory with markings of deep blue and cream clearly defined; cream blaze on the face desirable; nose leather and paw pads may be mottled; eyes brilliant copper or orange.

SILVER TABBY
Ground colour including lips and chin pale silver; markings dense black with no tawny shading; heels black; nose leather brick-red; paw pads black; eyes green or hazel.

SILVER PATCHED TABBY
Ground colour including lips and chin pale silver; markings dense black with patches of red clearly defined; red blaze on face desirable; nose leather and pads may be mottled; eyes copper or hazel.

HIMALAYAN OR COLOURPOINT LONGHAIRS

In the Himalayan pattern, the cat has a pale body and its extremities show the animal's true colour. The extremities are referred to as the cat's points, and include the face or mask, the ears, the tail, and the legs and paws. In all cases the points should match, with the tip of the tail being exactly the same intensity of colour as the tips of the ears. The forelegs are naturally slightly lighter in colour than the mask and tail, but even in the paler varieties the forepaws should show the correct colour. All Himalayan cats have blue eye colour, and the intensity generally complements the points colour.

SEAL POINT
Body pale cream shading to warm fawn on flanks, lighter on stomach; points very deep seal-brown; nose leather and paw pads dark seal-brown.

BLUE POINT
Body bluish white shading to slightly deeper tone on flanks and to white on stomach; points blue; nose and paw pads slate-blue.

CHOCOLATE POINT
Body ivory, unshaded; points warm-toned milk chocolate; nose leather and paw pads cinnamon-pink.

LILAC POINT
Body white, unshaded; points frosty grey of a pinkish tone; nose leather and paw pads lavender-pink.

RED POINT OR FLAME POINT
Body creamy white; points delicate orange; nose leather and paw pads coral-pink.

CREAM POINT
Body creamy white; points buff-cream; nose leather and paw pads flesh-pink.

TORTIE POINT
Body creamy white; points patched with dark seal-brown and red; red blaze on face desirable; nose leather and paw pads may be mottled.

BLUE-CREAM POINT
Body bluish white or creamy white; points blue with patches of cream; cream blaze desirable; nose leather and paw pads may be mottled.

Opposite top: Himalayan or Colourprint Persians are bred in a wide range of points colours. Here a Blue-cream Point contrasts well with her Seal-tortie Point cousin.

Opposite bottom: GCCF Grand Champion Frallon Creampoint Apache, an excellent example of his breed, is well boned, with a very good head and eyes correct for both shape and colour.

Right: Gently patched with blue and cream on her points and with a soft bluish white coat, Marisha Madresilva is a fine Blue-cream Point.

Below: This Seal-tabby Point clearly demonstrates the pale area separating mask and ears.

Bottom: The mostly recently recognized Colourpoints are the tabby points. This is a fine example of a Blue-tabby Point.

CHOCOLATE-TORTIE POINT
Body ivory; points chocolate with light red; light red blaze desirable; nose and paw pads may be mottled.

LILAC-CREAM POINT
Body white; points lilac with pale cream; cream blaze desirable, nose and paw pads may be mottled.

SEAL-TABBY POINT
Body cream or pale fawn, lighter on underparts; points seal-brown bars distinct and separated by lighter background colour; ears seal-brown with lighter 'thumbprint'; nose leather deep seal-brown or pink edged in seal-brown; paw pads deep seal-brown.

BLUE-TABBY POINT
Body bluish white, lighter on underparts; points deep blue-grey bars distinct and separated by lighter background colour; ears deep blue-grey with lighter 'thumbprint'; nose leather slate-blue or pink edged with slate-blue; paw pads slate-blue.

CHOCOLATE-TABBY POINT
Body ivory with no shading; points milk-chocolate bars distinct and separated by lighter background colour; ears milk chocolate with lighter 'thumbprint'; nose leather cinnamon or pink edged with cinnamon; paw pads cinnamon.

LILAC-TABBY POINT
Body glacial white with no shading; points frosty grey with pinkish tone bars distinct and separated by lighter background colour; ears frosty grey with pinkish tone, and lighter 'thumbprint'; nose leather lavender-pink; paw pads lavender-pink.

Inset far left: This shows the startling effect of good eye colour in the popular Black Persian.

Inset left: The dramatic coloration of an American Red Bi-color.

Below: Rare and exquisitely coloured, this is a Chocolate-tortie Persian queen. Light red patching breaks up the rich chocolate of the coat.

Inset right: A Seal-tabby Himalayan or Colourpoint Persian showing rather heavy shading on the body, a trait common to many Himalayan varieties.

Inset far right: The Chinchilla is a born extrovert and almost seems to appreciate the fact that his colouring and eyes are enhanced by posing on the green lawn.

SEMI-LONGHAIRS

Several very beautiful long-coated breeds of cat exist which cannot be grouped with Persians as their general conformation is unique to their individual breed. Some of the Semi-longhaired cats evolved as long-coated variations of established short-coated breeds, like the Somali and the Balinese; some are carefully protected breeds from ancient stock, like the Birman and the Turkish; while others, like the Angora, have been created by meticulous breeding.

THE BIRMAN

The Birman, or Sacred Cat of Burma, is a very old breed, said to have been the guardian of the temple of Lao-Tsun in Burma many years ago. An ancient legend tells a charming tale of how the Birman achieved its unique colouring.

Long ago, before the time of the great lord Buddha, the Khmer people raised a beautiful temple in honour of the goddess Tsu-Kyan-Kse, and here the High Priest Mun-Ha officiated, always accompanied by his favourite of the many white temple cats, the faithful Sinh. Bandits raided the temple one night and in trying to protect the golden statue of the goddess, Mun-Ha suffered a severe heart attack and sank to the ground. As his master lay dying, Sinh leaped onto his old master's head and hissed with such fury that the assailants left Mun-Ha alone. The junior priests rallied and fought off the bandits as Mun-Ha passed away. Sinh relaxed and gazed up at the sapphire eyes of the great gold statue, and as he did so, the perfect soul of his master suffered the miracle of transmutation and passed into the body of the white cat. As the transfer took place, the white cat seemed to shimmer and his body turned to palest gold as though absorbing the statue's reflected light; his face, legs and tail gradually took on the hue of the fresh brown earth at the base of the statue; and his yellow eyes, still locked with those of the goddess, gradually turned a brilliant sapphire blue.

Only the cat's four white feet, gently and protectively clasping the dead priest's snowy head, remained white and unchanged. As peace returned to the temple, the priests were astounded to see that all the temple cats had undergone the same transformation as Sinh, and from that day forward the cats were considered sacred, possessing the souls of dead priests. Sinh steadfastly refused all food and drink until on the seventh day after the loss of his beloved master he died, carrying with him the perfect soul of Mun-Ha to their eternal paradise.

At the turn of this century the temple was raided again, and this time was saved by Major Russell and Monsieur Pavie, who were later presented with a pair of the sacred temple cats in gratitude for their action. Though the male died on the way to the two gentlemen, who were then living in France, the female proved to be in kitten and her litter survived to become the first Birman cats seen in Europe. Despite wars and the usual difficulties in protecting and developing rare cat breeds, the Birman survived and prospered, and by the 1960s it was well established on the show benches in France. Here it was seen by British breeders, who, captivated by its charms and immaculate white gloves, soon arranged for the breed to be imported into Britain.

In 1960, a pair of Tibetan temple cats were imported into the United States, and proved identical to the Birmans. The breed soon established itself on both sides of the Atlantic, being officially recognized in Britain in 1966 and in the United States the following year.

CONFORMATION

Head Broad and round with a strong skull; forehead sloping back and slightly convex with a flat area just below ears; Roman nose of length proportional to head; nostrils set low; well-developed chin and strong lower lip forming straight line with upper lip; ears almost as wide at base as their length, with rounded tips set as much to the side as to the top of the head.

Eyes Wide set and almost round in shape; always blue in colour.

Body Long but stocky and substantial, with medium-length, heavy boned legs; large, round, firm paws, five toes in front, four behind.

Tail Of medium length and proportioned to balance the body; a kink considered a severe fault.

Coat Long and silky in texture; heavy neck ruff; slight tendency to curl on stomach; does not mat.

Faults Incorrect paw pattern; Siamese conformation; white shading on stomach or chest; kinked tail; any area of white except paws.

Right: The first Birman or Sacred Cats of Burma were Seal Points and, like all Birmans, were easily recognized by their startling white gloves. Today the Birman has been developed in a range of points colours, but the type has remained constant as breeders carefully selected against Persian conformation being introduced into the breed, particularly in the head type.

Opposite: The Blue Point Birman is a dilute version of the Seal Point, and differs only in colour. The mask, ears and tail are deep blue, in contrast to the bluish white body. The deep blue legs end in white gloves which should be exactly marked for showing. The front gloves end in a straight line across the third joint, and the hind gloves completely cover the paws.

COLOURS
The body should be evenly coloured, any shading being very subtle; strong contrast between body and points colour; all points except paws should be densely coloured and the mask, ears, legs and tail should all be of the same shade; mask covers the entire face including whisker pads and chin, and is connected by tracings to the ears; front paws have white gloves ending in a straight, even line across the paws at the third joint, hind paws have white gloves covering the entire paw and each must end in point that extends up the back of the hock (these points are called the laces).

SEAL POINT
Body pale cream of warm tone shading to fawn on flanks and to a lighter cream on stomach and chest; points deep seal-brown except for white gloves; nose leather deep seal-brown; paw pads pink.

BLUE POINT
Body bluish white shading to a lighter tone on stomach and chest; points deep blue except for white gloves; nose leather slate-blue; paw pads pink.

CHOCOLATE POINT
Body ivory with no shading; points milk chocolate except for white gloves; nose leather cinnamon-pink; paw pads pink.

LILAC POINT
Body cold glacial tone verging on white, no shading; points frosty grey of pinkish tone except for white gloves; nose leather lavender-pink; paw pads pink.

RED POINT
Body creamy white; points delicate orange except for white gloves; nose leather coral-pink; paw pads pink.

TORTIE POINT
Body creamy white; points patched with dark seal-brown and red except for white gloves; nose leather may be mottled seal or rosy pink; paw pads pink.

THE BALINESE

This is another Himalayan-patterned breed, being a long-coated version of the standard Siamese. The first of these kittens turned up unexpectedly in litters of normal-coated Siamese in the 1950s in the United States. At first the long-coated 'sports' were discarded as pets, but eventually they were kept to be raised as a separate variety, and named Balinese because their lithe beauty and grace were thought to be similar to that of the exquisite dancers of Bali. The Balinese should never be confused with the Himalayan or Colourpoint Persian, for that cat is a true Persian cat with Siamese colouring, while the Balinese is a Siamese cat with a long coat.

CONFORMATION

Head Medium-sized; long tapering wedge starting at the nose and flaring in straight lines to the ear tips, forming a perfect triangle with no whisker break; flat skull with straight side profile; no nose dip; long, straight nose; fine muzzle; medium-strength jaw; firm chin; tip of nose and chin line up in same vertical plane; large, pointed, wide-based ears continuing lines of wedge.
Eyes Of medium size; almond-shaped with at least an eye's width between the eyes; slanted towards nose to complement the wedge; no tendency to squint.
Body Of medium size; long, svelte and dainty; finely boned; well-muscled, tubular body; tight abdomen; hips never wider than shoulders; long, slender neck; long, slim legs, hindlegs higher than forelegs; small, oval paws,

five toes in front, four behind.
Tail Long, thin and tapered to a fine point; covered with long, fine, silky hair giving the tail a plume-like appearance.
Coat Long, fine and silky, with no downy undercoat.
Faults Unpigmented nose; weak hindlegs; kinked tail; double coat; white toes; incorrect number of toes; poor bodily condition.
Coat pattern is typical Himalayan pattern, with light body and well-defined contrast between body and points colour, though concession should be given for shading in older cats; mask, ears, legs, paws and tail should all be same shade; mask should cover entire face, including whisker pads and chin, and be connected to the ears by fine tracing except in kittens; mask must not extend over head.

Right: Cheldene Big Mac, a Lilac Point Balinese, is a cat which helped to popularize the breed in Britain, leading to its eventual recognition. This breed must not be confused with the Colourpoint Persian, which is a Persian cat with Siamese colouring. The Balinese is a Siamese cat with long silky fur. The aim of the developers of the Balinese is to produce cats of true Siamese show type, while retaining the coat of the first mutants. Balinese are also identical to Siamese in colour, and may be shown in the same series of show classes.

Opposite: In the Balinese kitten, the long coat takes some time to develop its full length and density. This young Seal Point has very good type and should develop into a pleasing adult.

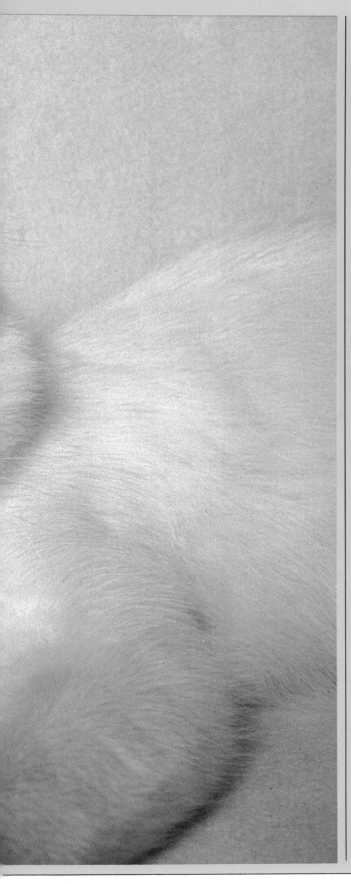

SEAL POINT
Body cream shading to warm fawn, lighter underparts; points deep seal-brown; nose leather and paw pads deep seal-brown; eyes deep vivid blue.

BLUE POINT
Body bluish white shading to white on underparts; points deep blue; nose leather and paw pads slate-blue; eyes deep vivid blue.

CHOCOLATE POINT
Body ivory with no shading; points milk chocolate; nose leather and paw pads cinnamon-pink; eyes deep vivid blue.

LILAC POINT
Body glacial white with no shading; points frosty grey with pinkish tone; nose leather and paw pads lavender-pink; eyes deep vivid blue.

RED POINT
Body clear white, any shading to tone with points; points warm orange-red (lack of barring desirable); nose leather and paw pads coral-pink; eyes deep vivid blue.

CREAM POINT
Body clear white, any shading to tone with points; points apricot (lack of barring desirable); nose leather and paw pads should be flesh-pink; eyes deep vivid blue.

SEAL-TORTIE POINT
Body cream shading to warm fawn, lighter underparts; points patched with seal-brown and red; red blaze desirable; nose leather and paw pads may be mottled; eyes deep vivid blue.

BLUE-CREAM POINT
Body bluish white, lighter underparts; points patched or mottled deep blue and cream; a blaze is desirable; nose leather and paw pads may be mottled; eyes deep vivid blue.

CHOCOLATE-TORTIE POINT
Body ivory; points patched or mottled milk chocolate and light red; a blaze is desirable; nose leather and paw pads may be mottled; eyes deep vivid blue.

LILAC-CREAM POINT
Body glacial white; points patched or mottled with frosty grey of pinkish tone and pale cream; blaze desirable; nose leather and paw pads may be mottled; eyes deep vivid blue.

SEAL-TABBY POINT
Body cream shading to warm fawn; points seal-brown barring clearly defined; ears seal-brown with paler 'thumbprint'; nose leather seal-brown or pink edged with seal-brown; paw pads seal-brown; eyes deep vivid blue.

BLUE-TABBY POINT
Body bluish white, lighter underparts; points deep blue barring clearly defined; ears deep blue with lighter 'thumbprints'; nose leather slate-blue or pink edged with slate-blue; paw pads slate-blue; eyes deep vivid blue.

CHOCOLATE-TABBY POINT
Body ivory; points milk-chocolate barring; ears milk chocolate with paler 'thumbprint'; nose leather cinnamon or pink edged with cinnamon; paw pads cinnamon; eyes deep blue.

LILAC-TABBY POINT
Body glacial white; points frosty grey of pinkish tone barring; ears frosty grey of pinkish tone with lighter 'thumbprints'; nose leather and paw pads lavender pink; eyes deep vivid blue.

RED-TABBY POINT
Body clear white, any shading to tone with points; points warm orange-red barring; ears with lighter 'thumbprint'; nose leather and paw pads coral-pink; eyes deep vivid blue.

CREAM-TABBY POINT
Body clear white, any shading to tone with points; points apricot barring; ears with lighter 'thumbprints'; nose leather and paw pads flesh-pink; eyes deep vivid blue.

TORTIE-TABBY POINT OR TORBIE POINT
Body white or cream depending on main tortie colour of points; points patched or mottled barring in seal-brown, deep blue, milk chocolate or frosty grey of pinkish tone with corresponding red, light red or cream; ears should show lighter 'thumbprint'; nose leather and paw pads to match main colour, may be mottled; eyes deep vivid blue.

THE SOMALI

Just as long-coated kittens appeared from time to time in Siamese litters and were eventually developed as a separate breed called Balinese, so the once-discarded long-coated kittens that arrived in Abyssinian litters were developed as a breed called the Somali. First recognized in the United States in October 1978, the breed quickly gained favour and continues to grow in numbers and popularity. Typically Abyssinian at maturity, the long fur masks and distorts the ticking in kittens and younger cats, and this is taken into account in judging at shows.

CONFORMATION

Head Modified, slightly rounded wedge without flat planes; brow, cheek and side profile all with gentle contours; slight rise from bridge of nose to forehead, which is broad; gently contoured muzzle, neither pointed nor pinched; firm chin; ears large and alert, broad and cupped at the base, moderately pointed and set well back on the skull with good width between; inner ear with long horizontal tufts.
Eyes Large, almond-shaped and accented by dark lidskin in turn outlined by lighter area; above each eye a short vertical line extends towards top of head, and a line from each outer eye corner extends towards the outer base of the ear.
Body Medium-sized, long, lithe and elegant with well-developed muscle; rounded ribcage; slightly arched back; level flanks; general conformation midway between svelte and cobby; legs in proportion to body; neat oval paws, five toes in front and four behind.
Tail Length proportional to body; thick at base and slightly tapered; covered with long, fine hair.
Coat Very soft and fine double coat, dense and of medium length except over the shoulders, where it may be shorter; full-coated on neck and hindlegs giving a definite ruff and 'breeches'; tufts of hair between toes.
Faults White marks anywhere other than the chin, nostrils and upper throat; unbroken necklace; any skeletal abnormality; incorrect colour of nose leather or paw pads; incorrect number of toes.

Top: The Sorrel or Red Somali. This variety derives its colour from the action of the light chocolate gene combined with agouti.

Above: This Brown, or Ruddy, Somali kitten is of pleasing type with a promising coat. Its eye and coat colour is good.

COLOURS
Coat should give a glowing impression and the adult should have two or three bands of ticking apparent in the hairs; underside of body evenly coloured without ticking, barring, necklaces or belly marks; tail should be unringed but carry a dark topline and tip corresponding with the cat's darker spine line; ears with darker tips and preferably tufted; dark toe tufts.

BROWN OR RUDDY
Body orange-brown or tawny base coat ticked with black banding; underparts of even, ruddy tone; darker spine shading allowed and continues along tail, which ends in a black tip; ears tipped black; black from heel towards hock; nose leather tile red; paw pads black; eyes gold or green.

SORREL OR RED
Body warm orange-red base coat ticked with chocolate banding; underparts of slightly lighter even tone; darker spine shading allowed and continues along tail, which ends in a chocolate tip; ears tipped chocolate; chocolate from heel towards hock; nose leather rosy pink; paw pads pink; eyes gold or green. Note: In line with the newer colours found in the Abyssinian breed, the Somali is also in the process of being developed in blue, fawn or lilac.

THE TURKISH OR TURKISH VAN CAT

The Turkish cat is a unique Semi-longhair breed which originated in the Lake Van area of south-eastern Turkey. An Englishwoman called Laura Lushington discovered the cats during her travels, and was presented with a breeding pair, which she carried home. During further trips, Miss Lushington was able to purchase further stock, and from her imports the breed was slowly developed in Britain. Eventually full recognition was granted to the breed as the Turkish cat in 1969, and exports were made to the United States, where the breed is called the Turkish Van. The cat is basically white with specific auburn markings but recently a natural dilute form with cream markings has appeared; no other colouring is allowed in the breed. In the United States the term Van is now applied to cats of other breeds which are predominantly white with discrete coloured areas on their coats.

CONFORMATION

Head Front profile presents a short wedge; side profile shows a medium to long nose with a slight downward curve; chin firm but gently curved; tapered jaw; level bite; ears large and upright, set rather close together, pointed at tips and inner ear with horizontal tufts.
Eyes Round and of medium size; lidskin pink; at least an eye's width between the eyes.
Body Of medium size, long and sturdy; particularly muscular in the neck and shoulder, especially

noticeable in the adult male; medium-length legs with neat, round paws and tufted toes, five in front and four behind.
Tail Of medium length, in proportion to the body; no abnormalities in bone structure allowed; covered with long, soft, silky hair giving a plume-like appearance.
Coat Very long, soft and silky to the roots, with no woolly undercoat.
Faults Persian type; undersize in adults; woolly undercoat; odd-eyes.

COLOURS
Chalk-white with no trace of yellow; distinct markings on the face, the forehead and around the base of the white ears; face has a white blaze; tail completely coloured and faint ghost rings are permitted in adults, more distinct rings in kittens; small, irregularly placed body markings, though not desirable, may be permitted in an otherwise excellent specimen.

Above and left: These two Turkish Van cats are basically white with deep auburn-red markings on the face and ears, and have matching red tails.

WHITE-AND-RED
Body chalk-white (small red markings not penalized); tail deep rich red; head chalk-white with deep red markings around base of ears and on forehead bisected by white blaze; ears white; nose leather, paw pads and inner ears shell-pink; eyes light, bright amber.

WHITE-AND-CREAM
Body chalk-white with no trace of yellow (small cream markings not penalized); tail light cream, head chalk-white with light-cream markings around base of ears and on forehead, bisected by white blaze; ears white; nose leather, paw pads and inner ears light shell-pink; eyes light, bright amber.

THE ANGORA

The Angora cat bred in Britain is the Semi-longhair version of the Oriental Shorthair (as the Balinese is to the Siamese), and for show purposes it is required to be of Oriental type but with a long, fine and silky coat.

CONFORMATION

Head Medium-sized; long, tapering wedge starting at the nose and flaring in straight lines to the ear tips, forming a perfect triangle with no whisker break; flat skull with straight side profile; no nose dip; long, straight nose; fine muzzle; medium-strength jaw; firm chin; tip of nose and chin line up in same vertical plane; large, pointed, wide-based ears continuing lines of wedge.
Eyes Of medium size; almond-shaped with at least one eye's width between the eyes; slanted towards nose to complement the wedge; no tendency to squint.
Body Medium-sized, long, svelte and dainty; finely boned; well-muscled, tubular body; tight

abdomen; hips never wider than shoulders; long, slender neck; long, slim legs, hindlegs higher than forelegs; small oval paws, five toes in front, four behind, all with tufts between.
Tail Long, thin and tapered to a fine point; covered with long, fine, silky hair giving the tail a plume-like appearance.
Coat Long, fine and silky with no downy undercoat; longer on ruff and underparts with a tendency to wave; coat length less on body than in the Persian, and tends to lie flat.
Faults Incorrect type; kinked or abnormal tail.
COLOURS
Identical to that of Oriental Shorthair.

THE TURKISH ANGORA

These cats were first known in Europe during the sixteenth century, but were gradually superseded by the Persians. In recent years, however, the breed has been revived in the United States from white cats imported direct from Turkey, and now a whole range of colours is accepted.

CONFORMATION

Head Of small to medium size; wedge-shaped, wide across the top and tapering towards chin; side profile medium length with a straight nose and a gently rounded chin, tip forming a perpendicular line with nose; ears wide at base, long, pointed and tufted.
Eyes Large, almond-shaped to round, slanted slightly towards nose.
Body Small to medium in female adult, male slightly larger; fine-boned; light-framed chest; long, fine legs, hindlegs higher than forelegs; paws small and round, five toes in front and four behind, all with tufts between.
Tail Long, thin and tapered, covered with fine, silky hair

giving it a plume-like appearance; generally carried lower than the line of the back, or held horizontally back over the body, the tip almost touching the cat's head.
Coat Long and fine with a silky sheen; medium-long on body, extra long at ruff, tending to wave on underparts.
Faults Persian type; kinked or abnormal tail.

COLOURS
White; Black; Blue; Black Smoke; Blue Smoke; Silver Tabby; Brown Tabby; Blue Tabby; Red Tabby; Calico; Bi-color. For full details refer to the appropriate Longhair or Persian entry on pages 112–115.

Above: Dark chocolate-brown cats of the Angora breed typify the breeders' intentions to produce long-coated cats of Oriental type and colour range.

Opposite and far left: Less extreme in type, with a head of medium length, the Turkish Angora has several features in common with the Angora, and similar coloration.

Left: This charming odd-eyed white kitten was one of the first Angora cats to be bred in the United Kingdom.

THE MAINE COON

A native of the state of Maine in North America, the Maine Coon has been recognized as a pure variety for well over a hundred years. It was very popular as a working cat, but also excelled on the show bench. A Maine Coon took Best in Show at Madison Square Gardens, New York, in 1895, and another, called Cosie, won top awards for neutered cats. Romantic legends abound to explain the origin of the breed, including the story that the cats resulted from a liaison between a farm cat and a raccoon, and another that the cats of the ill-fated Marie Antoinette were smuggled out of France and made landfall on the shores of Maine. It seems more likely, however, that Angora cats were landed as trade goods, and the breed became naturally established, being totally at home in the coastal environment.

From 1904, the breed's popularity declined until in 1953, the Central Maine Coon Club was established and researched pedigrees. By 1976, the International Society for the Preservation of the Maine Coon had been formed and this breed was once again given its rightful status by the Cat Fanciers' Association, America's largest registration body. It is interesting to note that the Maine Coon is very similar in all respects to a Scandinavian feline, the Norwegian Forest Cat. Today, the Maine Coon has regained its former popularity as a pet, working and show cat, and in 1983 the first imports were made into Britain.

WHITE
Body pure glistening white; nose leather and paw pads pink.

BLACK
Body dense black, sound to roots, no rusty tinge; nose leather black; paw pads black or dark brown.

BLUE
Body level shade of blue all over, sound to roots; nose leather and paw pads slate-blue.

RED
Body deep rich brilliant red, without shading, markings or ticking; lips and chin to match coat; nose leather and paw pads brick-red.

CREAM
Body buff-cream, sound to roots, without shading, markings or ticking; nose leather and paw pads pink.

BROWN TABBY
Body brilliant coppery brown; markings dense black; back of hindlegs black from paw to hock; white lips allowed; nose leather brick-red; paw pads black or brown.

CONFORMATION

Head Medium in width and length with a squared muzzle; high cheekbones; chin firm and in line with nose and upper lip; medium-length nose; ears wide at base, large, rather pointed, well tufted and set high and wide apart on the head.
Eyes Large and wide apart, set rather obliquely; may be any shade of green, gold or copper; white cats may have blue, copper or odd-eyes; otherwise, eye colour bears no relation to coat colour.
Body Medium to large, muscular and broad-chested; male larger than female; long and well proportioned, giving an overall rectangular appearance; substantial legs, length proportional to body; paws large, round and well tufted, five toes in front, four behind.
Tail Long and tapered; covered with long, flowing hair.
Coat Heavy and shaggy, shorter on the shoulders and longer on the stomach and hindlegs, giving the effect of 'breeches'; ruff desirable; texture of coat silky, and falls smoothly down body.
Faults Delicate bone structure; undershot chin; squint; kinked tail; incorrect number of toes; unwanted white spotting.

Above right and right: The Maine Coon cat is strong and sturdily built with a heavy, silky coat – short on the shoulders and longer on the ruff, stomach and breeches. It makes an excellent working cat.

BLUE TABBY
Body pale bluish ivory; markings very deep blue, giving good contrast; white lips and chin allowed; nose leather and paw pads rose-pink.

RED TABBY
Body red; markings deep rich red; white lips and chin allowed; nose leather and paw pads brick-red.

CREAM TABBY
Body very pale cream; markings buff or cream giving good contrast; white lips and chin allowed; nose leather and paw pads pink.

CAMEO TABBY
Body off-white; markings red; nose leather and paw pads rose-pink.

TORTOISESHELL
Body clearly patched in black and red; red blaze on face.

CALICO
Body white with clear patches of black and red.

DILUTE CALICO
Body white with clear patches of blue and cream.

BLUE-CREAM
Body clearly patched in blue and cream.

BI-COLOR
Body either black, red, blue or cream combined with white; solid colour predominates, the white portions being on the face, chest, stomach, legs and feet.

TORTOISESHELL-AND-WHITE
Body as for tortoiseshell, with or without white on the face; white on bib, stomach and all four paws; white on one-third of the body is acceptable.

TABBY-AND-WHITE
Body as for any tabby, with or without white on the face; white on bib, stomach and all four paws; white on one-third of the body is acceptable.

Above: This handsome tabby Maine Coon has the typical tufted ears and expressive eyes of the breed.

CHINCHILLA
Body has white undercoat tipped with black on back, flanks, head and tail, giving sparkling appearance; legs slightly shaded; chin, ear tufts, chest and stomach pure white; rims of eyes, lips and nose outlined with black; nose leather brick-red; paw pads black.

SHADED SILVER
Body has white undercoat tipped with black to give effect of mantle; general effect much darker than the Chinchilla; rims of eyes, lips and nose outlined with black; nose leather brick-red; paw pads black.

SHELL CAMEO OR RED CHINCHILLA
Body has white undercoat tipped with red to give sparkling appearance; face and legs slightly shaded with red; chin, ear tufts, chest and stomach pure white; rims of eyes, nose leather and paw pads rose-pink.

SHADED CAMEO OR RED SHADED
Body has white undercoat tipped with red to give effect of mantle; general effect much darker than the Shell Cameo; rims of eyes, nose leather and paw pads rose-pink.

CAMEO SMOKE OR RED SMOKE
Body has white undercoat deeply tipped with red; in repose cat looks red, white undercoat showing through in motion; points and mask red with hairs white at base; rims of eyes, nose leather and paw pads rose-pink.

BLACK SMOKE
Body has white undercoat deeply tipped with black, in repose cat looks black, white undercoat showing through in motion; points and mask black with hairs white at base; rims of eyes, nose leather and paw pads black.

BLUE SMOKE
Body has white undercoat deeply tipped with blue; points and mask blue with hairs white at base; rims of eyes, nose leather and paw pads slate-blue.

THE RAGDOLL

This breed is yet another Semi-longhair that owes its basic colouring to the Himalayan factor. It was developed in the United States from descendants of a White Longhair queen, and the breed is recognized in three main varieties – the Colorpoint, the Mitted and the Bi-color. The breed name aptly describes one of the cat's particular qualities – its ability to hang limply and relaxed in its owner's arms, just like a ragdoll.

CONFORMATION

Head Of medium size; side profile shows a gentle stop, medium-length nose, round, well-developed chin; front profile shows wide, modified wedge; medium-sized, round-tipped ears, wide-based and tilted slightly forward, set to continue line of wedge.

Eyes Large and oval, not Oriental in setting; outer aperture to fall level with base of ear; blue in colour.

Body Ideally very large and heavy, but full weight and size is not achieved for four years; male larger than female; overall impression of subdued power; deep chest; broad shoulders and hindquarters; long, heavy middle; all heavily muscled; short, heavy neck; heavy boned legs of medium length with large, round, tufted paws; five toes in front and four behind.

Tail Long and with a slight taper towards tip.

Coat Silky texture: medium to long, lies with the body and breaks as cat moves; longest around neck and framing the face, short on face and increasing in length from top of the head, through the shoulder-blades and down the back; medium length on sides, stomach and hindlegs; short to medium length on the forelegs.

Faults Short tail; pointed ears; eye colour anything but blue; kinked or abnormal tail; incorrect number of toes.

COLORPOINT
Body paler than points colour; cats over two years of age may be shaded; points darker than body and well defined on mask, ears, legs, paws and tail.

MITTED
Body paler than points colour; white stripe extending in width as it passes from the bib, down between the forelegs and along the stomach to the lower belly region; points (except paws) darker than body and well defined on mask, ears, legs, paws and tail; a white exclamation mark on nose and/or a white chin is also permitted; the paws carry white mittens, even markings preferred.

BI-COLOR
Underbody white; white legs preferred; some random white spotting accepted on back; mask marked with an inverted white 'V', points darker than body and well defined on the outer mask, ears and tail.

SEAL POINT
Body cream shading to warm fawn, lighter underparts; points deep seal-brown; nose leather and paw pads in keeping with colour/s of muzzle and paws.

BLUE POINT
Body bluish white, lighter underparts; points deep blue; nose leather and paw pads in keeping with colour/s of muzzle and paws.

CHOCOLATE POINT
Body ivory, lighter underparts; points milk chocolate; nose leather and paw pads in keeping with colour/s of muzzle and paws.

LILAC POINT
Body glacial white; points frosty grey of pinkish tone; nose leather and paw pads in keeping with colour/s of muzzle and paws.

SHORTHAIRS

This group consists of cats with short coats, but without the extreme body type of the Oriental and Foreign breeds.

The British, American and European Shorthairs are quite similar in conformation, and the Exotic resembles a short-coated Persian.

THE AMERICAN SHORTHAIR

There were no indigenous domestic cats in North America when the first settlers arrived, but over the years cats were introduced as trade goods, and were eagerly accepted because of their usefulness in controlling the vermin attracted by grain stored on farms. As pioneer families trekked inland, their cats accompanied them as part of their stock, and in this way the domestic cat gradually spread across the whole of the continent.

At the turn of the twentieth century, cats achieved added status with the advent of cat shows, and the domestic shorthair was upgraded by the infusion of pedigree Shorthair blood from animals imported from Britain. The first Shorthair to be registered in the United States, according to the Cat Fanciers' Association stud book, was an import from England called Belle of Bradford. Despite the feminine name, this was an Orange Tabby male, bred by Mr Kuhnel and imported by Miss Jane Cathcart. This lady was also responsible for importing the second cat in the registry, a Silver Tabby male named Pretty Correct, bred by Mrs Collingwood. These imports were made in the early 1900s, and in 1904 Miss Cathcart registered the third Shorthair, a Smoke male of unknown parentage called Buster Brown. These cats forged the way for the development of the American Shorthair, a breed of domestic cat with no extremes in either conformation or temperament, which has remained in favour to this day. The American Shorthair has very strong hunting instincts, and so is a superb working cat, while its even, placid nature also makes it an ideal pet and companion for small children and dogs. This is a very adaptable breed.

Below: The exhibition standard Silver Classic Tabby has distinctive black patterning on a clear silver ground. The patterning must conform to a set standard of points of perfection, which differs slightly in different countries.

On the opposite page is a superb Silver Classic Tabby American Shorthair: top winner and stud male Grand Champion Portrait's Romeow.

Below: This young American Shorthair pictured at ten months is a Brown Classic Tabby of very good colour and with superb markings in black on a tawny base.

Right: A Blue Mackerel Tabby American Shorthair.

Below right: The rare Silver-ticked Tabby has yet to be recognized.

CONFORMATION

Head Large, with a full-cheeked face, slightly longer than it is wide; squared muzzle; firm, well-developed chin forming perpendicular line with upper lip; medium-sized ears, slightly round at the tips, set wide apart and not too open at base.
Eyes Round and wide with slight slant to outer aperture; with at least one eye's width between eyes.
Body Medium to large; tightly muscled; powerful with well-developed chest and shoulders, but not coarse; legs of medium length, firm-boned and heavily muscled; firm round paws with heavy pads; five toes in front, four behind.
Tail Medium-length with heavy base, appearing to taper to an abrupt blunt end, though vertebrae taper normally.
Coat Short, thick and hard in texture; thicker and denser in winter.

Faults Excessive cobbiness or ranginess; very short tail; overweight or underweight for size; deep nose break; long or fluffy coat; mismarkings or undesired white spotting; hybrid appearance; incorrect number of toes.

COLOURS
White; Black; Blue; Red; Cream; Tortoiseshell; Blue-cream; Chinchilla; Shell Cameo; Shaded Silver; Shaded Cameo; Black Smoke; Blue Smoke; Cameo Smoke; Bi-color; Calico; Dilute Calico; Tabby (classic or mackerel) — Brown, Blue, Red, Cream, Silver, Cameo; Brown-patched Tabby; Blue-patched Tabby; Silver-patched Tabby.
N.B. For full descriptions of coats, together with eye, nose and paw pad colours, see pages 112–115.

THE BRITISH SHORTHAIR

In the first cat shows held in Britain at the end of the nineteenth century Shorthairs appeared in substantial numbers, but they soon lost their popularity in favour of the Persians being imported especially for the show bench. The decline continued until the 1930s, when a general resurgence began. From the cats of that time, evolved from the natural domestic cats found all over the British Isles, today's British Shorthair was developed and owes a great deal of its conformation to early infusions of Persian blood. Despite its humble roots, today's exhibition British Shorthair could never be mistaken for a non-pedigree domestic cat, though it has retained its keen hunting ability.

Top and above right: White British Shorthairs (a Blue-eyed and an Odd-eyed are shown) are very popular.

Above: Jet-black and with deep orange or copper eyes, the British Black is a popular breed.

CONFORMATION

Head Very broad and round from all angles; well-developed cheeks; good muzzle; short, broad, straight nose; small ears with rounded tips, set far enough apart for the outer edge of the ear base to be perpendicular to the outer corner of the eye.
Eyes Large, round and wide open; wide-set to accentuate the breadth of the nose.
Body Medium to large, well-muscled and powerful; broad, flat shoulders, hips same width as shoulders; short thick neck; short, strong legs with round paws; five toes in front, four behind.
Tail Short and thick but in proportion to body length; rounded tip.
Coat Short and dense, not double or woolly; the coat should be resilient and firm to the touch.
Faults Long, fluffy or open coat; light undercoat; tail defects; definite nose stop; incorrect eye colour; incorrect number of toes.

COLOURS UK and USA
White; Black; Blue; Cream; Tortoiseshell; Blue-cream; Black Smoke; Bi-colour; Tortoiseshell-and-white; Tabby (classic, mackerel or spotted) – Brown, Red, Silver.
UK only
Chocolate; Lilac; tipped (all colours); Himalayan or Colourpoint (all colours). For full descriptions see pages 110–115.

Left: Silver Tabby British Shorthairs may be Classic, Mackerel or Spotted in pattern, and have separate show classes for cats of each pattern. The Mackerel Tabby is rather rare today, but the Classic and Spotted varieties have increased in popularity during the past few years. In the shorthaired breeds the desired markings are very clearly defined and quite distinct from the base coat colour, with no diffusion.

Top: Silver spotted tabby is shown relaxing in this photograph.

Above: A red tabby lying playfully on the lawn. This cat is extremely popular with the British public.

All British Shorthairs are identical in type and bone structure, and the breed is found in several colour varieties like this appealing British Blue (main picture) and the brightly patched Tortoiseshell (inset).

This Exotic Shorthair (inset top) is a Cameo Mackerel Tabby, with red stripes on a silver base coat. His type contrasts well with the fine young British Cream pictured (inset above).

THE EXOTIC SHORTHAIR

Essentially an American breed but also raised in Britain from slightly different rootstock, the Exotic Shorthair is the ideal cat for those who require the conformation and temperament of the Persian without the hard work of keeping the long coat in perfect condition. The American Shorthair was mated to the Persian and then the kittens were backcrossed at maturity with further Persians. In Britain, the British Shorthair was used instead of the American Shorthair. The Exotics are sweet-natured cats of impressive stature and with superb coats. They are undemanding pets, ideal both with children and the show bench.

CONFORMATION

Head Round and massive, with good breadth of skull; round face and underlying bone structure; short, broad snub nose with definite break; full, round cheeks, broad, powerful jaw; firm, full and well-developed chin; small, round-tipped ears tilted slightly forward and not unduly open at the base, set wide apart, and fitting without distorting the rounded head.

Eyes Large, round, full and brilliant, set wide apart and imparting a sweet expression.
Body Medium to large, cobby but not coarse; firm, level back; deep chested, equally massive over shoulders and hindquarters, with short, strong middle; short, thick, strong legs with large, round paws; toes carried close, five in front and four behind.

Tail Short but in proportion to body length.
Coat Of medium length; soft and plush; standing out from body due to density; never flat or close-lying and never long enough to flow.
Faults Any skeletal defect; incorrect eye colour; incorrect coat pattern; incorrect number of toes; undesired white spotting. Any deviation from the accepted colour standards.

COLOURS

White; Black; Blue; Red; Cream; Tortoiseshell; Blue-cream; Chinchilla; Shell Cameo; Shaded Silver; Shaded Cameo; Black Smoke; Blue Smoke; Cameo Smoke; Bi-colour; Calico; Dilute Calico; Tabby (classic, mackerel or spotted) – Brown, Blue, Red, Cream, Silver, Cameo; Brown-patched Tabby; Blue-patched Tabby; Silver-patched Tabby. Descriptions on pages 112–115.

Exotic Shorthairs are spreading throughout the cat world, captivating cat lovers with their charm, and giving busy owners the chance to own a cat with all the characteristics of the Persian but with an easy-care coat. A wide range of colours and coat patterns is accepted, so there is an Exotic to suit everyone's taste, from the Tabby (top), to the little Red Mackerel kittens (above).

THE MANX

Many romantic legends exist to explain the lack of a tail in the Manx cat, and some of these may be very near the truth. As the taillessness is due to a dominant gene, only one parent needs to possess the characteristic in order to pass it on to the kittens, and just one mutant could easily found a strain of Manx cats in any favourable environment. In the late 1800s, Mr Gambier Bolton published an account of Spanish ships that were wrecked on the Spanish Rock, close to the Isle of Man, in 1558. It claimed that some tailless cats from the ship took refuge on the Rock, and then made their way ashore at low tide. These cats are purported to be the forebears of all tailless cats, known as Manx, which have now spread around the world.

In Frances Simpson's *Book of the Cat* published in 1903, six types of Manx cats are described: 'The long straight-backed cat, the long roach-backed cat, the long straight-backed cat with high hindquarters, the short straight-backed cat, the short roach-backed cat, and the short-backed cat with high hindquarters. The last type is the correct one, the first is the worst and commonest type, the others are intermediate and should be judged accordingly.'

The true, completely tailless Manx is called a Rumpy, that with a tiny vestigial tail is a Rumpy-riser, that with a short stump tail is a Stumpy, while the cat with all other Manx characteristics from Manx parentage but complete with a tail is a Tailed Manx. All Manx have the same conformation.

CONFORMATION

Head Large and almost round, slightly longer than it is broad; rounded forehead; pronounced cheekbones and jowls, especially in the male; definite whisker break; strong whisker pads; side profile gives fairly long nose with a gentle dip, and a strong chin; ears wide-based and tapering gradually to the tip, larger than the British Shorthair and set higher on the head.
Eyes Large, round and full, set at a slight angle towards the nose; colour in keeping with coat colour.
Body Solid, compact and as short as possible, of overall medium size; broad chest, deep flanks and short back rising to high, round rump; strong legs, with longer, very muscular hindlegs, causing the rump to be considerably higher than the shoulders; paws neat and round, five toes in front and four behind.
Tail Absolute taillessness in the perfect Manx, with a decided hollow where in a British Shorthair the tail would begin; rump extremely broad and round.
Coat Double coat, short and dense, giving a padded feel; guard hairs hard with glossy appearance, undercoat thick and close; coat thicker in winter.
Faults Definite tail joint; long or silky coat; poor condition; weak hindquarters; incorrect number of toes.

COLOURS

White; Black; Blue; Red; Cream; Tortoiseshell; Blue-cream; Chinchilla; Shaded Silver; Black Smoke; Blue Smoke; Bi-colour; Calico; Dilute Calico; Tabby (classic, mackerel, spotted or patched) – Brown, Blue, Red, Cream, Silver. For full descriptions see pages 112–115.

Two very good rumpies from the Calliope Cattery: a sturdy male (above right) and a finer female (right).

THE SCOTTISH FOLD

The first Scottish Fold was discovered in 1961 in Scotland in a litter of farm cats and was obviously the result of a simple mutation, which caused the normally upright attitude of the pinna to fold forward and down, rather like the ear of a puppy. A breeding programme was eventually instigated, and it was found that the folded ear was due to a dominant gene. By mating the Folds with cats of true British Shorthair type and normal ears at each generation, a proportion of Folds was produced with otherwise normal anatomy. When Fold with Fold matings were carring out, some of the kittens produced had other skeletal abnormalities and so this practice was discontinued. Because of difficulties in gaining acceptance from the only registration body in Britain at that time, breeders were so discouraged that most gave up their programmes for the Fold, and their stock was exported to the United States. The remaining breeders were forced to register their cats with foreign associations until early 1983, when the Cat Association of Britain opened its new register to Folds bred to certain requirements. Scottish Folds are quaint, charming and strong, and seem particularly disease-resistant. They make superb pets and working cats, and appear to enjoy the occasional appearance on the show bench.

CONFORMATION

Head Well-rounded with firm chin and jaw; short nose with gentle curve; muzzle with well-rounded whisker pads; prominent cheeks; pronounced jowls required in the male; ears folded forwards and downwards (small and tightly folded ears are preferable to large and loosely folded ears), and set in a cap-like fashion to expose a rounded cranium; ear tips rounded.

Eyes Large, round and set wide apart; wide open with sweet expression; eye colour to correspond with coat colour.

Body Short, rounded and evenly balanced with deep flanks; medium-length legs in proportion to body; neat, round paws with five toes in front and four behind.

Tail Medium to long but in proportion to body; flexible and gently tapered.

Coat Short, dense and resilient.

Faults Kinked, broad, thick or foreshortened tail; any skeletal defect or weakness.

COLOURS

White; Black; Blue; Red; Cream; Tortoiseshell; Blue-cream; Chinchilla; Shell Cameo; Shaded Silver; Shaded Cameo; Black Smoke; Blue Smoke; Cameo Smoke; Bi-colour; Calico; Dilute Calico; Tabby (classic, mackerel, spotted or patched) – Brown, Blue, Red, Cream, Silver and Cameo. For full descriptions see pages 112–115.

Above right and right: Scottish Fold cats have the most delightful temperaments.

Opposite top and bottom: The Japanese Bobtail has a short tail complete with thick hair, giving the effect of a pompon.

THE JAPANESE BOBTAIL

Known for centuries in its native Japan, the Bobtail was first exported from that country to the United States in 1968. Mrs Judy Crawford sent Madame Butterfly, a Calico or Mi-ke (pronounced mee-kay), and Richard, a Red-and-white male, to Mrs Freret, who took the queen and her kittens by Richard to a meeting of the Cat Fanciers' Association, where the breed was accepted for registration.

A shorthaired cat with a crooked tail, the Bobtail is not related to the Manx cat, and the typical rigid and shortened tail is caused by the action of a simple recessive gene, not a dominant one as in the Manx. It is necessary for both parents to carry the gene, therefore, in order for Bobtail kittens to be born, and when both parents are Bobtails, all the litter will resemble the parents. The traditional Mi-ke colouring describes that of a predominantly white cat with black or red markings (bi-colour) or black and red markings (tri-colour), but other related colours are allowed in the breed standard. The Bobtail is easy to care for and is an outgoing, loving, agile cat of great character.

CONFORMATION

Head Appears long and fine but in fact forms equilateral triangle with gentle curving lines, high cheek bones and a definite whisker break; long nose, well defined by two parallel lines from tip to brow, with a gentle dip at or just below eye level; broad, gently curved muzzle; large, upright ears, tilted slightly forwards, wide-set.

Eyes Large and oval, set at a pronounced slant when viewed from the side.

Body Medium-sized, slender but well-muscled; long, slender legs, hindlegs noticeably longer than forelegs, but generally flexed so that the back is level rather than rising at the rump; very straight shoulder in line with forelegs; oval paws, with five toes in front, four behind.

Tail Furthest extension of tail bone from body should be 5–7.5 centimetres (2–3 inches), though if straightened the tail may measure 10–12.5 centimetres (4–5 inches); carried upright; hair on tail longer and thicker than on body, growing outwards in all directions, creating a pompon effect; hair camouflages the structure of the tail bone, which is generally strong and rigid rather than jointed, and may be straight or angled and curved.

Coat Short to medium length, soft and silky, without noticeable undercoat.

Faults Short, round head; cobby build; tail bone absent or extending too far from body; tail lacking pompon; delayed bobtail effect – pompon preceded by a few centimetres of normal tail.

COLOURS

Traditionally Mi-ke, which is white with discrete red and black random markings, and only exhibited by the females, the males being white with either black or red random markings; preference given to dramatically marked cats; other colours allowed are those which tend to produce bi-colour or tri-colour cats: White; Black; Red; Black-and-white; Red-and-white; Tortoiseshell; Tortoiseshell-and-white; Tabby-and-white; Blue or Cream solid colours; Blue or Cream Bi-colour; Blue-cream-and-white; and variously patterned bi-colour and tri-colour combinations. N.B. See pages 112–115 for colour definitions.

REX CATS

In 1950, a curly coated kitten was born as one of a normal litter to a normal-coated female cat in a farmhouse in Cornwall, south-west England. At first the queen's owner, Mrs Ennismore, thought that the waviness of the coat was due to birth fluids, but when it dried out the kitten's curls remained. Her veterinary surgeon suggested that Mrs Ennismore contact some leading geneticists. Hair samples were examined microscopically and found to be similar to those of the Rex rabbit, and so it was suggested that the cat be described as Rex. When he grew up, the Cream male, christened Kallibunker, was allowed to mate with his mother, and this union resulted in a litter of three kittens, two of which were curly coated. The mating was repeated and more Rex kittens arrived, but sadly, Kallibunker died quite young, luckily leaving his son Poldhu to carry on the line. Poldhu sired a superb female called Lamorna Cove, who was exported to the United States to found the breed on the other side of the Atlantic.

Although it is now thought that Poldhu was a Blue Tabby, a theory strengthened by a study of the colours of his offspring, at the time he was considered to be Blue-cream, and a rare phenomenon, for most Blue-cream males, like Tortoiseshell males, are sterile. A tissue sample was taken from Poldhu, presumably for chromosomal analysis, and this operation rendered Poldhu sterile. Fortunately, another of Kallibunker's sons was still entire, and this Cream-and-white, registered as Sham Pain Chas, was outcrossed with three British Shorthairs and a Burmese queen, to form strong base lines for the development of the Cornish Rex as a breed.

The gene giving the curly Rex coat was found to be a simple recessive, which means that two cats carrying the gene must be mated together for Cornish Rex kittens to result, and when two Cornish Rex mate, the whole litter must consist of Cornish Rex. The original Cornish cats were varied in type, and breeders worked hard to attempt to standardize the breed, despite the diversity in conformation of the first outcrosses. This was achieved by breeding some lines from matings with Havanas and Shorthairs, and some other strains from descendants of Lamorna Cove, reintroduced from Canada.

Ten years after the discovery of Kallibunker, the Cornish Rex was well established and received a burst of publicity, with articles and photographs in the national press. An enchanting Blue-and-white kitten called Du-Bu Lambtex appeared in the *Daily Mirror*, published in London, and this was picked up by Beryl Cox, who lived in the county of Devon, adjacent to the county in which the first Rex cats were found. Miss Cox had heard of local feral cats which appeared to have curled coats, and a kitten of

Above: Coulamour William Whitesox is an aptly named Bi-coloured Cornish Rex. Here he demonstrates the breed's typical stance.

Opposite top: Garchell Dopey Dreamer was, despite his name, smart enough to win the admiration of many judges.

Opposite bottom: Devon Rex kittens, with their pixie faces, huge bat ears and wrinkled brows are the most appealing felines.

her own exhibited this unusual pelage. Miss Cox spoke on the telephone with Mrs Agnes Watts, the breeder of Lambtex, and as a result decided to keep the unusual kitten, now named Kirlee. He spent a happy kittenhood, and at puberty was mated with some Cornish Rex queens. To everyone's surprise, each resulting kitten proved to be flat-coated, not curly, and it was concluded that Kirlee's curls were due to a different gene. The gene for Cornish was labelled Rex gene [i], the gene for producing the Devon, Rex gene [ii], and the two Rex breeds were developed along separate lines.

The Cornish Rex has a short, plushy coat which curls, waves and ripples over the whole body, legs and tail, and even the eyebrows and whiskers tend to curl. The Devon Rex is a very striking and unusual cat, and would be considered so even without the addition of the wavy coat, with its pixie-like expression and huge bat ears. Both breeds of Rex make delightful pets and are very popular on show benches throughout the world. Rex cats are great characters, and are easy to keep in good condition by feeding a well-balanced diet and grooming regularly with suitable equipment.

Rex cats have appeared from time to time in other areas of the world, some of which proved genetically compatible with the Cornish Rex and had almost identical coat structures. Recently, yet another Rex mutation occurred, this time in Holland, and, unlike the two English breeds, proved to be due to a dominant gene which produces a fairly coarse, bristly, waved coat.

THE CORNISH REX

Cornish Rex cats often cause great interest at cat shows when their tightly waved coats are first noticed by novice visitors, who have been known to ask how the exhibitor manages to set the cat's coat in such close and even rows.

CONFORMATION

Head Small and rather narrow, length one-third greater than maximum width, narrowing to a strong chin; flat skull; in side profile a straight line can be seen from centre of forehead to end of nose, and a perpendicular line from nose tip to point of strong chin; lean cheeks; narrow muzzle narrowing to a rounded end, with whisker break; Large, wide-based ears tapering to rounded tips, set high on the head, and well furred.

Eyes Medium-sized, oval, with a full eye's width between them.

Body Medium-sized; hard and muscular; medium-length torso; tight abdomen; slender but strong on shoulders and rump; stands high on long, slender legs, with small oval paws; five toes in front and four behind.

Tail Long, fine, tapered and well furred.

Coat Short and plushy without guard hairs; relatively dense with uniform narrow waves extending from the top of the head across the back, sides and hips and continuing to the tip of the tail; fur on the underside of the chin, chest and abdomen is short and noticeably wavy, whiskers and eyebrows crinkled and of good length.

Faults Asymmetrical white markings *except* in Tortoiseshell-and-white, Calico and Harlequin; shaggy or too short a coat; bare patches; Shorthair type or too long a wedge; small ears; cobby build; lack of firm muscles; short or bare tail; kinked or abnormal tail.

COLOURS

Any recognized feline colour allowed, *except* that in the USA chocolate, lilac or Siamese markings, or any of these with white, are disallowed.

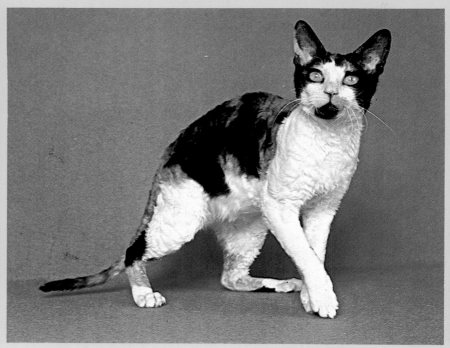

Above: Supreme Premier Cooli Iced Vanilla, a Cream Cornish Rex.

Above right: GCCF Grand Champion Senty-twix Jaspar, a famous male.

THE DEVON REX

Devon Rex cats may look very bare during or just after their moulting period, though a fine down usually covers the skin. Exhibitors have been asked why they clip their cats, and why they do not provide little coats.

CONFORMATION

Head Wedge-shaped with very full cheeks and pronounced cheek bones; short muzzle with strong chin and defined whisker break; side profile shows a forehead sloping back to a flat skull and a distinct stop at the bridge of the nose; large, very wide-based ears, tapering to rounded tips and well covered with fine fur, set wide apart and low; may have 'muffs'.

Eyes Large, oval and wide-set, slanted slightly so that the outer aperture is in line with the lower outer edge of the ear.

Body Medium-sized, slender, hard and muscular; tight abdomen; broad chest; firm rump; slender neck; hindlegs strong and longer than strong, straight forelegs; small, oval paws.

Tail Long, fine, tapering and well furred.

Coat Very short and fine, wavy and soft, without guard hairs; may have down on underparts, which should not be interpreted as bareness; crinkled whiskers and eyebrows of medium length.

Faults Straight or shaggy coat; white markings except in accepted patterns; bare patches; narrow, long or typically Shorthair head; cobby body; lack of firm muscles; small or high-set ears; short, bare or bushy tail; kinked or abnormal tail.

COLOURS

All feline recognized colours; some registering bodies disallow any white markings except in Tortoiseshell-and-white.

Opposite bottom: A Calico Cornish female with bright and sparkling patches of red and black, highlighted by the pure white of her underparts, limbs and mask, which added to her appeal.

Top: An appealing litter of Devon Rex kittens. At this tender age, kittens of this breed are covered with soft down rather than fur, though fur is generally visible on the nose, limbs and tail.

Above: Amaska Highlights, a Cornish kitten of good all-round type and with an excellent coat showing the close-waved effect. This kitten crossed the Atlantic to become a champion.

ORIENTALS

The Oriental group consists of the Siamese cats, as well as the range of whole-coloured and patterned varieties derived from Siamese stock that have been bred to recognition standard. All the Orientals have similar conformation, and are found in almost all known combinations of feline colours and patterns. They are interesting animals to own, being quite dog-like in their devotion to their owners and companion animals. Kept in isolation they may become morose and moody, but two or more Orientals will play together and remain firm friends.

The first Siamese cats were imported to Britain towards the end of the nineteenth century, and were first seen by an amazed British public at London's Crystal Palace in 1886. Though the first imports were rather frail and succumbed to disease, eventually the breed became acclimatized and increased in numbers. Initially only the Royal Cat of Siam – the Seal Point – was known, but from time to time a dilute kitten was born, and Blue Points were recognized in America during 1932 and in Britain in 1936. The Chocolate Point is another natural recessive form of Seal Point, and emerged quite naturally when cats carrying this elusive factor were unknowingly mated together. Regarded as poor Seal Points for many years, this variety was recognized eventually in Britain during 1950 and in America in 1951. Cats carrying the blue or dilute factor in addition to that for chocolate mated together produced the first Lilac Point Siamese. Again, these were often regarded as being 'sports' or 'poor blues', but eventually their true character was recognized, in the United States in the mid-50s under the name of Frost Point, and in Britain in 1960 as Lilac Point Siamese.

These four colours represent the natural set of Siamese varieties, produced without the necessity of outcrossing. The chocolate and its dilute, lilac, found originally only in Siamese, have been introduced by means of judicious outcrossing into several other breeds, including Persian, Shorthair, Rex and Angora. The semi-sex-linked orange gene and that for tabby markings were introduced into the Orientals by carefully selected outcrossings and, in some cases, by cats of impeccable breeding deciding to make their own mating arrangements. After the first cross, several back-crosses were necessary in order to regain the desired conformation of head and body. Pioneer breeders had much to put up with, first being denigrated by the purists for 'going against nature', and then having to find homes for kittens of poor type from the first, second and even third generations from the original cross. It is costly in time and money to follow breeding programmes in the quest for desired examples of a new variety, a fact often forgotten

Above: An Oriental Lilac or Lavender, also called Foreign Lilac in some associations, and Lavandel in Europe. Like all ideal Orientals, this young male is fine boned and elegant, and stands tall on slim legs and dainty paws.

Opposite: Siamese cats are members of the Oriental group, and are the forebears of the Oriental Shorthairs. This alert example is a Cream Point Siamese.

today, when almost the full possible range of conformation, coat and colour is available.

The introduction of the orange gene produced the Red Point, its dilute the Cream Point, and the range of tortoiseshell points – Seal-tortie Point, Blue-cream Point; Chocolate-tortie Point and Lilac-cream Point. A Siamese cat with tabby points was mentioned in 1902, and during the 1920s a breeder in Sweden carried out genetic tests in which tabby point Siamese were produced. However, it was not until a mismated Siamese queen's tabby kitten was bred with a good Seal Point stud and produced four tabby point kittens in a litter of six that the new variety caught the fanciers' imagination. Shown in public in 1961, the kittens aroused great interest, and several breeders decided to develop tabby points, preferring to call them lynx points. Over the following years, the whole range of tabby points were bred, and many of the cats were of such outstanding type that they took top show honours from the old-established varieties, such as Seal Points. Blue-tabby Point, Chocolate-tabby Point and Lilac-tabby Point all occurred as expected, but when Red-tabby Point and Cream-tabby Point

kittens arrived, it proved impossible to tell the difference between them and the standard Red Point and Cream Point Siamese. It was decided to register all such kittens as tabby points until breeding results proved them to be 'self' tabby points.

During the 1980s even more exotic colours appeared in Siamese, including subtle 'light' forms of the recessive colours, christened cinnamon and caramel. These were first identified in Siamese-derived varieties without the Himalayan pattern, and were more difficult to identify when restricted to the points only. Silver-tabby Points also appeared on the scene, and smoke points in several colours, all undershot with white and giving a silvered effect.

The first Siamese-derived variety to be recognized as a separate breed was developed in the 1950s. It was the self-coloured version of the Chocolate Point Siamese, emerging as a rich-brown cat with green eyes, and was given the name Havana, being the colour of a good Havana cigar. In 1956, the breed was officially recognized in Britain, and some kittens were exported to the United

Some of the author's Orientals which bear her renowned Solitaire prefix. Above are two Chocolate or Chestnut-spotted kittens, Sekmet and Kheta-Saru, pictured at eight weeks and already exhibiting excellent markings. On the right, effectively showing the difference between a Smoke and a Self-colour are Sobranie the Chocolate Smoke male – his silver undercoat shining through his dark chestnut mask – and Ala, an unrelated Havana queen.

States. There they formed the basis of a breed called the Havana Brown (see page 123), carefully selected and bred down to a standard that bears no resemblance to the Oriental. The Havana in Britain had its name changed by the Governing Council of the Cat Fancy and was required to be registered as the Chestnut Brown Foreign Shorthair for several years, after which the name Havana was allowed once more. In the meantime, some American fanciers, preferring the Oriental type of the 'new' Havana, imported more cats and registered these as Chestnut Orientals.

As some Havana cats carried the blue or dilute factor, it was only a matter of time before two such cats mated, and breeders were surprised, and usually delighted, to find self-coloured kittens of a delicate pinkish grey nestling among the expected chocolate-brown kittens. These cats were soon recognized as Foreign Lilacs by the Governing Council in Britain and Oriental Lilacs in America, terminology differing across the world in the Siamese-derived varieties. Today there is a wide range of colour combinations and patterns; almost all the possible permutations have been produced, and are recognized in New Zealand and by the Cat Association of Britain. It has been the tendency for other registering bodies to lag behind in their acceptance of separate colour varieties.

The Black and the White soon followed the Chocolate and Lilac selfs on to the show bench, but the self-blue, though equally easy to produce, was not developed until 1982, possibly because the niche was considered to be adequately filled by the Russian and the Korat, both self-blue breeds of Foreign type. At the same time, a group of breeders were developing 'self' tabby point Siamese, the author, in fact, attempting to re-create the cat of the kings of Ancient Egypt, worshipped and deified more than 2,000 years ago – the Egyptian Mau. Brown, Chocolate, Blue and Lilac Spotted Tabbies

CONFORMATION

Head Of medium size; long, tapering wedge starting at the nose and flaring out in straight lines to the tips of the ears, forming a triangle, with no whisker break; the muzzle fine and wedge-shaped; ears continue the wedge effect and are large, pointed and wide-based; in side profile the skull is flat and there is a straight line from the top of the head to the nose tip, with no bulge at the eyes and no dip in the nose; chin of medium strength, tip of nose in line with point of chin in same vertical plane; level bite.

Eyes Almond-shaped, of medium size; neither protruding nor recessed; with Oriental setting, slanting towards nose, in harmony with lines of wedge and ears; at least one eye's width between the eyes.

Body Of medium size, long, svelte and dainty – a well-balanced combination of fine bone and firm muscle; shoulders and hips continue the sleek lines of the tubular body; hips never wider than shoulders; tight abdomen; long, slim legs; hindlegs higher than forelegs, in good proportion to body; small, oval, dainty paws, with five toes in front and four behind; long, slender neck.

Tail Long, thin and tapering to a fine point at the tip.

Coat Very short, fine in texture, glossy and close-lying.

Faults Coarseness; weak hindlegs; kinked or abnormal tail; incorrect eye colour; white spotting; squint; incorrect number of toes; incorrect colour of nose leather or pads.

N.B. See pages 110–115 for colour definitions.

were produced with the desired conformation, looking very like the cats of the bronzes and papyri of those times, but they were slow to gain recognition in Britain. Exports were made to forward-thinking countries like New Zealand, where the cats took top awards and won great acclaim.

Today, the range of Oriental cats ensures that there is a colour and pattern to suit every taste, and as breeders continue to add and combine colours and patterns, all possible permutations will soon be available. The personality of the other Orientals is almost identical to that of the Siamese, except that with the loss of the restrictive Himalayan gene the cat also appears to lose a certain proportion of its vocalizing ability – quite an improvement in the opinion of some owners. Some strains have been bred particularly for sweet, even temperament, which is a boon on the show bench and an essential characteristic of cats destined to be family pets. All Orientals mature early and breed well, often producing larger than average litters of strong, healthy kittens. They are easy to care for and may be produced for show with the minimum of fuss.

COLOUR RANGE AND STANDARDS FOR THE SHORT-COATED BREEDS

Though the short-coated breeds are so diverse, their coat colours follow standard ranges and tones. In some cases the density, length and texture of the coat causes a slight variation in appearance, but a British Shorthair, for example, will be a similar shade to the corresponding Oriental variety.

SIAMESE AND HIMALAYAN-PATTERNED SHORTHAIRS

General colouring: light body with darker and well-defined points – mask, ears, legs, paws and tail; mask connected by fine tracings to the ears in adults; must have blue eyes.

SEAL POINT
Body pale cream of warm tone, shading to warm fawn; lighter underparts; points deep seal-brown; nose leather and paw pads deep seal-brown.

BLUE POINT
Body bluish white shading to lighter tone on stomach and chest; points deep blue; nose leather and paw pads slate-blue.

RED POINT
Body creamy white, any shading to tone with points; points warm orange-red (lack of barring desirable); nose leather and paw pads coral-pink.

'LIGHT' CHOCOLATE OR CINNAMON POINT
Body light ivory; points very light tan; nose leather and paw pads cinnamon-rose.

'LIGHT' LILAC OR FAWN POINT
Body glacial white; points very light pinkish grey; nose leather and paw pads rose-lilac.

CHOCOLATE POINT
Coat ivory; points milk chocolate; nose leather and paw pads cinnamon-pink.

LILAC POINT
Body glacial white; points frosty grey of pinkish tone; nose leather and paw pads lavender-pink.

CREAM POINT
Body clear white, any shading to tone with points; points apricot (lack of barring desirable); nose leather and paw pads flesh-pink.

BLUE-CREAM POINT
Body bluish white, lighter underparts; points patched or mottled, deep blue and cream, a blaze is desirable; nose leather and paw pads may be mottled.

SEAL-TORTIE POINT
Body cream shading to warm fawn, lighter underparts; points patched with seal-brown and red, red blaze desirable; nose leather and paw pads may be mottled.

Top: The Seal Point, or Royal, Siamese has dense points colour and the pale coat may darken to a deep warm fawn with maturity.

Bottom: Red mottles the seal-brown points in the Seal-tortie Point Siamese.

Opposite: In the Red Point Siamese, some slight barring is allowed.

CHOCOLATE-TORTIE POINT
Body ivory; points patched or mottled milk chocolate and light red, a blaze is desirable; nose leather and paw pads may be mottled.

LILAC-CREAM POINT
Body glacial white; points patched or mottled frosty grey of pinkish tone and pale cream, a blaze is desirable; nose leather and paw pads lavender-pink.

SEAL-TABBY POINT
Body cream shading to warm fawn; points seal-brown barring clearly defined, ears seal-brown with lighter 'thumbprint'; nose leather seal-brown or pink edged with seal-brown; paw pads seal-brown.

LILAC-TABBY POINT
Body glacial white; points frosty grey of pinkish tone barring, clearly defined, ears frosty grey-pink with lighter 'thumbprint'; nose leather lavender or pink edged with lavender; paw pads lavender.

BLUE-TABBY POINT
Body bluish white, lighter underparts; points deep blue barring clearly defined, ears deep blue with lighter 'thumbprint'; nose leather slate blue or pink edged with slate blue; paw pads slate blue.

CHOCOLATE-TABBY POINT
Body ivory; points milk-chocolate barring, clearly defined, ears milk-chocolate with lighter 'thumbprint'; nose leather cinnamon or pink edged with cinnamon; paw pads cinnamon.

RED-TABBY POINT
Body clear white, any shading to tone with barring on points; points warm orange-red barring, ears orange-red with lighter 'thumbprint'; nose leather and paw pads coral-pink.

CREAM-TABBY POINT
Body clear white, any shading to tone with barring on points; points apricot barring, clearly defined, ears apricot with lighter 'thumbprints'; nose leather and paw pads flesh-pink. (Forelegs only lightly marked.)

TORTIE-TABBY POINTS (TORBIE POINTS)
Body white or cream depending on main colour of points; points patched or mottled barring in seal-brown, deep blue, milk chocolate or frosty grey of pinkish tone, with corresponding red, light red or cream; ears should show lighter 'thumbprint'; nose leather and paw pads to match main colour, may be mottled. Though the main colour should be easily recognized on the points, forelegs may be lightly marked.

FULL-COLOUR SHORTHAIRS

The colour standards described here may be applied to all full-colour short-haired breeds in which the particular colour is recognized for show purposes. Coat length and density may slightly affect the overall appearance of some of the more subtle shades. (For eye colour, see table on page 127.)

WHITE
Coat pure glistening white, no yellow tinge; nose leather and paw pads pink.

BLACK = FOREIGN BLACK IN *UK*; EBONY IN *USA*
Coat jet black to roots, no rusty tinge; nose leather and paw pads black.

BLUE
Coat light to medium blue, very level in colour, with no barring, markings or shading; nose leather and paw pads slate-blue.

CHOCOLATE = ORIENTAL (HAVANA) IN *UK*; CHESTNUT IN *USA*
Coat rich chocolate brown, sound to roots, with no barring or markings; nose leather rich brown; paw pads cinnamon.

'LIGHT' CHOCOLATE OR CINNAMON
Coat light warm tan, sound to roots, with no barring or markings; nose leather and paw pads cinnamon-rose.

LILAC = FOREIGN LILAC IN *UK*; LAVENDER IN *USA*
Coat frosty grey of pinkish tone, sound to roots, with no barring, markings or shading; nose leather and paw pads lavender.

'LIGHT' LILAC OR FAWN
Coat very light pinkish grey; nose leather and paw pads rose-lilac.

RED
Coat rich orange-red, no barring or markings; nose leather brick-red; paw pads rose-red.

CREAM
Coat rich buff-cream, level in colour, with no barring or markings; nose leather and paw pads pink.

TORTOISESHELL
Coat clearly patched with black and red; red blaze desirable; nose leather and paw pads black, red or mottled.

BLUE-CREAM
Coat patched or intermingled, according to breed, with blue and cream; cream blaze desirable; nose leather and paw pads blue, cream or mottled.

CHOCOLATE-TORTIE
Coat patched with chocolate and light red; light red blaze desirable; nose leather and paw pads cinnamon, pink or mottled.

LILAC-CREAM
Coat patched or intermingled, according to breed, with pinkish grey and light cream; light cream blaze desirable; nose leather and paw pads lavender-pink or pink.

CHINCHILLA OR BLACK-TIPPED
Pure white undercoat, lightly tipped with black on back, flanks, head and tail, giving sparkling appearance; chin, ear tufts, chest and stomach pure white; eyelids, lips and nose outlined with black; nose leather brick-red; paw pads black.

SHELL CAMEO OR RED CHINCHILLA OR RED TIPPED
White undercoat, lightly tipped with red on back, flanks, head and tail giving sparkling appearance; chin, ear tufts, chest and stomach pure white; nose leather and paw pads rose-pink.

SHADED SILVER
Pure white undercoat with a mantle of black tipping, shading on face, sides and tail; white on chin, chest and stomach; eyelids, lips and nose outlined with black; nose leather brick-red; paw pads black.

Top: For show purposes the coat of the white shorthair, like this striking Oriental, must be pure, glistening white with no yellow tinges.

Opposite top: The kitten on the right is a rare Tortoiseshell Smoke.

Opposite bottom: Ebony male.

SHADED CAMEO OR RED SHADED

White undercoat with a mantle of red tipping, shading on face, sides and tail; white on chin, chest and stomach; nose leather and paw pads rose.

BLACK SMOKE

White undercoat, so deeply tipped with black that in repose the cat looks black with a little silvering just apparent on the mask; white base to all hair, more apparent on slightly longer-coated cats than the very short-coated Orientals; nose leather and paw pads black.

BLUE SMOKE

White undercoat, so deeply tipped with blue that in repose the cat looks blue with a little silvering just apparent on the mask; white base to all hair, more apparent on slightly longer-coated cats than the very short-coated Orientals; nose leather and paw pads slate-blue.

CHOCOLATE SMOKE

White undercoat, so deeply tipped with milk chocolate that in repose the cat looks chocolate with a little silvering just apparent on the mask; white base to all hair, more apparent on the slightly longer-coated cats than the very short-coated Orientals; nose leather and paw pads cinnamon.

LILAC SMOKE

White undercoat, so heavily tipped with pinkish grey that in repose the cat looks lilac with a little silvering just apparent on the mask; white base to all hair, more apparent on the slightly longer-coated cats than the very short-coated Orientals; nose leather and paw pads lavender-pink.

CAMEO SMOKE OR RED SMOKE

White undercoat so deeply tipped with red that in repose the cat looks red, white base to all hair, more apparent in the slightly longer-coated cats than the very short-coated Orientals; nose leather and paw pads rose. Barring or tabby markings undesirable.

BI-COLOUR (UK)

Coat of any recognized feline colour with white.

BI-COLOR (USA)

Coat black, blue, red or cream with white. Not more than half the coat should be white, and not more than two-thirds should be coloured; face to be patched with colour; white blaze desirable; symmetry desirable but not essential; nose leather and paw pads in keeping with colour of muzzle and toes.

HARLEQUIN OR VAN

Predominantly white cat with clear random marking of any recognized feline colour.

TORTOISESHELL-AND-WHITE OR CALICO

As the Bi-colour, but tri-coloured, being patched with black and red in the coloured areas.

BLUE-CREAM-AND-WHITE OR DILUTE CALICO

As the Bi-colour, but tri-coloured, being patched or intermingled with blue and cream in the coloured areas.

CHOCOLATE-TORTOISESHELL-AND-WHITE

As the Bi-colour, but tri-coloured, being patched with milk chocolate and light red in the coloured areas.

LILAC-CREAM-AND-WHITE

As the Bi-colour, but tri-coloured, being patched or intermingled with lilac and light cream in the coloured areas. Tri-coloured cats may be randomly marked, with less than half the coat white, and with less than two-thirds coloured.

TABBY SHORTHAIRS

Patterns All tabbies found in the American, British, Exotic and Oriental Shorthairs are found in the full range of colours, and both sides of the cat should be identically marked.

(For eye colour see table on page 127.)

CLASSIC, BLOTCHED OR MARBLED TABBY

Dense and clearly defined markings on lighter ground; head with 'M' on forehead; unbroken line runs back from outer corner of eye; swirls on cheeks; vertical lines run over head to shoulders; shoulders carry a distinct 'butterfly' with both upper and lower pairs of 'wings' well outlined and marked with clear spots inside each outline; back markings consist of three vertical, parallel lines from the 'butterfly' to the root of the tail, which is clearly ringed; on each flank a large solid blotch is encircled by one or more unbroken lines forming oyster-shaped patterns; several unbroken necklaces encircle the neck, and the legs are evenly barred right down to the paws; the chest and stomach are both spotted.

MACKEREL TABBY

Head, legs and tail as the classic tabby; body is marked with dark spine lines running together to form a dense saddle from which finely pencilled lines run down the body.

SPOTTED TABBY

Head, lower limbs and tail as for the classic tabby; body is marked with numerous, clearly defined spots; spots should not run together to form lines or solid areas.

PATCHED TABBY

A patched tabby or torbie is a brown, blue, chocolate, lilac or silver tabby with patches of red or cream.

Above right: Even non-pedigree tabby cats often have the strong markings set out in pedigree standards.

Right: In the blue tabby, shown here with its black litter mate, slate-blue markings pattern a bluish ivory base coat.

Opposite: The lilac tabby colour, as seen in this Oriental variety, has rich lavender markings on a paler lavender base.

BROWN TABBY
Base rich coppery brown; markings dense black; nose leather brick-red; paw pads black.

BLUE TABBY
Base pale bluish ivory; markings deep blue giving good contrast; nose leather old rose; paw pads rose pink.

CHOCOLATE TABBY
Base warm fawn; markings bright chestnut; nose leather chestnut or cinnamon rimmed with chestnut; paw pads cinnamon.

CINNAMON TABBY
Base light fawn; markings bright tan; nose leather and paw pads cinnamon-rose.

LILAC TABBY
Base pale lavender; markings rich lavender; nose leather and paw pads lavender-pink.

FAWN TABBY
Base light pink-beige; markings light, warm lilac; nose leather and paw pads rose-lilac.

RED TABBY
Base red; markings deep, rich orange-red; nose leather and paw pads brick-red.

CREAM TABBY
Base very pale cream; markings buff-cream, giving good contrast; nose leather and paw pads pink.

SILVER TABBY
Base pale clear silver; markings black; nose leather black or brick-red rimmed with black; paw pads black.

Note: there are Blue-silver, Chocolate-silver, Cinnamon-silver, Lilac-silver and Fawn-silver Tabbies in the Oriental group, and in each case the first colour describes the markings, which are clearly defined on a silver-white base coat; nose leather and paw pads are in keeping with the main colour.

CAMEO TABBY
Base off-white; markings red; nose leather and paw pads rose.

FOREIGN SHORTHAIRS

Though the first Abyssinian cats were found only in the colour now called either Brown, Usual or Ruddy, kittens of a second colour began to appear in occasional litters. These paler, reddish-gold cats were called Sorrel or Red Abyssinians and won recognition. In recent years, the Blue – a simple dilute version of the Brown Abyssinian – has appeared on the show scene, and the Fawn or Cream – a dilute version of the Sorrel Abyssinian – has also been produced by dedicated breeders.

THE ABYSSINIAN

One of the oldest domesticated breeds, the distinctively ticked Abyssinian was first recognized in 1882. An Abyssinian-type cat called Zula was brought out of Abyssinia (now Ethiopia) in 1868, at the end of a war in that country, and some believe that this cat was the forebear of the breed in Britain. Whether or not this is the case, by the turn of this century the Abyssinian cat was being seen at every cat show. John Jennings, writing in *Domestic and Fancy Cats* in 1893, states, 'whether imported or a manufactured cross hardly matters, as it [the Abyssinian] now breeds fairly true to point ... no variety has yet rejoiced in such varied names, several countries claiming it as their own.' In Frances Simpson's *Book of the Cat* published in 1903, colour plate 12 is from a painting by W. Luker Junior, captioned 'Abyssinian and Indian Cats'. Both cats are ticked and show heavy barring on the head, legs and tail, and while the cat on the left is a Brown Abyssinian, the 'Indian' cat on the right of the picture is a Sorrel.

In Britain the breed was variously known as the Russian, the Spanish, the Bunny Cat, the Hare Cat and the Ticked. The ticked coat closely resembles that of the wild rabbit or the Belgian hare, and some people insisted that the coat was produced by a cross between a cat and a rabbit!

Abyssinian cats are not very easy to breed as they are slow to mature and generally produce small litters at long intervals. Exceptionally loving and affectionate to those they know, they can be rather shy with strangers, and, therefore, do not always appear to advantage on the show bench. The short, close coat is easily maintained with a minimum of grooming.

Two or three bands of black or dark brown colour on each hair give the Brown, Usual or Ruddy Abyssinian its characteristic ticked coat. The underside of the body is a rich orange-brown colour, and free from markings. Fairly short, fine and close-lying, the coat is dense.

CONFORMATION

Head Medium-sized, modified wedge with brow, cheek and profile all showing gentle contours; gently pointed muzzle and rounded brow, with slight rise from bridge of nose to forehead; firm chin; level bite; large, pricked ears, broad at base and cupped as though listening, set well apart and preferably tufted at the pointed tips.

Eyes Large, bright and almond-shaped; very slightly tilted towards the nose, but neither Shorthair nor Oriental in effect.
Body Medium build; firm, lithe and muscular; between Shorthair and Oriental in overall conformation; legs proportionately slim and fine-boned with small oval paws, five toes in front and four behind.

Tail Thick at base, fairly long and tapering.
Coat Fairly short, close-lying, of fine texture but dense to the touch.
Faults Unbroken necklet; white locket or white anywhere other than at the nostrils, chin and upper throat; kinked or abnormal tail; greyish hair with no ruddy undercoat in a Brown; any black hair on Sorrel.

COLOURS

Coat pattern: Hairs to show two or preferably three bands of colour; dark colour should extend well up the back of the hindlegs towards the hocks, and should also be apparent at the tail tip; barring on the legs, tail and chest is undesirable.

BROWN, USUAL OR RUDDY

Coat ruddy brown ticked with dark brown or black with orange-brown undercoat, sound to roots; underside to harmonize with base hair of rest of body; any spine shading to be of deeper colour; nose leather brick-red; paw pads black, eyes: *USA* – rich gold or rich green; *UK* – amber, hazel or green.

SORREL OR RED

Coat warm copper-red distinctly ticked with chocolate, and base hair deep apricot; underparts deep apricot or harmonizing with base hair; any spine shading to be of deeper colour; tip of tail and heels chocolate; nose leather and paw pads rose-pink; eyes: *USA* – rich gold or rich green; *UK* – amber, hazel or green.

BLUE

Coat soft warm blue ticked with deeper steel-blue, and base hair warm oatmeal; underparts warm oatmeal, harmonizing with base hair; any spine shading to be of deeper colour; tip of tail and heels steel-blue; nose leather deep rose; paw pads lavender-blue; eyes amber, hazel or green.

FAWN OR CREAM

Coat light mushroom-beige distinctly ticked with lilac, and base hair light beige; underparts beige, harmonizing with base hair; any spine shading to be of deeper colour; tip of tail and heels chocolate; nose leather and paw pads lavender-pink; eyes amber, hazel or green.

Note: As the Sorrel or Red Abyssinian is produced by the action of the 'light' chocolate gene, and the Fawn or Cream Abyssinian is its dilute form, the names Red and Cream are misnomers; true chocolate and lilac Abyssinians have also been bred and are ticked milk chocolate and ticked pale lilac respectively. Sex-linked red, cream and various tortoiseshell Abyssinian cats have also been produced, as well as a whole range in the silver series, with various coloured ticking on a silver base coat.

Above: Though some Abyssinians tend to show reserve or some shyness with strangers, they can be exceptionally loving towards their owners. Many males, like The Wild One, a Brown champion shown here, enjoy attention and respond to quiet, considerate handling with a typically friendly, tail-up gesture.

Left: In the Blue Abyssinian a warm oatmeal-coloured base coat shades to blue and is double or trebly ticked with deep steel blue to give the unique 'Aby' effect. The nose leather is deep rose-pink and the paw pads lavender-blue.

THE BURMESE

This cat is closely related to the Siamese, sharing the same genetic series, and if the two breeds are mated together an interesting intermediate variety, the Tonkinese, is produced. When Tonkinese are mated together the kittens may be Siamese, Burmese or Tonkinese. In 1930, the forebear of the Burmese breed, Wong Mau, arrived in the United States, having been given to a retired ship's doctor, Joseph C. Thompson, in the East and taken home with him as a much-loved pet. Wong Mau resembled a dark-coated Siamese but was in fact Tonkinese, for when she was mated to a Siamese male she had some Siamese kittens and some just like herself. Later, the darker of her offspring were mated together to produce America's first Burmese cats, and the breed was eventually recognized in 1936.

Burmese cats were imported to Britain from America during 1949, and the breed steadily grew in popularity. The first cats were Sable or Brown Burmese, but beneath the dark, glossy coats lurked recessive genes, and before many years had elapsed, Blue, Chocolate and Lilac Burmese began to appear. In Britain, judicious outcrosses were made to introduce the sex-linked orange gene into the breed, which now contains the whole red series.

Type in the United States differs from that in Britain, but character and temperament remain similar. Burmese are extroverts, and should be kept in pairs, for as single pets they may feel lonely and morose at times. Often mischievous and very intelligent, Burmese are easy to groom and to maintain in perfect health, and are very good with children and dogs.

Above: Cream Burmese.

Above right: Chocolate-tortie Burmese kitten.

Right: The Red Burmese has a light tangerine coat.

Opposite: Chocolate Burmese.

CONFORMATION

Head
USA Rounded without flat planes in both front and side profiles; full face tapering to short, well-developed muzzle, visible nose break; medium-sized ears set well apart on rounded skull, tilting slightly forward, broad-based with slightly rounded tips.

UK Slightly rounded on top, with wide cheek bones and a short blunt wedge; jaw wide at the hinge and with firm chin; distinct nose break; medium-sized ears set wide apart, broad-based with slightly rounded tips, outer line of ears continuing the shape of upper part of face.

Eyes
USA Set far apart and with rounded aperture, ranging from yellow to gold; the greater the depth and brilliance the better.

UK Large, lustrous and set wide apart; top line showing Oriental slant towards nose, the lower line rounded. Any shade of yellow from chartreuse to amber, with golden-yellow preferred.

Body
USA Medium-sized, muscular and compact; ample, round chest; level back from shoulder to tail; legs in proportion to body; round paws with five toes in front, four behind; male larger than female.

UK Medium size and length; hard and muscular, feeling heavier than expected; strong, rounded chest; straight back; legs slender and in proportion to body; neat, oval paws with five toes in front, four behind.

Tail
USA Straight and of medium length.

UK Slightly tapered and of medium length.

Coat
USA Fine, glossy, satin-like texture, short and close-lying.

UK Short, fine, satin-like texture, close-lying and glossy.

Faults
USA Green eye colour; kinked or abnormal tail; white locket or button; incorrect number of toes.

UK Siamese or Shorthair type; kinked or abnormal tail; round or Oriental eyes; incorrect eye-colour, white spotting.

CONFORMATION

COLOURS
In the United States of America, the various registering bodies recognize only certain Burmese colours, and most consider only the Sable or Brown as the true Burmese. In Britain and other European countries the full range of colours in the natural and the red series are accepted.

SABLE OR BROWN
Coat rich, warm sable or seal-brown, gradually shading to a slightly lighter colour on the underparts; ears and mask may be very slightly darker but no other markings or shadings; nose leather and paw pads brown.

BLUE
Coat soft silver-grey with distinct silver sheen on highlighted areas – ears, face and feet; slight shading gives darker tone on back and tail, lighter underparts; nose leather dark grey; paw pads grey.

CHOCOLATE
Coat warm milk chocolate; evenness of colour desirable, but mask and ears may be slightly darker; legs, tail and lower jaw should be of matching shade; nose leather warm chocolate; paw pads brick-red to chocolate.

LILAC
Coat pale dove-grey with slight pinkish cast; ears and mask may be slightly darker; nose leather and paw pads lavender-pink.

RED
Coat light tangerine; ears slightly darker; small, indeterminate markings may be allowed on face and elsewhere except the sides and belly of an otherwise excellent cat; nose leather and paw pads pink.

CREAM
Coat rich cream, ears very slightly darker; small indeterminate markings may be allowed on face and elsewhere except the sides and belly of an otherwise excellent cat; nose leather and paw pads pink.

BROWN TORTIE
Coat a random mixture of dark brown and red without any obvious barring; nose leather and paw pads brown and/or pink, plain or mottled.

BLUE TORTIE
Coat a random mixture of blue and cream without any obvious barring; nose leather and paw pads blue and/or pink, plain or mottled.

CHOCOLATE TORTIE
Coat a random mixture of chocolate and light red without any obvious barring; nose leather and paw pads chocolate and/or pink, plain or mottled.

LILAC TORTIE
Coat a random mixture of lilac and cream without any obvious barring; nose leather and paw pads lilac and/or pink, plain or blotched.

119

THE BOMBAY

This American breed was produced by outcrossing Burmese to Black American Shorthairs. It has become popular in the United States, and is recognized by some associations.

CONFORMATION

Head Pleasingly round, without flat planes, in both front and side profiles; full face with breadth between the eyes, tapering slightly to a short, strong muzzle; visible nose break; medium-sized ears set well apart and tilted slightly forward; broad-based and with slightly rounded tips.

Eyes Set far apart, with rounded aperture.

Body Medium-sized and muscular, neither compact nor rangy; legs in proportion; male larger than female.

Tail Straight and of medium length.

Coat Fine, short and satin-like, very close-lying, with a patent-leather sheen; unlike the coat of any other black cat.

Faults Kinked or abnormal tail; white spotting; incorrect number of toes; incorrect colour of nose leather or paw pads; green eyes.

COLOUR

Coat jet black to the roots, with a high-gloss like patent leather (kittens may be slightly less dense and sleek); nose leather and paw pads black; eyes ranging from gold to deep copper.

Above and left: These two fine jet-black cats aptly live up to the American description of the Bombay breed – they are said to be 'patent leather kids with the new penny eyes'.

CONFORMATION

Head From the front the head appears heart-shaped with breadth between and across the eyes, the eyebrow ridges forming the upper curves of the 'heart' and the sides of the face curving down to the chin; side profile shows a flat forehead and a slight stop between it and the nose; the nose tip has a slight downward, lion-like curve; jaw and chin strong and well developed; all planes smoothly curved; large, round-tipped ears, flared at the base and set high, giving an alert look, with short, close hair on the outside of the pinna and very little hair inside.

Eyes Large, luminous and rather prominent; open and over-sized for face; when partially closed, present an Asian slant, when open, appear well rounded; brilliant luminous green colour preferred, but amber cast accepted; cats under two years of age may have yellow, amber or amber-green eyes.

Body Of medium size and semi-cobby; medium bone structure; curved back; legs in proportion to body, with length of back equal to height from rump to floor; hindlegs very slightly longer than forelegs; oval paws with five toes in front and four behind.

Tail Medium in length, tapering to a rounded tip.

Coat Medium-length, single coat, glossy and fine; close-lying except along the spine, where it is inclined to break as the cat moves.

Faults White spotting; incorrect eye colour; incorrect coat colour; visible kink; incorrect number of toes.

COLOURS

Silver-blue all over, without shading or any tabby markings but with silver tipping to all hairs at maturity; nose leather and paw pads dark blue or lavender with rosy tinge.

Above: Large, luminous, brilliant green eyes are a feature of the silver-blue shorthaired Korat, the 'lucky-charm' feline breed.

THE KORAT

One of the most ancient of all feline breeds and unadulterated by any outcrosses, the Korat originated in Thailand (formerly Siam). There it is known as Si-sawat, a compound word referring to its evocative colouring of silver-grey coat and light green eyes. In the *Book of Cat Poems*, probably written in the thirteenth century and preserved in the National Library of Bangkok, the Si-sawat is illustrated with the caption: 'The cat Mal-ed has a body like Doklao, the hairs are smooth with roots like clouds and tips like silver, the eyes shine like dewdrops on a lotus leaf.' Mal-ed is the word for seed, and refers to the seed of the Look Sawat, which has a silver-grey fruit, lightly tinged with green. Dok means flower and lao is a plant with silver-tipped flowers. Rare and highly prized in Thailand, the Si-sawat is considered a good-luck charm, and a pair of such cats is a traditional wedding gift, intended to bring prosperity and long life to the couple.

A Korat was exhibited at the National Cat Club Show, London, in 1896, but was disqualified because the judges considered that all cats from Siam should be fawn with dark brown points. In 1959, Korat cats reached the United States and were officially recognized there in 1966. South Africa accepted the breed in 1968, Australia in 1969 and Britain's Governing Council of the Cat Fancy in 1975, though it denied the breed championship status. In 1983, the Cat Association of Britain accepted the Korat for full status, and Britain's first Champion was made up at the Association's first show in Esher on 2 October, when Thai-Wun-On won certificates in her three rings, under judges from England, Belgium and Australia. All Korat cats must be bred from Korat stock, and are thus able to trace their pedigree back to Thailand. They are excellent in the house, being quiet-voiced and dainty in all they do, but they are not prolific breeders, and it is often necessary to wait for some time before kittens are available for sale. The short, dense coat is kept immaculate by weekly brushing and combing to remove dust and loose hair, and the silver sheen may be enhanced by buffing with a silk scarf or chamois leather. This makes the Korat an easy cat to prepare for the show ring.

THE RUSSIAN BLUE

This breed is said to have originated in Archangel in north-west USSR and to have been transported as trade goods to England. Russian Blue cats were shown quite extensively at the early cat shows in Britain, but differed from those of the breed today in having orange eyes. The fortunes of the breed suffered greatly in Britain during the two world wars, when breeders were hard pressed to find cat food, but a nucleus of breeding stock was maintained. A retrograde, but probably necessary, step was taken in the post-war years, when Russians were outcrossed to Siamese to enlarge the gene pool. Today breeders test mate their stock for freedom from the undesirable recessive Himalayan factor.

Russian Blues are very popular in the United States, which has a slightly different breed standard, while in Britain breeders have worked for some years on the production of the Russian Black and the Russian White. Whatever their conformation, Russian cats are loving, quiet-voiced and generally very hardy. They are easy to groom and make excellent family pets.

CONFORMATION

Head
USA Broad across the eyes; top of skull long and flat; medium-length nose; level chin; large, wide-based ears, tips more pointed than rounded; short fine hair on outside of pinna, very little hair inside; ears set far apart as much on the side as on the top of the head.

UK Short wedge with flat skull; straight nose forming an angle with flat forehead in side profile; strong chin; prominent whisker pads; large, pointed, wide-based ears, set vertically on the head with little hair inside pinna.

Eyes
USA Wide-set; rounded in shape; vivid green in colour.

UK Wide-set; almond in shape; vivid green in colour.

Body
USA Fine-boned, long, firm and muscular, lithe and graceful; long, fine-boned legs with small, slightly rounded paws; five toes in front and four behind.

UK Long, lithe and graceful in outline; medium-boned; long legs with small oval paws; five toes in front and four behind.

Tail
USA Long in proportion to body, and tapering from a fairly thick base.

UK Fairly long and tapering.

Coat
USA Short, dense, fine and plush double coat stands out from body due to density, and has distinct soft and silky feel.

UK Short, dense, fine and plush double coat, standing up soft and silky, unlike that of any other breed.

Faults
USA Kinked or abnormal tail; white spotting; incorrect number of toes. Siamese type; incorrect eye colour.

UK White or tabby markings; cobby or heavy build; square head; Siamese type; incorrect eye colour.

Above and left: Like the Korat, the Russian Blue has an easy-care coat which may appear silver at the tips. Here, however, the similarity ends for the Russian Blue is typically long and lithe, with an angular skull, almond eyes, distinctive ears and prominent whisker pads.

THE HAVANA BROWN

In the United States of America, the Havana Brown is a unique breed, developed from imports from Britain in the 1950s. While the same rootstock has led to the Oriental Chestnut or Havana in Britain, the American breeders selected for different characteristics. One of the original imports, Roofspringer Mahogany Quinn, bred by Baroness von Ullman in London, became the first Grand Champion Havana in the United States following full recognition by some associations in 1959. Never crossed with other breeds, the Havana Brown has established a permanent niche in the cat world. It makes a delightful, intelligent and active pet, is less vocal than the Siamese, and its richly coloured glossy brown coat glows with a minimum of grooming.

CONFORMATION

Head Slightly longer than it is wide with a distinct stop at the eyes and a strong chin forming a straight line with the nose; decided whisker break; large wide-set, round-tipped ears, tilted slightly forward; very short fur on outside of pinna and very little inside.
Eyes Oval-shaped; colour ranging from chartreuse to green, greener shades preferred.
Body Medium in length, firm and muscular, midway between Siamese and Shorthair in type; medium-length legs with oval paws.

Tail Medium in length, tapering.
Coat Medium in length, smooth and lustrous.
Faults Kinked tail; incorrect colour of eyes, whiskers, nose leather or paw pads; white spotting.

COLOURS
Coat rich mahogany toned brown, solid to roots and with no tabby markings or barring in adults; brown whiskers; nose leather brown with rosy tone; paw pads with rosy tone.

Left and above: The American Havana Brown has a puppy-dog face and modified foreign type, even though it was bred from the same stock as the Oriental Chestnut or Havana which were British breeds.

Though the Foreign and Oriental Shorthairs are alike in having short, fine coats and light, elegant conformation, they differ considerably in the points laid down for their judgement in the show ring. The Blue Point (inset above left), like all Siamese, must be long, lithe and svelte. Its colouring is restricted to the points, and it has blue eyes.

The Havana or Oriental Chestnut (inset above right) has similar conformation to the Siamese but is coloured all over and has green eyes. The Foreign Shorthairs have specialized type according to their breeds, and here we see a typical Russian Blue (main picture), contrasted with a superb Blue-cream Burmese (inset opposite).

Good contrast must exist between pale ground colour and deeper markings; forehead barred with characteristic 'M' and frown lines forming lines between the ears which continue down the back of the neck breaking into spots along the spine; spine lines merge into dorsal stripe over haunches and along the length of the tail to dark tip; tail also carries bands of dark colour; cheeks have two lines outwards; chest carries one or more, preferably broken, necklaces; shoulder markings transient between spots and stripes; front legs barred; body randomly spotted and two sides do not need to match; spots must not form mackerel lines; haunches transiently spotted and striped; underbody with 'vest button' spots.

SILVER
Base pale silver, brighter underparts; white throat, chin and nostrils. Markings charcoal, showing good contrast; back of ears greyish-pink, tipped black; nose, lips and eyes outlined in black; black heels; nose leather brick-red; paw pads black.

BRONZE
Base light bronze, lighter underparts; creamy white throat, chin and nostrils; markings dark brown showing good contrast; back of ears tawny pink tipped dark brown; nose, ears and eyes outlined in dark brown; bridge of nose ochrous; black or dark brown heels; nose leather brick-red; paw pads black or dark brown.

SMOKE
Coat charcoal grey with silver undercoat across head, shoulders, legs, tail and underside; light throat, chin and nostrils; markings jet black, pattern to be clearly visible; black heels; nose leather and paw pads black.

THE EGYPTIAN MAU

Said to be the only natural breed of domesticated spotted cat, and probably directly descended from the cats of Ancient Egypt, the Mau was first brought to the United States of America by Princess Natalie Troubetskoye in 1956, from her cattery in Italy. The Princess obtained her first Mau, called Baba, from Cairo and by 1955 the breed was on show in Rome. Some associations recognized the breed as early as 1957, but the Cat Fanciers' Association only granted Championship status in 1977. The Egyptian Mau, unlike any other breed in conformation and with distinctive markings, makes a fine pet, being robust, playful and having a dog-like devotion to its owners.

CONFORMATION

Head Modified, slightly rounded wedge without flat planes; brow, cheek and profile all show gentle contours; slight rise from bridge of nose to forehead,which then flows into arched neck without a break; large, moderately pointed ears, broad at base and with good width between; hair on outside of pinna very short and close; inside pinna delicate, almost translucent shell pink (may be tufted).
Eyes Large, almond-shaped, with slight slant towards nose; colour gooseberry green, amber cast accepted. Correct colour must be present in adults.

Body Of medium length and muscular; legs in proportion to body, hindlegs longer than forelegs; small, almost oval paws, five toes in front, four behind; overall conformation midway between Siamese and Shorthair.
Tail Of medium length, thick at base, with slight taper.
Coat Silky and fine but dense and resilient to touch, with a lustrous sheen; medium in length.
Faults Incorrect eye colour or coat pattern; short or round head; pointed muzzle; small ears; small, round or Oriental eyes; incorrect conformation; short or whip tail; poor condition.

Eye-colour chart for shorthaired breeds

Basic coat colour	American shorthair & Scottish fold	British shorthair	Exotic shorthair & Manx	Oriental USA	UK
White	deep blue or orange/copper or one eye of each colour	deep blue or orange/copper or one eye of each colour	deep blue or orange/copper or one eye of each colour	deep blue or green, amber permitted	vivid blue
Black, blue	brilliant gold	orange/copper	brilliant copper	green preferred, amber permitted	green
Chocolate, cinnamon, lilac, fawn	—	—	—	green preferred, amber permitted	green
Red, cream, tortoiseshell, blue-cream, calico*, dilute calico*, shell cameo*, shaded cameo*, black smoke, blue smoke, cameo smoke*	brilliant gold	orange/copper *not accepted	brilliant copper	green preferred, amber permitted	green preferred, amber permitted
Chinchilla, shaded silver	green or blue-green	green or blue-green	green or blue-green	green	green
Silver tabby	green or hazel	green or hazel	green or hazel	green	green
Silver patched tabby	green or hazel	—	brilliant copper	green preferred, amber permitted	green preferred, amber permitted
Brown tabby	brilliant gold	orange, hazel or deep yellow	brilliant copper	green	green
Blue tabby	brilliant gold	—	brilliant copper	green	green
Chocolate tabby, cinnamon tabby, lilac tabby, fawn tabby	—	—	—	green	green
Red tabby	brilliant gold	brilliant copper	brilliant copper	green preferred, amber permitted	green preferred, amber permitted
Himalayan	—	vivid blue	—	vivid blue	vivid blue

BREEDING

Though it is usually considered that cats have kittens easily, without fuss and often too frequently, the production of pedigree kittens following controlled mating, and in a controlled environment, can prove difficult. Despite its generations of domestication, a cat can resent the unnatural restrictions placed upon her during conception, pregnancy and parturition. She may be difficult to mate and, after a troublesome gestation period, she may have a stressful delivery. She may reject her kittens, fail to lactate, or spend all her time anxiously moving her kittens from one place to another.

In this book we explain at length how cats used for breeding purposes should be kept and cared for, the psychological needs of the entire male and the brood queen, what happens at each stage of mating, pregnancy and birth, and how to cope when things go wrong. With luck, with this book at the ready in case of problems during your first attempt at cat breeding, your cat will perform beautifully and prove to be a perfect mother.

A litter of beautiful Foreign Lilac kittens: a credit to their mother.

Like any serious hobby, that of cat breeding should not be entered into lightly or for the wrong reasons. You must desire to breed cats for personal satisfaction rather than financial gain, and you must have sufficient funds available to feed and house the cats adequately and safely, and be prepared to gain enough knowledge to care for your felines in sickness as well as in health, as newborn babies and as geriatrics. Breeding pedigree cats is a hobby full of rewards, even though these will never be financial. There is a great sense of pride and achievement in planning a litter and then rearing it, and great happiness may be derived from caring for the brood queen and her kittens from birth through weaning. Later, when your kittens grow and develop into prize winners on the show bench, your pride may know no bounds, and you will feel well on the way to the establishment of your own distinctive bloodlines in your chosen breed.

While it seems logical to the novice to buy a breeding pair of cats, this is impractical; a male is not content with one queen, and is a nuisance as a pet due to his adult habit of spray-marking his territory. Keeping a stud male is a job for the experienced fancier. So, once you have chosen the breed in which you want to specialize, buy one or two of the very best females that you can afford. Two kittens will keep each other company and will provide healthy competition for one another during their formative months of growth. It is quite a good idea to buy unrelated female kittens if you can, so that in later years, having kept further stock, you can mate together unrelated offspring with your own cattery name. You will find suitable cats at stud, with experienced owners full of useful advice, when your females are ready for mating.

THE QUEEN

A kitten for eventual breeding should be purchased at about three months of age, though if you have the chance to buy an older kitten that has already proved its potential in the show ring so much the better. It is not necessary for her to have taken the top honours so long as she is sound and has an impeccable pedigree. She should be properly registered with a bona fide body that registers cats and runs cat shows, and have had a suitable course of vaccinations. She should be well grown, healthy and free from parasites, and come from a cattery or home where a programme of testing for freedom from feline infectious leukaemia is carried out.

A novice breeder should join a breed group and attend as many seminars and teach-ins as possible while the kitten is young. Cat shows are held around the country and at such events the novice can meet and talk with other fanciers of his or her chosen breed.

From the age of three months the female kitten may be allowed to live a fairly normal life within the family, though she should usually be kept safely indoors away from health hazards and traffic. The little female should be fed a sensible, well-balanced diet, and encouraged to play in order to keep fit. Daily grooming will help to keep her coat in good condition and her muscles toned, and such sessions also help to strengthen the bond between cat and owner.

Though the kitten's first period of heat or oestrus may occur at any time from four months onwards, most young queens of Siamese or Oriental breeds start to 'call' at about nine months of age, while the Persians and Shorthairs may not 'call' until well over one year old. A full description of the outward signs of a queen in oestrus is given in the chapter on cat behaviour, on page 45.

It is best to merely observe the young cat during her first period of heat, and to make sure

Most female cats mature and have their first period of heat, or oestrus, at about nine months of age.

that she is safely confined indoors or in a secure pen until the oestrus has passed. By noting her symptoms and behaviour you will be able to monitor subsequent periods of oestrus. At her next 'call' you may wish to have her mated, and if so you must make arrangements with the owner of a suitable stud cat, found by visiting cat shows or by reading relevant advertisements in the cat press.

Some cats mature early and may 'call' at three- or four-week intervals from a very young age. In this case your veterinary surgeon may advise early mating rather than risk a setback in your kitten's health, for frequent 'calling' can cause loss of appetite and, therefore, loss of condition at a critical period in the cat's development. Continued periods of heat without conception can also lead to sterility in later life. Your veterinary surgeon will check your kitten to make sure that she is physically fit for motherhood. Pregnancy often completes the growth and maturity of well-grown youngsters if they are well fed and correctly cared for during this important stage.

THE STUD MALE

Though the brood queen plays a vital part in the breeding programme, the stud male's role is perhaps even more important, for he may be responsible for hundreds of kittens during his working life, while even the most fertile queen is likely to produce a maximum of one hundred. For this reason the stud male must be an excellent example of his breed, selected for his good looks, which should approximate closely to the breed standard of points of excellence, for his general health and stature, and for his gentle temperament.

The responsible breeder will ensure that all kittens that are produced have the very best start in life.

The ideal stud quarters for the male cat, providing warmth, comfort and fresh air within a safe enclosure.

He should have been well reared and from a strong litter that suffered no setbacks during the kittens' early days. The qualities and fertility records of both his parents should be known.

Keeping a stud male properly requires experience and understanding. Such cats are generally loving and affectionate, but their habit of spray-marking their territory and possessions means that they usually have to be housed well away from the family's rooms. It is important, however, for the stud cat to be kept occupied and interested in life during the periods between visiting queens. He will need lots of affection and daily handling, even short-coated cats benefiting from daily grooming. His accommodation should be as pleasant and spacious as possible, with plenty of exercise areas and access to suitable spots for sunning and running.

Each owner has his or her own ideas about the ideal construction of stud accommodation, but its siting is very important and should be adjacent to areas of general daily activity. Kennels, stables, summerhouses and workshops have all been successfully converted into stud homes. The basic requirements are a building tall enough to allow you to stand inside and with a large enough floor area to enable you to comfortably attend to the daily needs of the male and his visiting females, and to adequately supervise matings. It should be large enough also for the male cat to take exercise during long winter months when he may not wish to use his outdoor run. All interior walls should be lined and insulated, and all the surfaces should be completely washable. The floor, in particular, will receive very hard wear and be subjected to urine spray. The walls may be lined with laminated board or may be sealed and painted with washable paint. The floor may be tiled or fitted with impervious, vinyl-coated material, and all cracks and crevices should be adequately sealed.

A pen or cage must be provided for the visiting queens, and opinions vary as to the ideal size for this. Some catteries provide very large pens and runs, but the queen is at stud for a limited time, during which she is likely to be very preoccupied with the important matter in hand. It seems more logical, therefore, to make most of the stud-house space available to the male cat, who is in occupation at all times. The queen's pen should be draughtproof and cosy, with one side of wire mesh so that the two cats can get to know one another. It must be large enough to hold the visiting queen's bed and toilet tray, and have room for her to exercise and for her food and water bowls. It is perhaps best sited well above the floor, unless it is of walk-in height, for the stud male may try to spray the queen's bedding and belongings if these are at floor level.

The stud house should be enclosed in a pleasant, safely wired run. The floor should be paved or concreted, for grass soon becomes soiled and is impossible to sterilize. It is a good idea to have part of the run covered to give exercise space in inclement weather, and the door to the stud house should be angled to avoid prevailing winds. Logs and shelves provide climbing and sunning facilities. The entrance gates must be well constructed and fasten securely.

A cat chosen as a potential stud will be shown to championship status in order to prove his quality and may even go on to become a grand or supreme champion. He will be carefully reared through kittenhood, and be fed to grow strong and healthy. His vaccination programmes will be meticulously carried out and regular booster injections given. He will be regularly dosed against internal parasites and his teeth, ears and claws will be examined weekly. His owner will arrange for regular swabs to be taken to check his freedom from any viral infections brought in by visiting queens, and for regular blood testing for feline leukaemia virus.

When a stud cat loses his popularity, the caring owner will have him neutered rather than let him become more and more morose living in a state of frustrated boredom. Though many neutered ex-studs continue to spray, and are, therefore, unable to become house pets, their busy youth should have

entitled them to a long and peaceful retirement. Ex-stud cats, which would have fought each other to the death during their working lives, often settle down to live out their days together.

SUPERVISED MATINGS

The first queens mated by a young stud should be steady and experienced. Feline mating procedures often seem quite terrifying to the casual observer as the mated queen quickly and sometimes viciously attacks the male, who must be quick enough to jump sharply out of reach of her flashing claws. A quieter, older queen may growl and hiss, but her swiping paws will be merely feints and not intended to hurt. It is important that the male's first sexual encounters are well supervised to guard against him being injured or frustrated.

When the visiting queen is delivered by her owner, she should be put quietly and gently into the special queen's pen in the stud house. Her owner may be allowed to put the queen into the pen and to settle her down. If this is permitted, the stud cat should be shut out in his run while the human visitor invades his territory for he may decide to mark the visitor in the friendliest way he knows – with a well-directed spray of urine.

Once the queen is settled, the stud cat will show great interest in her. Though she is likely to

Though well into her period of oestrus, a queen may at first resent the male's eager advances.

133

spit, snarl and growl at his advances, he is well protected from her teeth and claws by the wire-mesh partition. The stud should have been given a really good meal before the queen's arrival, for he may refuse all food from the time she is in residence until he has successfully mated with her. The cats must be kept apart until the queen shows signs of being ready for mating. This can take up to thirty-six hours with the maiden queen, and less than one hour with a more experienced one. The signs of readiness include vigorous rolling and stretching, the queen's growls and hisses stopping or becoming rather half-hearted, and she may make welcoming cries in answer to the stud male's encouraging crooning.

Before the queen is released a coarse woven rug should be placed on the floor and the stud house door closed. Most stud owners keep a special mating rug for their cats. It is taken away when not in use so that it does not become impregnated with spray, and brought in specially for mating times. The stud soon recognizes the appearance of his rug and fully realizes its implication. Closing the door cuts down the area in which the queen may run around, pretending to avoid the stud cat's advances, while the rug gives her a warm place on which to roll and provides her with a surface to grip for stability during mating. The stud's owner should sit quietly and not interfere with the mating, which may take some time while the stud manoeuvres the queen into position. After mating, the male cat will leap away from the queen on to his shelf or stool, and the queen should be allowed to settle down. Then she should be replaced in her pen to rest before a repeat mating is allowed.

THE BROOD QUEEN

A queen can breed quite satisfactorily for a number of years provided that she is kept fit and well fed and not allowed to produce and rear too many kittens each year. A queen that starts breeding at about ten months of age and then has one or two litters each year will probably breed successfully until the age of eight or nine. Lactating to feed a litter of five or more kittens takes much more out of a queen than the process of pregnancy and birth, and too frequent or too lengthy periods of lactation can seriously deplete the mother's calcium reserves. A breeder must be watchful, and ensure that an adequate level of calcium is present in an easily assimilable form in the queen's diet and, if in any doubt, should seek veterinary advice.

The cat does not have a specific breeding season, and may be in breeding condition for most of the year, with peaks in early spring, early summer and occasionally at the onset of autumn. Cats kept indoors with longer than natural periods of white light tend to breed more frequently than those kept in a cattery with normal hours of daylight and darkness. Kittens born in the spring are generally easier to rear and often appear more robust than those born at other times, and spring and summer kittens are able to spend time in the sunshine, which is of definite benefit to them.

During oestrus the queen must be carefully confined. If she is to be mated to a pedigree stud, she will be taken for service on the second or third day, but may try to get out of the house before this. Queens have been known to jump from very high windows and escape through very narrow apertures to gain their freedom while on heat, so extra vigilance is essential. Even if the calling queen does not mate with a stray tom, she may well pick up an infection or parasites, or could be killed or injured on the road. Some female cats call at regular, well-spaced intervals, while others seem to be perpetually in some stage of heat unless pregnant or lactating. Cats of Foreign and Oriental breeds seem to call more frequently than Persians or Shorthairs.

A rather strange phenomenon that occurs in some cats is the urge to mate again after three or four weeks, even though safely and sometimes obviously pregnant. Cats kept in small breeding colonies for research and study have been observed to do this, and some breeders have been caught out by it. Seeing a queen rolling and calling again, the obvious response is to assume that the first mating was unsuccessful and arrange for the queen to go back to the stud male and mate again. The breeder will then be taken completely by surprise when the queen produces normal kittens some sixty-five days after the first mating! No one is quite sure why some queens act in this way, but one theory suggests that the act of mating again stimulates certain hormone production, and may help with the processes of birth and subsequent lactation.

Occasionally a queen will appear to come into heat almost immediately after giving birth, rolling and calling in a manner typical of oestrus. She is unlikely to mate, however, and the scent of her lactation appears to repel other cats, including entire males, which tend to spit at her and keep their distance. Even when a queen nursing young kittens does mate, she rarely conceives, possibly because her hormone balance prevents implantation of the fertilized ova.

GOING TO STUD

The young queen must be treated kindly and tenderly during her first period of oestrus. She will be under considerable stress and may react in uncharacteristic ways. She may be extra-affectionate, and also hypersensitive to being touched – purring and rubbing one moment, spitting, scratching and biting the next. She should, therefore, be kept as calm and quiet as possible, and should not be subjected to any unnecessary strain. It is unwise to mate the young queen, for she should be allowed

to use this period to become acccustomed to the new sensations within her body without the added stress of travel and confinement with a strange male cat in an unknown environment.

The breeder should make the necessary arrangements with the stud owner for the queen to mate on her second heat. It is usual to telephone on the first day of the queen's oestrus, arranging to transport her on the second or third day. The queen should be rolling as well as calling before she is taken to stud. The journey may upset her sufficiently to stop the calling, but once she is actually rolling it is unlikely that any minor upset will interfere with the natural breeding process. During her trips to and from stud, the queen should be transported in a wicker, wood or plastic-covered mesh carrier, which must fasten securely and be escape-proof.

It is usually necessary to leave the queen at stud for three or four days. The first day is spent becoming acclimatized to both the stud quarters and the close proximity of the male cat, separated from her by a wire-mesh grille. The queen is generally ready to mate by the following day, and the two cats are allowed together. Mating may be repeated two or three times before the cats are separated, and the process is repeated again the following day. Some stud owners allow the two cats to live together once the first successful mating has been observed and the animals have shown themselves to be totally compatible. They will mate many times during their time together, and will curl up in the same box to sleep. As the act of mating stimulates the release of the queen's ova, repeated matings generally ensure that the queen is safely in kitten before she returns home. When collected by the breeder, the queen will still be well in heat and must be safely confined indoors or in a pen until the oestrus diminishes. During the period she should be kept as quiet as possible and fed her normal nourishing meals.

An Oriental Tabby queen in the typical mating position.

GESTATION TABLE

JANUARY | 1 | 2 | 3 | 4 | 5 | 6 | 7 | 8 | 9 | 10 | 11 | 12 | 13 | 14 | 15 | 16 | 17 | 18 | 19 | 20 | 21 | 22 | 23 | 24 | 25 | 26 | 27 | 28 | 29 | 30 | 31
| 7 | 8 | 9 | 10 | 11 | 12 | 13 | 14 | 15 | 16 | 17 | 18 | 19 | 20 | 21 | 22 | 23 | 24 | 25 | 26 | 27 | 28 | 29 | 30 | 31 | 1 | 2 | 3 | 4 | 5 | 6
MARCH .... *APRIL*

FEBRUARY | 1 | 2 | 3 | 4 | 5 | 6 | 7 | 8 | 9 | 10 | 11 | 12 | 13 | 14 | 15 | 16 | 17 | 18 | 19 | 20 | 21 | 22 | 23 | 24 | 25 | 26 | 27 | 28
| 7 | 8 | 9 | 10 | 11 | 12 | 13 | 14 | 15 | 16 | 17 | 18 | 19 | 20 | 21 | 22 | 23 | 24 | 25 | 26 | 27 | 28 | 29 | 30 | 1 | 2 | 3 | 4
APRIL .... *MAY*

MARCH | 1 | 2 | 3 | 4 | 5 | 6 | 7 | 8 | 9 | 10 | 11 | 12 | 13 | 14 | 15 | 16 | 17 | 18 | 19 | 20 | 21 | 22 | 23 | 24 | 25 | 26 | 27 | 28 | 29 | 30 | 31
| 5 | 6 | 7 | 8 | 9 | 10 | 11 | 12 | 13 | 14 | 15 | 16 | 17 | 18 | 19 | 20 | 21 | 22 | 23 | 24 | 25 | 26 | 27 | 28 | 29 | 30 | 31 | 1 | 2 | 3 | 4
MAY .... *JUNE*

APRIL | 1 | 2 | 3 | 4 | 5 | 6 | 7 | 8 | 9 | 10 | 11 | 12 | 13 | 14 | 15 | 16 | 17 | 18 | 19 | 20 | 21 | 22 | 23 | 24 | 25 | 26 | 27 | 28 | 29 | 30
| 5 | 6 | 7 | 8 | 9 | 10 | 11 | 12 | 13 | 14 | 15 | 16 | 17 | 18 | 19 | 20 | 21 | 22 | 23 | 24 | 25 | 26 | 27 | 28 | 29 | 30 | 1 | 2 | 3 | 4
JUNE .... *JULY*

MAY | 1 | 2 | 3 | 4 | 5 | 6 | 7 | 8 | 9 | 10 | 11 | 12 | 13 | 14 | 15 | 16 | 17 | 18 | 19 | 20 | 21 | 22 | 23 | 24 | 25 | 26 | 27 | 28 | 29 | 30 | 31
| 5 | 6 | 7 | 8 | 9 | 10 | 11 | 12 | 13 | 14 | 15 | 16 | 17 | 18 | 19 | 20 | 21 | 22 | 23 | 24 | 25 | 26 | 27 | 28 | 29 | 30 | 31 | 1 | 2 | 3 | 4
JULY .... *AUGUST*

JUNE | 1 | 2 | 3 | 4 | 5 | 6 | 7 | 8 | 9 | 10 | 11 | 12 | 13 | 14 | 15 | 16 | 17 | 18 | 19 | 20 | 21 | 22 | 23 | 24 | 25 | 26 | 27 | 28 | 29 | 30
| 5 | 6 | 7 | 8 | 9 | 10 | 11 | 12 | 13 | 14 | 15 | 16 | 17 | 18 | 19 | 20 | 21 | 22 | 23 | 24 | 25 | 26 | 27 | 28 | 29 | 30 | 31 | 1 | 2 | 3
AUGUST .... *SEPTEMBER*

JULY | 1 | 2 | 3 | 4 | 5 | 6 | 7 | 8 | 9 | 10 | 11 | 12 | 13 | 14 | 15 | 16 | 17 | 18 | 19 | 20 | 21 | 22 | 23 | 24 | 25 | 26 | 27 | 28 | 29 | 30 | 31
| 4 | 5 | 6 | 7 | 8 | 9 | 10 | 11 | 12 | 13 | 14 | 15 | 16 | 17 | 18 | 19 | 20 | 21 | 22 | 23 | 24 | 25 | 26 | 27 | 28 | 29 | 30 | 1 | 2 | 3 | 4
SEPTEMBER .... *OCTOBER*

AUGUST | 1 | 2 | 3 | 4 | 5 | 6 | 7 | 8 | 9 | 10 | 11 | 12 | 13 | 14 | 15 | 16 | 17 | 18 | 19 | 20 | 21 | 22 | 23 | 24 | 25 | 26 | 27 | 28 | 29 | 30 | 31
| 5 | 6 | 7 | 8 | 9 | 10 | 11 | 12 | 13 | 14 | 15 | 16 | 17 | 18 | 19 | 20 | 21 | 22 | 23 | 24 | 25 | 26 | 27 | 28 | 29 | 30 | 31 | 1 | 2 | 3 | 4
OCTOBER .... *NOVEMBER*

SEPTEMBER | 1 | 2 | 3 | 4 | 5 | 6 | 7 | 8 | 9 | 10 | 11 | 12 | 13 | 14 | 15 | 16 | 17 | 18 | 19 | 20 | 21 | 22 | 23 | 24 | 25 | 26 | 27 | 28 | 29 | 30
| 5 | 6 | 7 | 8 | 9 | 10 | 11 | 12 | 13 | 14 | 15 | 16 | 17 | 18 | 19 | 20 | 21 | 22 | 23 | 24 | 25 | 26 | 27 | 28 | 29 | 30 | 1 | 2 | 3 | 4
NOVEMBER .... *DECEMBER*

OCTOBER | 1 | 2 | 3 | 4 | 5 | 6 | 7 | 8 | 9 | 10 | 11 | 12 | 13 | 14 | 15 | 16 | 17 | 18 | 19 | 20 | 21 | 22 | 23 | 24 | 25 | 26 | 27 | 28 | 29 | 30 | 31
| 5 | 6 | 7 | 8 | 9 | 10 | 11 | 12 | 13 | 14 | 15 | 16 | 17 | 18 | 19 | 20 | 21 | 22 | 23 | 24 | 25 | 26 | 27 | 28 | 29 | 30 | 31 | 1 | 2 | 3 | 4
DECEMBER .... *JANUARY*

NOVEMBER | 1 | 2 | 3 | 4 | 5 | 6 | 7 | 8 | 9 | 10 | 11 | 12 | 13 | 14 | 15 | 16 | 17 | 18 | 19 | 20 | 21 | 22 | 23 | 24 | 25 | 26 | 27 | 28 | 29 | 30
| 5 | 6 | 7 | 8 | 9 | 10 | 11 | 12 | 13 | 14 | 15 | 16 | 17 | 18 | 19 | 20 | 21 | 22 | 23 | 24 | 25 | 26 | 27 | 28 | 29 | 30 | 31 | 1 | 2 | 3
JANUARY .... *FEBRUARY*

DECEMBER | 1 | 2 | 3 | 4 | 5 | 6 | 7 | 8 | 9 | 10 | 11 | 12 | 13 | 14 | 15 | 16 | 17 | 18 | 19 | 20 | 21 | 22 | 23 | 24 | 25 | 26 | 27 | 28 | 29 | 30 | 31
| 4 | 5 | 6 | 7 | 8 | 9 | 10 | 11 | 12 | 13 | 14 | 15 | 16 | 17 | 18 | 19 | 20 | 21 | 22 | 23 | 24 | 25 | 26 | 27 | 28 | 1 | 2 | 3 | 4 | 5 | 6
FEBRUARY .... *MARCH*

This table allows a ready reference for calculating the date on which kittens are due to be born. To use the table, first look up the date on which the queen was mated, then read off the date below. For example: a cat mated on April 1 will be due to have kittens on June 5.

THE PREGNANT QUEEN

It may be difficult to tell whether or not a queen is safely in kitten, but careful inspection of the nipples each day will reveal the condition known as 'pinking-up' – the nipples look slightly enlarged and very pink on about the twenty-first day after conception, having looked normal the previous day – and this is a very hopeful sign that a cat is pregnant. Gestation in the cat seems to average sixty-five days, though kittens may survive if born fifty-nine to seventy days after mating. Throughout the gestation period the queen should be treated quite normally and should not be fussed, for over-humanized queens usually make dreadful mothers. The spoiled queen may refuse to wash or nurse her kittens unless her owner stays beside her and lends a hand; she may be constantly stressed and therefore produce acid milk, which adversely affects the litter; and she may constantly carry the kittens in and out of the nest box, becoming more and more distressed and agitated and perhaps lacerating their necks in the process. The normal, well-balanced and properly treated queen will sail through her period of pregnancy, birth and mother-hood without encountering any serious problems, and will, in turn, rear normal, healthy, well-balanced youngsters.

As the queen becomes heavier she takes less exercise, but still enjoys leisurely walks in the garden.

WEEKS ONE TO THREE

Appearance Normal, no increase in girth apparent. Nipples may look pink and enlarged on twenty-first day.

Behaviour Normal, except that some morning sickness may be noticed on queen's return from stud.

Treatment Normal, except that the diet may be changed slightly, giving easily digested, nourishing meals on her return from stud. If the queen runs a temperature, seems listless or is off her food, verterinary advice should be sought straight away.

WEEK FOUR

Appearance Abdomen appears slightly swollen. A veterinary surgeon may be able to feel the tiny embryonic kittens by palpation, but this must *not* be attempted by the inexperienced, as careless probing can cause the queen internal damage.

Behaviour Calm and very relaxed. The queen may seek out and chew special grasses if allowed her freedom to roam in the garden.

Treatment Normal; careful grooming helps to keep the coat and skin in good condition and the muscles toned.

WEEK FIVE

Appearance Abdomen is visibly swollen in action and repose, and nipples are definitely enlarged.

Behaviour Very calm and relaxed.

Treatment Normal; careful grooming continues and an extra high-protein meal should be added each day.

WEEK SIX

Appearance Queen looks obviously pregnant, even to the casual observer.

Behaviour Seems less inclined to exercise and takes extra care when jumping up or down; appetite increases.

Treatment Extra calcium may be given; some cats can assimilate milk, and evaporated milk is easier to digest than fresh cow's milk. Encourage the queen to take exercise through play – for example, get her to chase a feather tied to string – but do not allow her to become overtired or to jump and twist her body too vigorously.

WEEK SEVEN

Appearance The kittens may be seen moving in the queen's abdomen.

Behaviour Seems to enjoy the process of 'quickening' and rolls and stretches herself sinuously along the floor. The quickening also appears to trigger off the nesting instinct, and the queen may start to search out a suitable place for giving birth.

Treatment Careful feeding of three good meals a day, continuing to ensure that adequate minerals and vitamins are provided. Daily grooming to tone the body and to remove dead hairs and flakes of skin should continue. A large cardboard box should be provided, with a hole cut in the side for the queen's access, and a pile of newspapers and pieces of kitchen paper placed inside for her to tear up to form a soft bed. Special heated pads can be purchased, which are perfectly safe and can be placed under the bedding, giving a low, gentle heat, ideal for kittening and during the first few weeks of rearing the litter. Some breeders use special kittening boxes of wood or plastics, but the humble cardboard box is cheap and ideal, for it may be discarded when soiled and replaced by another, eliminating the risk of any build-up of infection.

WEEKS EIGHT AND NINE

Appearance The queen's abdomen becomes hard and rather pear-shaped. Her breasts are noticeably enlarged. Her coat should be in very good condition, but with small flakes of dandruff apparent in darker-coated breeds.

Behaviour The queen spends extra time in self-grooming, paying particular attention to her breasts. She is extra-affectionate, and goes to her box from time to time, tearing the paper into shreds with her teeth and claws as her time draws nearer. A few days prior to kittening, the queen's voice changes dramatically, and this is particularly noticeable in the vocal Foreign and Oriental breeds. Just before birth, the queen will refuse her food and become restless; she may get up and flop down several times as if trying to find a comfortable position. When the birth is imminent, she may go repeatedly to her toilet tray.

Treatment The queen should be lovingly cared for, groomed daily, and fed on four small, very nourishing meals of her favourite foods, with suitable vitamin and mineral supplements. As she may be too bulky to attend properly to her anal area, this region should be gently cleansed every day with soft tissues, soft soap and warm water, then dried carefully, and talcum powder may be applied. The nipples should be checked, and if dry or cracked they should be gently massaged with vegetable oil. In the Longhair queen, the hair should be gently clipped away from around the nipples and the genital area, using blunt-ended scissors. Check the queen's coat for parasites by using a very fine-toothed metal comb (never use pest powder on pregnant cats). Ensure the ears are clean and her teeth are in a healthy condition. It is often advisable to have the queen checked by the veterinary surgeon to make sure all is well prior to the birth.

THE BIRTH

First-stage labour When the queen's labour starts her rectal temperature drops from its normal 38–38.6°C (100.4–101.5°F) to 36.6–37.2°C (98–99°F). She may pace the floor, wail continuously, groan, growl, go in and out of her kittening box, tear paper, go in and out of her litter tray and vomit. Instead, however, she may just sit quietly, purring and kneading with her forepaws.

Slight uterine contractions may be noticed as ripples along her flanks when the first kitten moves from the uterine horn to the uterus, and these contractions may be accompanied by a break in the rhythm of the queen's breathing or purring. The queen may pant, growl or tremble with the contractions. This stage can last up to twenty-four hours.

Second-stage labour Most queens go into their nesting box as second-stage labour commences. Some want to be with their owners during this stage, while others are happier left alone in the dark, and in this case the breeder should look into the box from time to time to check that everything is going well.

Fierce contractions are seen as the first kitten moves into the birth canal. Contractions may occur every half-hour at first, increasing to every thirty seconds just prior to the birth. Kittens may be born in rapid succession, or with long intervals between, and the queen usually deals with cleaning away the membrane, severing the cord and disposing of the placenta. When the last kitten is born she settles down to rest and to nurse the litter.

A normal birth The kitten is normally delivered in its sac within twenty minutes, and immediately it is expelled it flexes its neck to free its head from the membranes and takes its first gulp of air. The mother licks the kitten quite roughly, drying its body, and eats the membranes. As the kitten's breathing reflex is stimulated, it squeaks and flexes its body. The placenta is attached to the kitten by the umbilical cord, and as the queen moves, or gives another contraction, the placenta passes out of her vagina. The queen normally eats the placenta and along the cord, stopping a couple of centimetres from the kitten's body.

THE KITTENING KIT

Small squares of terry towelling, boiled to sterilize, and then air dried and stored in a polythene bag.
A bottle of astringent antiseptic, obtained from the veterinary surgeon, to seal the kittens' umbilical cords.
A pair of blunt-tipped scissors, sterilized by boiling and stored in a polythene bag.
Cottonwool.
Roll of absorbent paper towelling.
Hot-water bottle or electric heating pad, wrapped in clean linen towel.
Bag or bin for soiled equipment.

As the birth approaches, it may be advisable to confine the queen and her kittening box within a portable pen.

Left to right: As the queen contracts, the kitten passes down the birth canal and slowly out through the vagina. The mother cat licks and pulls at the kitten, helping it into the outside world. The kitten is born encased in a transparent foetal sac and surrounded by clear fluid, and is attached by the umbilical cord to a placenta, still inside the mother cat's body.

Left to right: The queen licks vigorously at the membranous sac over the kitten's face as it kicks and arches its back struggling to break free and, as the nose and mouth is exposed, the kitten takes its first dramatic breath of air. The mother cat licks away and swallows the shreds of sac and the birth fluids, and chews through the cord, expelling and eating the nutritious placenta.

Left to right: Finally the kitten is licked all over to remove every trace of the birth secretions and their characteristic odours, the cord is trimmed close to the kitten's body and the cat clears up soiled areas of her own coat. The kitten, now strongly stimulated and breathing evenly, crawls towards the warmth of its mother's body as she begins to contract once more.

An assisted birth Human intervention in the kittening process is only necessary when things go wrong, or if the queen gives birth so quickly that she is unable to cope with each kitten in turn. Too many breeders fuss and interfere, pulling each kitten into the world, cleaning it, tying and cutting the cord, and disposing of each placenta. This is quite inexcusable, for it has been proved that naturally delivered animals fare far better than those assisted into the world. The breeder should be on hand, prepared and ready to help in an emergency.

If a kitten remains in a half-presented position for some time, despite constant straining by the queen, you are justified in lending a hand. The kitten born safe inside its sac usually slides easily through the birth passage like a well-lubricated capsule. If the sac has ruptured and the fluid expelled, the kitten begins to dry out and it may become stuck. Put a square of terry towelling over the exposed portion of the kitten, and wait until the queen contracts. Then, gently ease the small body out and down, in a curved movement between the queen's hindlegs towards her belly. Do not pull hard, and make certain that you get the angle correct so as not to hurt the queen, timing the tension to coincide with her straining. The queen may growl or cry out, and will then rest once the kitten is freed. Do not pull on the umbilical cord until the next contraction, and hold it with a piece of terry towelling rather than in the fingers. Be careful not to pull on the umbilicus, or the kitten may develop a hernia at the navel.

Put the kitten near the queen's head so that she can clean it, but if she refuses, clean its face, nostrils and mouth with some kitchen tissue. The kitten should breathe before the cord is broken or cut. With luck, the placenta will pass easily, and the queen should be encouraged to eat it. If you need to dry and clean the kitten, use kitchen tissue to mop up the amniotic fluid and to wipe away the membranes from its body, and then rub it dry with a square of terry towelling. If its breathing sounds bubbly, hold the kitten firmly in the hand and swing it head down in a smooth arc from waist height to your knee two or three times to clear the mucus from its lungs and nasal passages. Then, with its head still lower than its body, hold it on one hand while you rub the body from tail down to head with the towelling square.

There is no urgency about severing the umbilical cord and, in fact, it is best to wait as long as possible in case the cat decides to take over once more. If you do have to deal with the cord, use the sterilized scissors to cut it a couple of centimetres from the kitten's body. There is no need to tie the cord first, just dip a piece of cottonwool into the astringent antiseptic lotion and use this to hold the cord between the thumb and forefinger of one hand, near the kitten's body. Cut the cord close to your fingers and press the cottonwool over the cut end, squeezing tightly for a moment or two while the end seals to ensure that bacteria cannot enter the stump. Within a few days the cord will dry and fall away leaving a neat navel.

If the queen needs assistance with all the kittens, deal with each in the same way, putting one kitten on a wrapped hot-water bottle or heated pad while you deal with the next. The chances are that after the last kitten is born the queen will contentedly gather them to her to nurse.

If you cannot deliver a kitten, or the queen strains to no avail and no portion of the kitten can be seen, you should call your veterinary surgeon for assistance. It is normally advisable to take the queen, in her maternity box if possible, to the veterinarian, in case surgery is required. Try to get someone else to drive so that you are free to comfort your cat during the journey.

In some cases, matters may be righted by a hormone injection to encourage contractions, while in others, the veterinary surgeon needs to manipulate a tiny limb into a better position to allow natural birth. The best presentation for a kitten is the 'diving' position, where it comes head first with its forepaws tucked up under the chin. The normal tail-first presentation causes few difficulties either, as the kitten's tail and extended hindlegs are presented first and the rest of the body follows quite easily. The butt presentation is fairly easy to deal with, the tail and rump coming first with the hindlegs pointing towards the kitten's head. Problems mainly occur when the kitten is turned so that the back of its neck is presented first and the shoulders cause a blockage, and manipulation can often rectify the kitten's position. However, when the queen's pelvis is small and the kitten large, any but the best presentation can prove impossible.

Caesarian section When there is no alternative, the veterinary surgeon will deliver the kittens by opening the queen's abdomen. This operation is known as a Caesarian section and is carried out under general anaesthetic. Unless affected by the anaesthetic, the kittens are usually quite strong and may be passed to the breeder waiting in the anteroom to be dried and stimulated, while the queen is stitched up and brought round. The queen may be allowed home, but if she has reacted badly to the operation she will be kept in the veterinary hospital under observation, and the breeder may be asked to take the kittens home without the mother. The kittens need not be fed for several hours, by which time the queen may be ready to accept them.

Some queens resent kittens born by such unnatural means, and need great encouragement before they will nurse their litter. The hormone balance is very disturbed at this time, so patience is needed. As soon as the milk supply starts, the queen's natural instincts should prevail, but it may

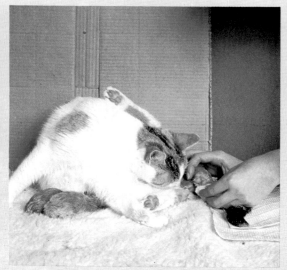

Left to right: After prolonged labour it may be necessary to assist the queen in producing her first kitten. She must be kept calm at all times and nothing must be done to alarm or injure her. Once the kitten has been eased through the well-lubricated vaginal opening, its mouth and nostrils must be cleared without delay and the queen must see the kitten to ensure bonding.

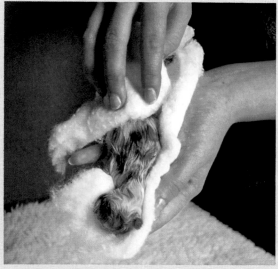
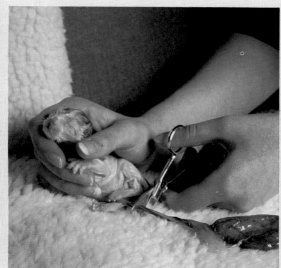

Left to right: It is vital that the kitten breathes properly before the cord is severed, as its only oxygen supply at this time passes through the blood from the placenta. If the kitten is weak, it can be held, head down, on the palm while it is quite vigorously rubbed to stimulate the lungs and the breathing response, then the cord is cut 1 inch from the kitten's body, using blunt, sterilized scissors.

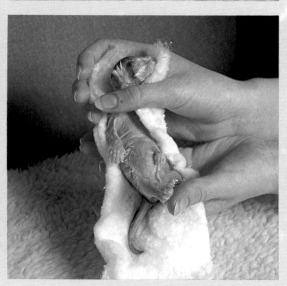

Left to right: The cut end of the cord is pinched for a moment or two to stop the bleeding. It is best to do this by dipping a small piece of cotton wool into an astringent antiseptic solution, placing this on the cut stump and holding it between the thumb and forefinger. This helps to avoid infection entering the body, and within a few days the cord dies and drops off, leaving a small, neat navel.

be necessary to hold the queen firmly while the kittens are encouraged to suck, after which she should be petted and fussed. Within a week matters are usually normal, but in rare cases it is necessary to treat the kittens as orphans, fostering them with another queen or hand-rearing them. The queen's stitches are removed after seven to ten days.

HAND-REARING KITTENS

While the best way of rearing orphan or rejected kittens is to find a foster mother, this is not always easy. A foster queen needs to have had her litter as near to the kittens' birth as possible so that the milk will be at the right strength. Sometimes veterinary surgeons can help, having been asked for euthanasia for an unwanted litter. The newborn kittens are first rubbed all over with the foster mother's bedding and then are placed between her hindlegs to crawl forward towards her stomach. It can take some time before the foster mother will accept the youngsters, and great patience is re-

quired on the part of the breeder. The kittens should not be left alone at this time in case they are rejected and injured, but once they have nursed and the queen has cleaned them, they will be all right and can safely be left.

If no foster mother is available, the litter may be hand-reared, but this is not a task to be undertaken lightly. The kittens must be kept at a constant temperature of 27–30°C (81–86°F) for the first two weeks, gradually reducing to 21°C (70°F) by the age of six weeks, when they are well furred, and moving around and playing during waking hours. The best bedding is torn kitchen tissue, which is absorbent and comfortably warm if laid in a thick layer. The pieces should be torn so that they are not likely to entangle the kittens' legs, and any soiled pieces removed at each feeding time.

The breeder must mimic the mother's cleaning technique by using a piece of cottonwool or tissue, moistened with warm water, to clean the genital regions of the kittens after each feed. The queen would lick this area to stimulate urination and

The mother cat is fastidious in the way in which she cleans away the kitten's faeces and urine. She stimulates and cleans each kitten after feeding, and continues this regular routine until weaning.

defecation, and it is important to ensure that each kitten empties itself. At birth, the kitten's bowel is filled with a dark sticky substance called meconium, and this can cause problems unless passed within the following three or four days. Such stools will be almost black in colour, and the breeder should note which kittens have passed them. Normal stools are yellow-orange in colour. After washing the kittens, dry them carefully and use a little talcum powder if necessary to keep them dry and fresh. Any soreness can be treated with a light smear of petroleum jelly.

Feeding the kittens is done at two-hourly intervals day and night for the first week. It is possible to leave a four-hour break from midnight to 4 a.m. during the second week, stretching this from midnight to 6 a.m. during the third week unless the kittens' digestions seem to be suffering, or they wake and are fretful. All the other milk feeds should be given every two hours without fail, even if the kittens have to be wakened for them. This is obviously a demanding time, requiring patience and fortitude. Luckily, from three to four weeks of age the kittens will show an interest in solid food, and gradually the milk feeds can be spread apart. By six weeks, they will be having five small meals daily and the breeder is able to catch up on all that lost sleep.

The most important aspect of bottle feeding is the maintenance of strict hygiene. Kittens feeding from their mother obtain antibodies in her milk to fight off infection, while bottle-reared youngsters have no such protection. All their feeding equipment must be properly cleaned and sterilized every time it is used. The milk feeds should always be freshly made and be at the correct temperature. Kittens may be bottle fed with a syringe or dropper, with a short piece of rubber tube over the tip to encourage the kitten to suck, but by far the best utensil is a proper kitten-feeding bottle, complete with correctly shaped teats.

The feeds can be made up using specially formulated powdered milk, which simulates the queen's milk, or, in an emergency, evaporated cow's milk may be used diluted with an equal quantity of boiled water. During the first week, 3 to 5 millilitres are sufficient for each kitten at each feed, increasing to about 7 millilitres at two weeks of age and 10 millilitres at three weeks. The kittens must be allowed to suck at their own speed and not hurried in any way. While feeding they should be encouraged to knead with their forepaws, and this can be done by allowing the kitten to feed with its stomach and chest across the bare forearm, giving warmth and comfort, as well as supplying a suitable surface for the tiny kneading paws. At first the sucking reflex may be difficult to stimulate, and the teat should be put into the kitten's mouth and gently lifted upwards before starting to withdraw it again. If a drop of milk is expressed before this is done, the kitten should soon start to suck.

REARING KITTENS

The normal litter will settle down immediately after birth, and the queen, having cleaned the kittens and her own flanks and legs, will rest. She should be given a nourishing drink at this time, and most acceptable is a concoction made from one beaten egg, one teaspoon of glucose and two tablespoons of boiling water. Most queens will gulp this down with relish before settling down with the litter, and will then be happy to rest undisturbed for several hours. When she stirs, the queen should be encouraged to stretch her legs and to use her litter tray, but she may be reluctant to leave her kittens.

Many breeders change the nest material at this stage, and the easiest way is to use a firm pad of paper or blanket covered with a smooth pillowcase or sheet, all folded to the size of the base of the box. The kittens can be lifted quickly on to the fresh bedding, the soiled bedding removed from the box, and the kittens and new pad placed back in the nest. As kittens 'home in' on the scent of the birth excretions, it is advisable to put a little of the pink-stained papers back on top of the clean bedding, and this also helps the queen to relax. She may become distressed at having the bedding changed, and it is vitally important to keep her as calm and relaxed as possible during this stage. A fraught or upset queen may decide to move the kittens, or she may lose her milk. The soiled paper bedding should be taken well away for disposal, because the queen may try to take her kittens to the bedding if she can scent the nesting material.

The queen must pass water within twenty-four hours of the birth. If she is reluctant to do this, lift her and place her in a clean litter tray at regular intervals until she gets the message and performs. Each kitten should be lifted and examined every day. The breeder must have clean, well-rinsed, carefully dried and warm hands, and a kitten should be lifted by enclosing its body in the hand, raising it gently and firmly, and holding it securely so that it feels safe. The body should feel firm and plump if the kitten is feeding well. Its face should be clean, there should be no stains under the tail, and the cord should have dried up and the navel area look normal. Danger signs include: noisy, squealing kittens which feel bony – these are not feeding well and may need supplementary meals until the queen's milk adjusts to the litter's needs; a raised, angry rim around the navel – this could mean that infection entered the severed cord and veterinary attention is required; yellow-orange staining down the kitten's hindlegs – this should be wiped away with warm water to encourage the queen to clean the region.

Most queens enjoy having the breeder examine and admire the kittens, but too many visitors, or inquisitive family pets, may upset her so much that she carries the kittens in and out of the box, possibly damaging them, so peace and quiet is the order of the day. The queen rarely seems hungry after the birth if she has eaten the placentas and been given the nourishing milk, egg and glucose drink. Light feeds are best at this time – steamed fish, meat jelly and a little raw minced rabbit or other white meat, with a pinch of sterilized bonemeal for its calcium content.

For the first few days of life the kittens sleep and feed. Each kitten selects its own nipple and will prefer that feeding position from then on. Kittens may be seen to scrabble at one another's heads and shoulders, apparently fighting for a nipple, and this is quite normal behaviour. The queen's nipples must be examined on the day after the birth to ensure that milk is flowing properly and that there are no 'blind' breasts. Blocked breasts can be eased by gently bathing with hand-hot water and then massaging with warmed olive oil. If this treatment proves ineffective, veterinary advice is necessary to prevent milk fever or the formation of a breast abscess. A queen may have one or two permanently blind breasts, but as no milk is formed they cause little or no trouble and are usually superfluous, for the queen normally has eight breasts.

The queen can develop acid milk if her diet is unsuitable, or if she is continually stressed, worried or harassed. The litter may be lost if this condition is not recognized and treated in time. The first sign is that the kittens become increasingly restless and noisy. Veterinary treatment is required for the queen, and this combined with the feeding of a carefully chosen, bland diet should adjust the acid balance of the milk, resulting in contented kittens once more.

Kittens vary considerably in birth weight. Some Foreign and Oriental kittens may weigh as little as 57 grammes (2 ounces) at birth, while a Persian kitten can weigh double that. A small litter usually has bigger kittens than a large litter. Kittens born weighing less than 57 grammes (2 ounces) rarely survive to adulthood, even if they live through to weaning, and sickly kittens are often rejected by the queen, who may push them to the back of the nest and lie on them. Kittens increase in weight rapidly and should gain the equivalent of their individual birth weights each week, so a kitten weighing 85 grammes (3 ounces) at birth should weigh 255 grammes (9 ounces) at three weeks, provided the queen is adequately fed.

The kitten's eyes remain sealed for the first few days after birth, and the little animal sleeps for much of the time.

Breeders are usually eager to determine the sex of newborn kittens, and it is quite easy for even the novice to tell males from females while the kittens are still damp, particularly if both sexes are present for comparison. In the female kitten the two tiny orifices – the round anus and the small, slit-shaped vagina – are close together, resembling an inverted exclamation mark. In the male, the tiny round anus is separated from the dot which indicates the end of the penis by two small swellings, which are the testes. As the kittens grow it is sometimes possible to mistake their sex, but this can always be confirmed by the veterinary surgeon at vaccination time.

During the first ten days of its life, the kitten's eyes open. In some breeds, such as the Siamese and its derived varieties, the eyes may start to open on the second or third day, while in Persian and Shorthair breeds the eyes may remain tightly sealed until well after the first week has passed. A tiny slit appears as the eyelids begin to part, and then both eyes may open simultaneously or one eye may open, followed by the other the next day. Occasionally, the eyes water and the exudate seals the lids again. If this happens, the eyes should be gently bathed with warm water, and on no account must the eyes be manually opened. A smear of cod-liver oil may be applied to the eyelids if they tend to reseal. This is soothing and healing for the kitten and encourages the mother cat to lick the eyelids, keeping the eyes open and clean. At first the kittens' eyes should be protected from bright light, as their structure is at a delicate stage of development. If the eyes seem full of matter, even after bathing, seek veterinary advice.

During the first four weeks the kittens make progressively greater demands upon their mother, as their appetites increase and they grow bigger and stronger. With a large litter, the strain begins to show on the queen and she may become thin and gaunt, even though she eats and drinks well. The lactating cat needs four good-quality meals each day, served in spotlessly clean dishes, preferably made of china or glass rather than plastic. She needs constant access to fresh water, and this should also be served in a clean bowl. It is important to take the residue away after feeding so that the queen learns to eat a proper meal and then to rest and digest it. This aids the lactation process, and also helps to prevent diarrhoea and vomiting.

Newborn kittens scrabble and jostle for their mother's milk while she rests, contentedly kneeding her paws.

Meat takes several hours to digest so it should be fed at midday and at night, with lighter meals consisting of fish, cheese or other milk products in the morning and early evening.

At four weeks of age the kittens start to show an interest in the queen's food, and this is the time to commence the long weaning process. The queen's food is not altogether suitable for kittens of this age, and so it is a good idea to prepare a special mixture. Put some raw white meat or cooked and boned white fish into an electric blender with a little water, reduce this to a creamy consistency and then add a pinch of bonemeal. Offer this to the kittens in the absence of the queen, because otherwise she will devour the lot before the kittens get the chance to taste it. Present a little of the mixture to each kitten in turn, using a small spoon, and if the taste seems acceptable, the kitten will follow the spoon with its nose as it is lowered to the shallow dish. It takes only two or three such lessons before the kittens learn to lick and eat the semi-solid meal.

Some breeders feed milk and baby cereal to their kittens, and while this does help them to put on weight quite rapidly, it does nothing for the development of their digestive systems and, in some breeds, may lead to diarrhoea or gastritis. As the kittens grow they will eat more and more solid food, and they should be offered a great variety so that they do not develop into fussy adults. The texture should vary too, strips of raw meat and some crunchy cat biscuits helping with teething and the development of strong gums and jaws. The queen must be fed extremely well at this stage, so that she maintains her body weight until the kittens are independent. Apart from the sterilized bonemeal added to her meals to keep her calcium level high, she may benefit from a vitamin supplement recommended by the veterinarian.

The young kittens must be carefully watched as they learn to eat. Sometimes a lump of food becomes wedged across the palate, and the kitten paws frantically at its mouth to dislodge it. A matchstick can be used to gently prise the food off the roof of the mouth, and the kitten should be comforted. Food should be forked into little pyramids to make it easier for small kittens to eat, and care should be taken to ensure that it does not contain fragments of bone or indigestible skin. The young kitten's stomach is very small, only about the size of a walnut, and so small meals at regular intervals are preferable to large meals. As kittens drink so little, water can be mixed with most meat meals, gravy being added to meat and boiled water to canned food. The food should not be made too mushy, but warm water tends to make the food more palatable. Offer the kittens drinking water at room temperature, as cold water may cause tummy upsets. For the same reason food should never be served straight from the refrigerator.

While the kittens are fed only on their mother's milk, the queen cleans away all their excretions, licking and swallowing both urine and faeces. The moment the kittens start on other foods, however, this behaviour ceases, and she expects them to make alternative arrangements. Some queens actively encourage their kittens to use the toilet tray by nudging them and mewing whenever they go to her to be relieved. If a kitten soils the nest a queen will occasionally lift it bodily and put it in the tray. Some trays are rather too tall for small kittens to get into. A sheet of newspaper can be spread under and around the tray, and some litter sprinkled on this. Most kittens learn house manners very fast, but any mistakes should be swiftly and efficiently cleaned away to prevent dirty habits becoming implanted at an early age.

Above left: At six weeks of age these Abyssinian kittens eat small amounts of their mother's food, though still suckling at intervals through the day.

Above: The mother cat encourages her kittens to explore and play while she keeps a watchful eye for any sign of danger that may threaten her family.

Though any form of litter may be used to house-train kittens, it must be remembered that at the sensitive nest-leaving period, from four to five weeks of age, kittens vigorously lick any newly encountered surface or object, and this can include litter. If quantities of granular litter are ingested gastritis may follow, which could kill a small kitten. Torn kitchen tissue makes suitable litter for very young kittens, and large, coarse wood shavings are absorbent but cannot be swallowed. The litter tray should be kept scrupulously clean, and sterilized with a solution of ordinary household bleach, not disinfectants, many of which are toxic to kittens (see page 184). No cat or kitten can be expected to use a wet or foul litter tray, so change the contents frequently. Many cats labelled as dirty are merely fastidious cats which have rebelled against using a dirty tray.

The kittens may be completely weaned at eight or nine weeks of age, although the mother will be quite willing to continue feeding them. The breeder usually settles the queen in a pen far away from the kittens, either in the cattery or in an upstairs room. Some breeders prefer to make a clean break, while others will separate the queen and kittens for longer and longer periods each day. The kittens do not seem to mind being deprived of their mother, and eat well, play hard and sleep for long periods. The queen does miss the kittens, and must be carefully watched to ensure that she does not suffer discomfort from swollen breasts.

When two clear weeks have elapsed since taking their mother's milk, the kittens may receive the first injections in their vaccination programme. Once immunity to feline infectious enteritis and cat 'flu is assured, they are ready to go to their new homes complete with diet sheets and, if they are pedigree kittens, with all relevant papers.

THE KITTEN

A kitten is a very special little creature, and when you decide to take one into your home, you must be prepared to accept full responsibility for its care and welfare for the next twelve years or more.

You must be knowledgeable about its general health and maintenance, its dietary requirements, how to groom and clean its coat and how to provide the correct toilet facilities and training. You must be prepared to obtain the necessary bedding, carriers and equipment, and to provide a warm, safe environment in which the small animal can grow up. You must provide toys, and learn how to play with your kitten to develop its reflexes and motor co-ordination. You should be prepared to have the kitten fully vaccinated, not only as a young animal but at regular intervals throughout its life, and if it is not to be bred from, to arrange for neutering at the correct age. You will need to find a cat-sitter or a boarding cattery for when you take your holidays, and you will need a cat-loving veterinarian to attend your charge in an emergency. Above all, you will need to provide a great deal of love, and this will prove to be your best investment, for however much you give will be repaid with interest.

Kittens need correct care and handling from an early stage for a proper development.

PREPARATION

Before collecting a new kitten, you should ensure that your home is free from hazards and that you have purchased all the items necessary for its health and well-being. It is best to arrange for the kitten to be confined to one room only, at first. This should have a washable floor covering, and if there is a fireplace the chimney should be temporarily blocked off. Fires must be guarded and inviting trailing electric wires looped up high or disconnected at the socket. If the kitchen is selected, make sure that the large gaps commonly found at the back of equipment, such as the tumble drier and the refrigerator, and blocked off. Many a missing kitten has been finally discovered squeezed into such seemingly impossible apertures. Whatever its temperament, it is never possible to guess what a kitten's reaction will be to a brand new environment, and it is up to the owner to make its introduction to its new home as calm, safe and happy as possible. A little thought at this stage pays dividends.

Bedding A kitten needs its own private bed into which it can retire to rest at any time, and where it soon learns that it will be left undisturbed. A small cardboard box makes an ideal bed for the young kitten, being cheap, draughtproof and totally disposable. A thick layer of newspaper can be laid in the bottom for insulation, and an old warm sweater makes a perfect mattress. The weanling kitten may still be teething and will chew the edges of the box to relieve the gums, especially if a round or oval entrance hole is cut in one side. It is pointless to buy an expensive wicker basket at this stage, for a kitten-sized one will be quickly outgrown and a cat-sized one will be too large for comfort. Wickerwork is difficult to clean, too, and the kitten could make some errors in house manners when first in its new home. A plastic bed is suitable for the older kitten – and cat – being easy to clean, and soft, washable linings can be provided to give the cat warmth and comfort.

Toilet tray The kitten also needs a shallow toilet tray, and a supply of litter similar to that used at its breeder's. The tray should be placed on a large sheet of newspaper in a convenient corner, fairly near to the kitten's bed. The tray should always be located in the same place so that the kitten does not become confused and dirty the floor. The tray should be kept clean and dry at all times and, again, it should be stressed that care should be taken in the choice of disinfectant (see page 184). As the kitten grows, you can buy a deeper toilet tray, complete with a hooded lid and an entrance hole at one end.

Feeding bowls The kitten should have its own food and water bowls, and these need to be shallow so that the little animal does not have to dip its nostrils into its meals. It is vital that the kitten learns to like and lap water from a very early age in order to prevent kidney disease in later life. Deep water bowls, causing it to choke and splutter, may discourage the kitten from drinking its full liquid requirement at a time when habits are forming fast. Change the water every morning, and let the bowl stand until the water reaches room temperature, or add a little boiled water from the kettle, before offering it to the kitten. Water should be available

Right: A Cat Sac makes an ideal toy and bed for young kittens. It is warm, easily washed and provides hours of fun, as well as a comforting retreat.

at all times. Dishes, bowls and plates should be carefully washed after use, well rinsed in running water to remove all detergent, and then allowed to dry naturally. Never offer the kitten stale food, and never leave food down. Give a normal portion at each meal and allow the kitten a reasonable amount of time to eat it in peace without distractions. When it has finished and sits back to wash its face and paws, remove the dish and discard any residual food.

Carrying equipment Every cat needs its own safe carrier, and it is advisable to buy a suitable one before you collect your new kitten. Carriers are available in several shapes and designs, and of various materials. Wicker baskets are traditional and aesthetically very pleasing, but are difficult to clean after a cat has had an infectious illness or has been travel sick. Plastic-covered mesh carriers are very eash to clean, and can be totally immersed, if necessary, in a bath of disinfectant, but they need some form of covering to keep out draughts, cold and rain. Fibreglass and plastic carriers are easy to clean, warm and draughtproof, and they look good, too, their only drawback being that they tend to attract condensation if the cat is confined within them for too long. For emergency use, disposable carriers made of thick card are available from pet stores and veterinarians. Sold folded and flat, these are easily stored and quickly assembled, but they will not contain a strong cat determined to escape for long. Whatever type of carrier is chosen, its opening should be a lift-up lid and not a door at one end. A nervous or frightened cat is more easily lifted straight out of a top-opening carrier than pulled out of a front-opening one.

Above: A hooded wicker basket provides an elegant and very acceptable bed for the older kitten, and has a cushion in the base for added comfort.

Far left: Most kittens quickly learn to use their litter trays.

Left: Though not ideal for transporting cats on long journeys, this feline 'holdall' is fine for short trips.

Toys Kittens need to play in order to fully develop their co-ordination and reflexes. Play builds up a good relationship between owner and pet, keeps the kitten fit and encourages a good, healthy appetite. Simple toys seem to be preferred to some of the more complicated, often more expensive, ones. Table-tennis balls, golf balls, large feathers, lengths of thick string, foam hair rollers and furry pipe-cleaners twisted to resemble leggy spiders are all thoroughly appreciated by kittens. They also love to dive into large paper bags and under sheets of lightly crumpled newspaper laid on the floor. Never let the kitten play inside a plastic bag, however, for it could suffocate or chew fragments, which could block its intestines. Especially good toys made for kittens and cats include a sausage-shaped 'tiger's-tail' with a tufted end, complete with a very securely fastened bell. This toy is easily tossed around by kittens and greatly appreciated. Little mice made of tough material and stuffed with the irresistible catnip herb are also great favourites.

Collars and leads If the kitten is allowed to wander freely in the garden it should be encouraged to wear a lightweight elasticated collar bearing its address and telephone number, just in case it gets lost. The leather collars made for puppies are quite unsuitable for kittens; if they get caught on twigs or spikes the kitten could be strangled within moments. Elasticated collars pull off over the kitten's head should this occur.

Though you can attach a lead to a cat's collar, you will never teach it to walk on the lead like a dog. When walking a cat, you must follow where the cat chooses to go rather than vice versa. Special elasticated cord harnesses are made for cats, and these are very useful for cats and kittens that must travel a great deal with their owners. The harness is comfortable to wear and an attached lead means that the animal can be restrained without having to be confined within a carrier. Collars and harnesses should never be left on the kitten as the coat will quickly rub away, leaving bare skin.

THE NEW ARRIVAL

Introducing a kitten into its new home is really a matter of common sense. It should be taken in its carrier into the room prepared for its reception, where there should be no other pets present and any humans should keep as still and quiet as possible. The kitten should be lifted out of the carrier and placed in its bed. A nervous kitten may

Young cats often adopt toys as their special favourites, and these may range from the giant furry spider adored by the tabby, to the lightweight plastic ball (opposite top).

Opposite bottom: A kitten in a new environment must be given time to settle down and gain confidence. The shy tabby uses the space beneath a bed, the Burmese prefers the rockery.

huddle down, while an extrovert one will jump out and immediately start exploring the room. In any case, it should be given time to settle, and made a fuss of from time to time. After about half an hour, a small meal should be offered, consisting of one of the kitten's favourite foods as indicated on its diet sheet. It may eat, or it may prove to be still unsure of itself. If the kitten eats, it will then need to be shown the toilet tray. When a young kitten wants to use the tray it will sniff along the floor, perhaps mewing plaintively, and should be placed firmly on the litter. This may need to be repeated several times before the kitten is confident enough to use the tray, but once it has it will not need reminding.

Allow the kitten to settle in before attempting to introduce it to other pets. It is important to build up confidence slowly and steadily, and to ensure

that the kitten is not frightened. At night, a well-wrapped hot-water bottle or a heated pad in its bed will help to comfort the kitten, and if it is particularly upset and wailing, a loudly ticking clock sometimes has a relaxing effect on the little animal, which probably relates the beat to that of its mother's heart.

During the first few weeks in its new home the kitten should be fed exactly as instructed on its diet sheet in order to avoid gastric disturbances, which can seriously debilitate a young animal. At this time it will spend its waking hours exploring, and will taste and test all manner of objects and surfaces. Great care must be taken with all cleaning materials, which could prove toxic, and avoid the use of pest and air-freshener sprays and any other possibly harmful products.

Above: Bright eyes, an alert expression and a soft, clean coat are signs of good health in the young kitten.

Previous pages: Burmese kittens are naturally playful and inquisitive, and make ideal pet cats.

A young weanling kitten will probably need five small meals a day, and as it grows and its capacity increases it may have four slightly larger meals. Gradually the number of meals is decreased and the quantity of each increased, until at nine months the well-grown semi-adult has two meals, each about 110 to 140 grammes (4–5 ounces) in weight, of good-quality canned or fresh meat or fish.

Health checks You should give your growing kitten a routine weekly health check. The ears should be examined and any dark wax removed from the inner ear flaps with a cottonwool bud. Never probe into the ear canal, but if any dark, gritty specks are apparent have the ears checked for possible infestation by ear mites. The claws should be checked, and overlong or torn ones gently smoothed with an emery board. Cats and kittens living indoors should have the very tips of the claws removed with nail clippers, and the veterinarian will demonstrate how this should be done. Scissors must never be used as these crack the claw sheath. All cats need to strop their claws regularly, and a catnip-impregnated scratching board can be bought, or any log or piece of unplaned timber will do. It is more likely to be used by the cat or kitten if it is fixed vertically to a wall or table leg. Carpet-covered scratch posts are often used, but these are inclined to indicate to the kitten that carpet is for scratching and this is not really the case!

The kitten's mouth should also be examined weekly to check that the secondary teeth are coming through correctly and are not causing soreness, for this may make the kitten reluctant to eat and so cause weight loss. If the milk teeth are being retained instead of being pushed out by the secondary teeth, the veterinary surgeon may need to do some extractions. The gums should be pink and healthy, and the tongue free from any sign of ulceration. Any deviation from this should be treated as a danger sign and veterinary advice sought without delay.

Grooming In addition to feeding your kitten and providing toilet facilities and toys you will need to introduce a grooming routine suitable for the little cat's breed and coat type. The Persian kitten needs a stiff brush to part and untangle the hairs all over its body and tail. A wide-toothed metal comb is useful, too, and it is usual to start at the hind end of the kitten and work in gradual layers towards its head, finishing with the ruff around the neck and the tail. Special grooming powder, or unscented powder designed for use with human babies, may be sprinkled into the coat before you start, and this is allowed to absorb any grease before being carefully brushed out again. Powder helps to clean and separate the hairs, and also inhibits the formation of mats. After thoroughly brushing and combing through the long coat, a final brush the 'wrong way' – that is, from tail to head – fluffs out the coat, and then the tail is taken gently by the tip and given a slight shake to separate the hairs, completing the Persian's toilet.

Semi-longhaired breeds are treated in a similar way, except that the coat is allowed to flow down the body rather than standing away as it does in the Persian. Grooming powder helps to keep the longer hair of the ruff and tail clean and well separated. Extra care should be taken with the long tufted hairs inside the ears, as these soon attract grease and dust and may need gentle washing with mild soap and water before being rinsed and carefully dried.

Shorthaired kittens rarely need brushing as the

coat is short and dense. A fine-toothed comb soon removes any dust and loose hairs, and then the kitten can be buffed up with a warmed pad of cottonwool, a silk scarf or a chamois leather kept specially for this purpose. Siamese, Oriental and Foreign kittens may also be groomed with a fine-toothed metal comb to remove dust and loose hairs, and then a soft bristle brush can be used to tone up the muscles and impart a sheen to the coat, a final buffing with warm cottonwool producing a satin-like feel.

Left: Toys of all kinds are eagerly accepted by the lone kitten. They act as a substitute for a playmate and develop its motor skills.

Above: The healthy kitten is always inquisitive, alert and responsive to the various stimuli present in the wide world of the garden.

During grooming the coat and skin can be checked for any sign of parasites, though it is highly unlikely that a cat kept in the house will have picked up fleas or other offenders. The excreta of the cat flea appears as tiny black grits found in clusters in the coat near the skin. If wetted with water, these specks turn red. Flea-dirt is mainly found at the base of the ears and the tail – the places where these parasites prefer to bite the cat and feed on its blood. Fleas transmit several diseases and can cause unpleasant conditions in the cat, including dermatitis, so they should not be tolerated under any circumstances. If you find that your kitten has fleas, obtain a safe pest spray made specifically for cats – any other spray could prove toxic and may be fatal. Use the spray *exactly* according to the instructions, and use a special metal comb to groom out the fleas and excreta from the coat. A comb manufactured for dealing with human head lice is best for this purpose and can be obtained from any chemist.

COMPANION KITTENS

Kittens are far happier if they have company and, hence, greater play opportunities. When two kittens are bought together, they settle quickly into their new environment and provide healthy competition for one another at mealtimes. Introducing two kittens from different homes may cause a few initial problems, but after a little hissing and half-hearted shows of strength, the two will normally become firm friends and cuddle up together for comfort on the very first night. When a new kitten is introduced to an established family pet cat, a satisfactory relationship may take a little longer to emerge, possibly a week or so. It is quite a good idea to sprinkle some talcum powder into the coat

Left: In play, all kittens learn to use various innate skills to their best advantage. Here a kitten practises the pounce and neck-bite to be used later not only in hunting but in mating behaviour patterns.

Above: It is rare for young animals of different species to fight one another. You must remember, however, that their visual signals are so different that they might not, at first, easily recognize each other's body language.

Far left: Play fighting between kittens is a natural learning process.

Left: Natural play behaviour soon develops motor skills and sharpens reaction times.

of both animals before they are introduced to help mask some of their individual odours. The cat and kitten should not be left alone together until you are confident that no harm will be done to the kitten.

The procedure is similar when the new kitten has to be introduced to a family dog. The dog should be kept safely on a lead when it first meets the kitten, and should be constantly petted and reassured so that it does not feel that its position in the family has been usurped. The body language of dogs and cats is very different, and the kitten will not appreciate a wagging tail but will only perceive a large, threatening, strange-smelling monster, while the dog will not recognize the kitten's threat display of fluffed-out fur, bushed-up tail and flattened ears. The owner must be the mediator until a common language is learned, and the animals should not be left together unsupervised until they are totally compatible. It is a popular myth that cats and dogs are sworn enemies. Provided that they are introduced correctly, they will normally accept each other happily.

VACCINATIONS

If your new kitten was not vaccinated before you acquired it, then you should arrange an appointment with a local veterinarian. The kitten should be protected against feline infectious enteritis and cat 'flu, and combined vaccines are readily available, usually administered in two separate doses given two or three weeks apart. Before giving the first injection, the veterinary surgeon will thoroughly examine the kitten and ask for details, such as its age. You can ask for advice on the routine dosing procedures to prevent intestinal worms and, unless your kitten is intended for breeding, decide on the best time for neutering. Your veterinary surgeon will play an important part in your kitten's life, and early visits should form the basis of a lasting happy relationship.

Kittens rarely have any adverse reaction to vaccination. Some may go off their food for a few hours, or have a short spell of diarrhoea, but rest, warmth and quiet soon restore them to normal.

A contented cat rolls over to show that it is happy in its new and temporary holiday home.

HOLIDAYS

If cats are to travel frequently, they should be accustomed to car journeys from a very early age. It is best to take the kitten out every time you are going on a short journey in the car – for example, to post a letter or to the local store. For such trips, either pop the kitten in a mesh carrier so that it can see all that is going on, or fit its collar or harness and lead. For longer journeys, a folding pen may be fitted into the back of the car with a litter tray. If this training programme has been carried out adequately, at holiday times your kitten will be quite unconcerned by being popped into its accustomed pen, with its own bed and favourite toys, and will not be travel sick or discomfited on the journey.

Kittens and cats adapt well to holidays afloat, and in campers and trailers, but it is sensible always to have a folding pen in case the animal needs to be confined during an emergency. Adequate supplies of the cat's favourite food should be taken along as well as cat litter and all its normal belongings. Be sure that the cat is wearing a collar with details of your holiday address, just in case your pet goes missing. It is not unknown for cats to try and get back home to more familiar surroundings.

Alternatively, there are excellent boarding catteries which care for cats and kittens although the accommodation they offer and their prices vary considerably. It is advisable to visit selected catteries before making your booking to ascertain whether the facilities offered are exactly right for your pet, and whether you will be allowed to take your kitten's bed and toys for its comfort during your holiday. Most catteries insist on the production of a current certificate of vaccination, and may not take a male cat over one year old unless it

Do Not Touch The Cats

In this spacious cattery, two Seal-point Siamese companions are allowed to share their safe, enclosed accommodation.

has been neutered. Always make proper appointments to visit catteries, and make firm bookings for the times and dates that you wish to deposit and collect your kitten. Make friends with your cattery proprietor for, like your veterinary surgeon, he or she may become an important factor in your kitten's life.

When you visit a cattery, there are certain important features to look for. The cat houses should be sited out of doors and have high, safely wired runs. You should ask about diets and ensure that your kitten can have its usual food even if you have to pay an extra fee. Make sure your kitten can

have a litter tray and that this will be changed frequently. Pay particular attention to the runs, which should be paved or concreted and never grassed or earthed, for it is impossible to clean and sterilize the latter between inmates. If the cattery has an attached kennels, make sure that the dogs do not run in close proximity to the cats. The cattery you choose will have high standards and will probably be at the upper end of the price range, but the extra money will be well spent, for a cheaper cattery with lower standards could result in veterinary fees being incurred on your return from your holiday.

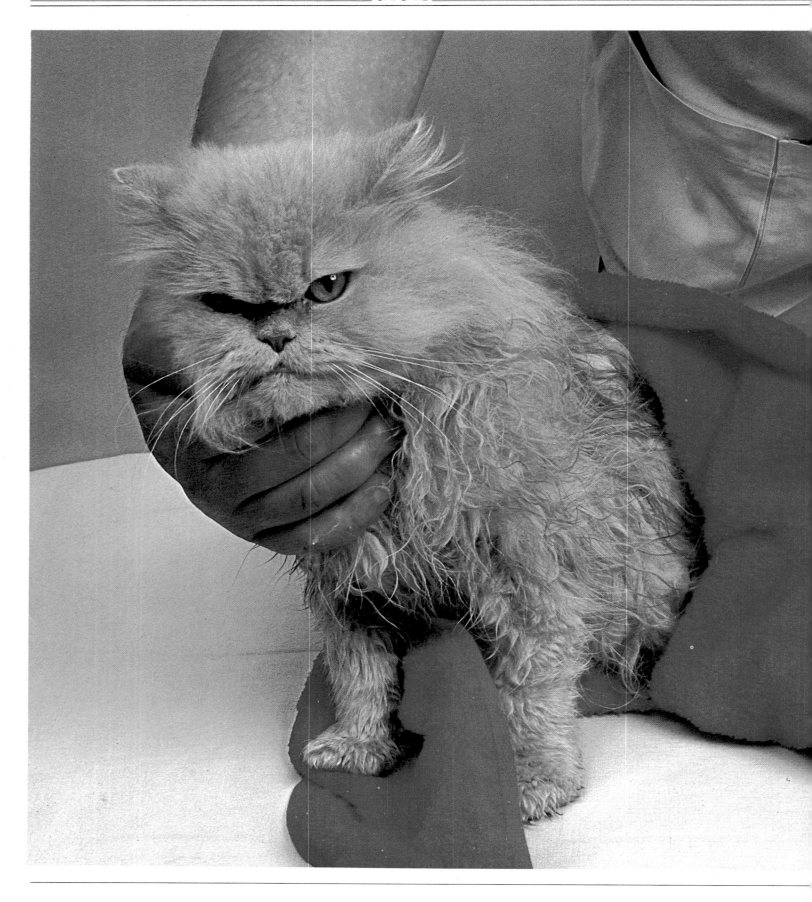

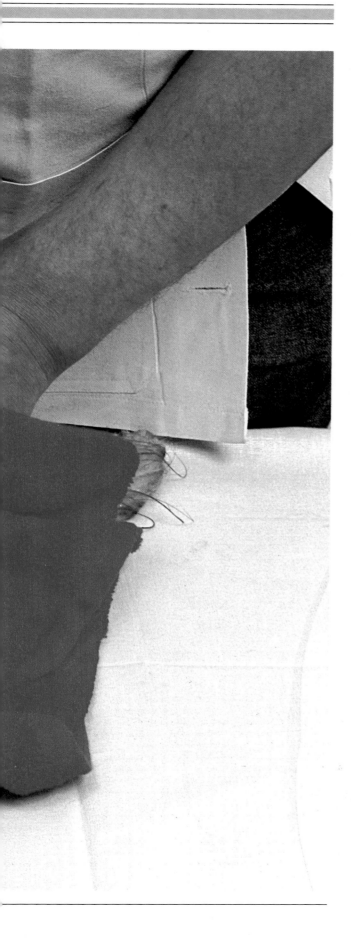

CAT CARE

The care of the cat in sickness and in health is usually a matter of plain commonsense. However, this section of the book will help you to keep your cat in top condition, and to nurse it through sickness should it become ill. You will learn the best way to keep a normal cat healthy by providing the correct environment, a balanced diet, sufficient exercise and proper grooming. The establishment of routines are explained both for standard health checks and for veterinary attention. The control of parasites is also explained and the main feline diseases are described.

In serious cases, though the veterinarian will do his best to treat the disease with antibiotic treatment, it will be the efficacy of the nursing that you carry out which decides whether or not your cat makes a full recovery, and home nursing is carefully explained. A feline first-aid kit can be prepared and kept ready for use as directed. We explain how to bath a cat in the conventional way, and how to give a dry shampoo using hot bran. The emphasis is always on keeping your cat healthy and happy for, as in all spheres, prevention is better than cure.

As this photograph shows the cat is very much part of the family.

TOYS AND EQUIPMENT

If your cat was obtained as a kitten, many of its toys, as well as its general feeding and grooming equipment, will stand it in good stead in adult life – although most cats appreciate the novelty of a few new toys, and you should of course replace worn or damaged items of equipment. However, if your cat was obtained as an adult, it is advisable to refer to the chapter on the kitten to ensure that the correct items of equipment – particularly those for grooming – are available for your type of cat.

KEEPING YOUR CAT HEALTHY

Daily: Observe your cat's general appearance and behaviour – any dramatic change may indicate a need for veterinary attention.
Feed a sensible, well-balanced diet and provide fresh, clean water.
Change soiled litter, clean toilet tray, check the cat's stools (and urine, too, if possible) for normality.
*In free-ranging cats, check the coat for abnormal staining, and paws for sore or cracked pads and foreign bodies such as splinters or thorns. Check for signs of skirmishes such as bites and scratches. These can turn septic if not treated with antiseptic.
Groom your cat according to its coat length and habits.
Weekly: Examine ears and coat for parasites and treat

as necessary. Check the mouth and clean the teeth if necessary.
Fortnightly: Check claws and trim tips if required.
Monthly: Check your cat from head to tail for any abnormalities. Any unexplained lumps, bumps or lesions should be discussed with your veterinarian.
Six-monthly: If your cat contacts other cats arrange to have a blood sample taken and tested for presence of feline leukaemia virus. If your cat free-ranges, have a sample of faeces tested for parasitic worms and treat the condition accordingly.
Yearly: Have a complete veterinary check on your cat and arrange for booster vaccinations as required.

Scratching/stropping posts All cats need to strop their claws, and if not provided with a suitable post or board they will use the furniture. Most cats prefer to stand on their hindlegs to strop, so the post or board should be vertical, or very nearly so. Coarse-grained wood is the ideal stropping surface, though many cats love to scratch at the reverse side of good-quality carpet. Powdered catnip sprinkled on the post or board helps to train the cat to strop in the required place.

Cleaning the cat's ears The inside of the ear is easily cleaned with a cottonwool bud. Used dry, the bud lifts offending material away leaving the ear and its lightly oiled inner surface intact. Particularly dirty ears may need washing or swabbing, and the cottonwool bud may then be dipped in warm water and lubricated with a smear of unscented baby soap. If the ear has mites, then a suitable lotion must be administered deep into the ear, and the veterinarian will demonstrate the correct method of doing this. Never put powders or potions into your cat's ears unless you know exactly what to use and how to apply it.

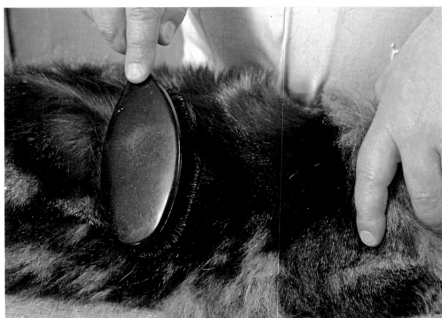

Top: Even in the adult cat kept apart from other animals, toys often provide an important stimulus and interest.

Above: Grooming helps to form a bond between pet and owner as well as keeping the coat clean and healthy.

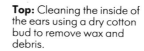

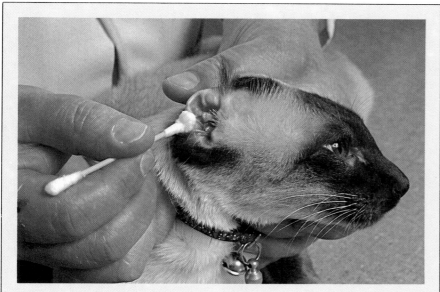

Top: Cleaning the inside of the ears using a dry cotton bud to remove wax and debris.

Centre: Claws must only be clipped with nail clippers, never scissors, which may splinter or fray the claw.

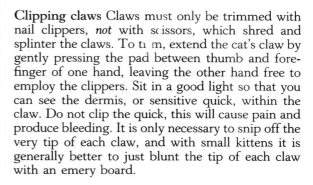

Bottom: The cat's teeth may be kept free from a build up of tartar by regular cleaning with a cotton bud dipped in a solution of hydrogen peroxide.

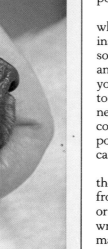

Clipping claws Claws must only be trimmed with nail clippers, *not* with scissors, which shred and splinter the claws. To trim, extend the cat's claw by gently pressing the pad between thumb and forefinger of one hand, leaving the other hand free to employ the clippers. Sit in a good light so that you can see the dermis, or sensitive quick, within the claw. Do not clip the quick, this will cause pain and produce bleeding. It is only necessary to snip off the very tip of each claw, and with small kittens it is generally better to just blunt the tip of each claw with an emery board.

Caring for cats' teeth Due to the unnatural texture of the domestic cat's diet, problems may develop in the mouth. Tartar deposits accumulate, generally on the molar and premolar teeth, and may be seen as hard yellow or grey deposits along the gum margins. Tartar is best removed with surgical instruments by the veterinarian, although it is possible to learn how to do this yourself.

Plaque may be removed in several ways, all of which help to avoid the build-up of tartar. For instance, your cat may be encouraged to chew on some non-splinter bones that are too hard to break and too large to swallow. From an early age, offer your cat such bones with a little meat still attached to encourage the habit of bone chewing. Chicken necks may be baked in a very hot oven until completely crisped. A cat may crunch these to powder, cleaning the teeth and providing valuable calcium.

You may also clean your cat's teeth if you wish, though it is essential to accustom your cat to this from an early age. You can use a small toothbrush or a cottonwool bud, or even your own finger tip wrapped round with rough gauze or bandage. You may use plain warm water, or 3 per cent (10 volume) hydrogen peroxide, with a final rinse of salt water to neutralize.

FEEDING YOUR CAT

An adult cat requires about 50 Calories per 450 grammes (1 pound) of body weight each day, though a very active cat may need more calories, and a sedentary one may exist on less and still remain healthy. Neutered cats require less food than entire cats, and the lactating female will probably require 125 to 150 Calories per pound of her body weight while feeding an average litter of kittens.

Most cats seem to thrive best on two regular daily meals and, as cats age, they often require smaller meals at fairly frequent intervals, rather like young kittens. Certain conditions found in the old cat, such as kidney disease or constipation, may require special diets, and your veterinarian will advise.

A cat's general appearance can help you determine whether or not the diet you feed is adequate in terms of content as well as quantity. Signs that the diet is lacking in certain nutrients include a dry, scurfy coat, dull eyes, warm, dry nose, flaking claws, bad breath and offensive stools.

Nutritional requirements The following are the essential foodstuffs for a healthy cat.

Proteins The building blocks of the cat's body, proteins are essential substances for growth and repair. Suitable proteins for feeding to cats are found in muscle meat, fish, eggs, milk and cheese. At least 35 to 40 per cent of the cat's diet should be made of protein, unless it is neutered, when it can survive adequately on a 25 per cent protein level. Some cats cannot digest milk or milk products, and such foods produce diarrhoea. Some of these cats can, however, digest yoghurt, with its lower lactose content.

Fats Fats provide concentrated forms of energy for the cat and, contrary to popular belief, the cat can digest a diet high in fat; in fact feline nutritionists often recommend diets containing 25 to 30 per cent fat for young, growing cats. Fats contain fatty acids necessary for healthy skins and coats as well as the fat-soluble vitamins A, D, E and K. To promote growth and a healthy appearance, your cat's diet may be supplemented with bacon fat, butter, margarine or any of the pure vegetable oils used in domestic cooking.

Carbohydrates If carbohydrates are fed, these are usually designed to bulk out a protein-rich diet, and in this case should consist of cooked grains and vegetables.

Vitamins and minerals Cats have a high requirement for Vitamin A, and are unable to convert this from vegetables so other sources must be found. Too much Vitamin A can be as dangerous to the cat as too little, so it is advisable to either use a proprietary brand of food with the Vitamin A level clearly stated, or feed a general diet and add 28

grammes (1 ounce) of lightly cooked liver on one or two days only per week.

Vitamins of the B group are very important to the cat, which requires approximately twice the quantity needed by a dog of equivalent size. Some of the B vitamins are destroyed by heat, so care must be taken when selecting canned foods to ensure that those vitamins lost during processing have been replaced. Liver is high in B vitamins, and several of the B group are synthesized by bacteria in the cat's intestines.

Vitamin C is considered unnecessary in the diets of most cats, though it has been discovered that during stress or illness the addition of Vitamin C to the diet, or with antibiotic treatment, aids and accelerates recovery. Most cats readily accept Vitamin C in the form of orange-flavoured syrup as sold for human babies.

Though Vitamin D is an essential component of the cat's diet, the animal's requirements are very low compared to those of the dog and man, and the vitamin is required to allow correct absorption of calcium from the gut.

Cats rarely exhibit symptoms of an imbalance of the important Vitamin E provided they are fed a normal, varied diet.

The other vitamins and minerals are required in such tiny amounts that they are easily provided in virtually any diet. Great care should be exercised when feeding the various vitamin supplements, especially those prepared for humans or for dogs, and it is best to seek veterinary advice if you have any worries or fears over your cat's diet.

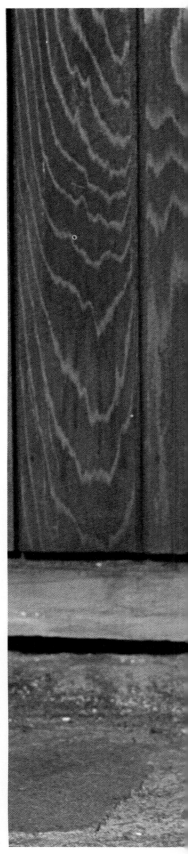

A cat will ask to go out when it needs to (opposite), but the fitting of a cat-flap (left) will enable your pet to come and go as it pleases.

Selecting the right foods Apart from fresh food, three types of diet are available to your cat.

Canned Probably the most expensive; may consist of meat; meat and cereal; or as a complete diet – meat and vitamins carefully balanced to provide the correct level of nutrients required by the average cat.

Semi-moist Highly acceptable to most cats and very convenient to store and serve, these foods do, however, contain humectants and preservatives, which may produce gastric disturbances in some cats. Most cat owners feed these products as part of their cat's diet – usually giving one canned meal and one semi-moist meal each day. A little less expensive than canned food, the semi-moist diet is carefully formulated, but may prove to be slightly deficient in fat, in which case a little bacon fat, butter, margarine or vegetable oil may be added.

Dry The least expensive and perhaps the best in terms of balance, except that the fat content may be too low. Cats on a basic diet of dry food must be seen to drink extra water.

Processed cat foods may be categorized in two ways. *Complete food* is carefully formulated and rigorously tested, and has proved to be adequate for the average cat's needs. It contains sufficient vitamins and minerals to allow reproduction. *Balanced food* is carefully formulated to contain all nutrients necessary for the health and well-being of the average cat. Commercial cat foods should indicate whether or not they are complete or balanced. If not, check the label for added vitamins A, B and E, and for a calcium to phosphorus ratio of 1:1.

Price is often an indication of quality; very cheap food is generally produced from poor-quality protein and indigestible filler; very expensive foods may contain high-quality ingredients, but are intended to appeal to your 'tastes' rather than those of your cat. Use your discretion to choose the product that has good-quality protein, no filler, and is in the medium to high price range, and you will probably make the right choice for your cat. Feed a wide variety of flavours and textures to your cat to prevent the formation of feeding fads. Examine your cat's litter tray to determine what effect the food has. If the result of feeding a new product is diarrhoea or an offensive stool, it might prove to be an unsuitable diet and should be discontinued. The production of a voluminous stool indicates an excessive amount of filler.

TRAVELLING

Cats expected to travel with their owners should be accustomed to such journeys from as early an age as possible, but no matter how seasoned a traveller your cat becomes, you should always keep it confined within a suitable, comfortable carrier. An unconfined cat can be a hazard when driving, and

OUTLINE FEEDING PLAN FOR THE AVERAGE ADULT CAT

Daily: a.m. Normal ration of complete or balanced commercial dry food with a dessertspoon of fat (see page 166).
p.m. Normal ration of complete or balanced canned food (add fat if label indicates that the can contains less than 5 per cent fat); vary the flavours daily. ENSURE THAT FRESH, CLEAN DRINKING WATER IS ALWAYS AVAILABLE

Weekly or Twice-weekly: Feed 28 grammes (1 ounce) lightly cooked liver; one or two crisp-baked chicken necks.

Occasional treats: Cottage cheese; grated hard cheese; cooked vegetables; cooked fish (remove skin and bones); cooked poultry (remove skin and bones); raw or lightly cooked strips of muscle meat; cooked cereals; brewer's yeast; milk, cream or yoghurt if these do not give your cat diarrhoea.

These bowls contain suitable foods for the average cat. Cat food varies considerably in calorific value, so it is important to check quantities against the manufacturer's directions — usually found on the packet or can — and feed accordingly. The cat itself is the best indicator of the adequacy or otherwise of its diet, and a sleek, lively cat with bright eyes and an interest in everything around it is almost certain to be having a good varied and balancing diet. Clockwise from the left: sardines in tomato sauce; fresh, lean minced beef; complete dry diet; beef and rabbit canned food; semi-moist diet; sliced lamb's liver. Centre: cooked white fish.

may run off when the car door is opened. Start training by popping the kitten or cat into its carrier, warmly lined with a favourite blanket, and take it with you on short journeys. On your return, give your cat a favourite treat while it still remains in the carrier, then take it out for a petting. Many owners make the mistake of using the carrier only for trips to the veterinarian, instead of making riding in the carrier a pleasant experience. If you habitually take your cat on very long journeys, obtain a carrier large enough to hold a small litter tray and hook-on food and water containers, as well as providing sufficient room for the cat to settle down in comfort.

Sending your cat by air It is normal for cats to travel in the specially licensed, heated and pressurized holds of certain aircraft, but they should be confined in specially designed containers. Each country has its own regulations for the movement of all livestock, and if you are taking your cat to another country it is essential to check with the local ministry, embassy or airline to ensure that you are in possession of all the correct documents and certificates.

Your cat should be allowed to get accustomed to its airline kennel well before the flight. The kennel should be lined with a warm, soft blanket, and left around with the door ajar so that the naturally curious cat will go inside from time to time and gradually impregnate the kennel with its personal odour tag. The kennel must meet certain specifications, which may be checked with the airline, and should preferably be manufactured by a specialist company (ordinary show carriers are inadequate).

Avoid feeding your cat within six to eight hours of travel, and do not put food and water containers in the air kennel. On long flights arrangements are made for routine watering and/or feeding of cats in transit, and the airlines are very caring in this respect. Rather than trying to fit a litter tray into the air kennel it is better to put a thick layer of torn sheets of absorbent kitchen paper in the bottom.

Quarantine Several countries, especially those closely surrounded by sea, have restrictions on the importation of animals, and control rabies by enforcing a period of quarantine. In the British Isles all animals subject to this control, including cats, have to have an import permit and, on arrival, are taken by licensed carriers to an approved quarantine cattery for a period of six calendar months. Such catteries are run under government control and have high standards of care and hygiene. Owners are able to visit regularly, and the confined cats soon settle down to the routine, so that the six months seem to pass quite quickly. Regulations change frequently, and should be checked at the embassy of the country to which you are travelling or exporting.

Above: A Cameo kitten securely packed in its air kennel waits for a flight to a far-off land.

Left: Even when travelling in a car the cat is safer when securely enclosed within a carrier.

Below: In the quarantine cattery, an Abyssinian import responds to a visit from his new owner.

PREVENTING ACCIDENTS AND DISEASE

Most accidents happen to the cat allowed free range, though some accidents can occur in the home. Neutering helps to lessen the roaming tendency. A free-ranging cat should wear an elasticated collar bearing a name tag, never a leather or other firm collar which will not give if the cat becomes entangled or hung up by the neck. In the home, the cat should be kept away from potentially dangerous equipment.

Vaccinations are vital for the well-being of your pet, and are available against the deadly disease feline infectious enteritis, or panleukopenia, and respiratory viral infections, collectively called cat 'flu and including rhinotracheitis and calicivirus. In countries with a risk of rabies, vaccination against this deadly disease is important and, when available, vaccination against feline leukaemia virus will save the lives of many cats. Kittens receive antibodies against disease in their mother's milk, but the immunity afforded diminishes around ten to twelve weeks of age. Kittens should be vaccinated at this age, and then receive regular booster doses as recommended by the manufacturers or the veterinarian. It is particularly important to vaccinate regularly cats at particular risk, such as free-ranging cats and those being exhibited at cat shows or being placed in a boarding cattery. Any form of stress increases the susceptibility of the cat to infection, and all changes in routine and environment, and the close proximity of other cats, produce some stress.

THE SPREAD OF DISEASES

Cat diseases may be either infectious or non-infectious, and infectious diseases may also be contagious or 'catching', whereas non-infectious diseases are not. The non-infectious diseases include those caused by the malfunction of certain organs, resulting in, for example, heart, kidney or liver disease.

Diseases may be transmitted in various ways. Viruses tend to spread through droplets sneezed or breathed out by an infected cat, which are then breathed in by the susceptible cat, so entering its lungs. Food, drink, bowls, or the cat's fur, may become contaminated directly, or through transmission by flies, with faeces, urine, vomit, pus or saliva from an infected cat, which are ingested by the susceptible cat, entering its stomach and bloodstream. Cats may eat disease-carrying insects, birds or small animals, or may be bitten by disease-carrying parasites. Direct contact between cats, without inhalation or ingestion, is responsible for the spread of some diseases.

From cats to humans Zoonoses (pronounced zoo-oh-no-sees) are diseases capable of transmission from animals to humans, but luckily very few diseases pass to humans from cats. The most deadly zoonosis, rabies, occurs on the continents of America, Africa, Asia and Europe.

Ringworm is a fungal disease of cats readily transmitted to human contacts, and certain mites and fleas will pass from cats to humans. Bacteria from a cat may infect open wounds on humans, and scratches and cuts should be carefully cleaned and covered to avoid contact with the animal's breath, saliva or coat. Bites and scratches inflicted by cats on humans should also receive careful treatment, including a thorough cleansing of the wound and application of antiseptic.

Perhaps the most worrying zoonosis is toxoplasmosis, a disease caused by a microscopic single-celled organism or protozoan called *Toxoplasma*. This parasite can affect many animals, but only the cat spreads its infective cysts by voiding them in its faeces. The disease often produces no symptoms in the cat, but in a pregnant woman it may affect her unborn child by causing congenital defects. Humans can also contract the disease by eating or handling raw or undercooked meat. The normal way to prevent toxoplasmosis in the cat is to feed only heat-processed canned foods and well-cooked fresh meat, and not allow the cat to catch or eat wild prey. You should always wash your hands after handling raw meat in any case, and pregnant women should avoiding changing the cat's toilet tray in case they pick up any germs from it.

A young kitten just opening its eyes may have a mild form of conjunctivitis, which needs careful treatment.

SYMPTOMS OF ILLNESS

Generally speaking, an ailing cat loses its appetite, either partially or completely, and when this happens, the caring owner should always check for an obvious cause. Most cats eagerly wait their regular meals, and consume the entire contents of their dish within a few minutes. While a finicky cat may have slightly different feeding habits, there will still be a pattern, and any change in this should sound a danger bell in the owner's mind.

The incubation of an illness can also be indicated by changes in appearance and behaviour. The cat's coat may be held slightly erect, giving it an open or spiky look. The eyes may look rather dull, and the third eyelid may appear in the inner corner of each eye. The cat may seem to be thirsty but be reluctant to drink, crouching with its head over its water bowl, or it may drink copiously with gulping movements. It may go repeatedly into its toilet tray, but seem unable to pass urine or faeces, despite straining. It may resent handling and spit when touched, it may stop cleaning its fur and become odorous, and its breath may smell unpleasant. Other symptoms include sneezing, drooling, vomiting, diarrhoea and discharges from the eyes or nose.

The veterinarian will want to have accurate details of the onset and timing of any symptoms, to help him diagnose and treat the illness.

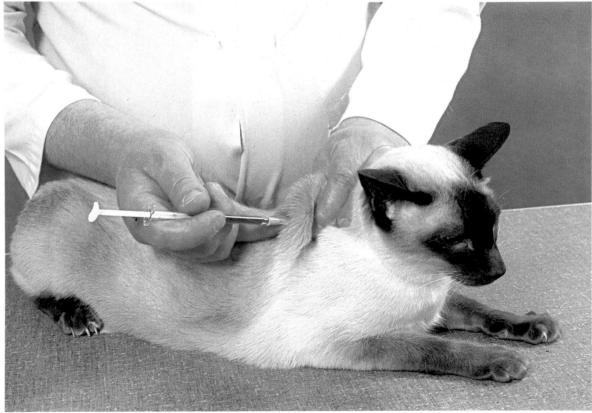

Above: When the nictitating membrane, or haw, shows at the inner corner of the cat's eye, a careful watch should be kept for further symptoms of illness.

Left: Subcutaneous injections are usually quite painless.

Temperature It is useful to be able to take your cat's temperature, as this can be a very good indication of when to seek help. The normal temperature of an adult cat varies between 38 and 38.6°C (100.4 and 101.5°F) and it may rise one degree through excitement, fear or stress. A low body temperature should be treated with as much alarm as a high one, for a subnormal rectal temperature is indicative of some of the more serious feline diseases.

It is best to have an assistant to hold your cat when taking its temperature, and the animal should be lying or standing in a relaxed manner. You should have a special small-bulbed rectal thermometer in your cat's first-aid kit. Shake this sharply once or twice to lower the level of the mercury, lubricate the bulb with a little vegetable oil and insert it for one-third of its length into the cat's anus. Be firm but gentle, rotating the thermometer if necessary and aiming the tip in a line towards the cat's head. Hold the instrument in place for at least one minute, remove it, wipe it with a tissue and read off the level.

Pulse The pulse rate for an adult resting cat is between 110 and 120 beats per minute. High on the inside of the cat's thigh the femoral artery passes close to the surface of the skin. If you place your middle finger lightly on the artery you should be able to feel the pulse. Count the beats for thirty seconds and then double this number to obtain the pulse rate per minute.

Taking samples of urine and faeces To collect samples of your cat's urine or faeces prepare a clean, sterilized toilet tray. There must be no trace of disinfectant or detergent, so after washing and disinfecting rinse it copiously with cold running water and dry it with kitchen or toilet tissue. Place the tray in its normal place and put two or three small sheets of toilet tissue inside. Confine the cat, but otherwise treat it quite normally. It may be reluctant to use the sparsely furnished tray, but eventually will find it unavoidable. When the cat has urinated, pour the liquid into a clean glass jar ready to take to the veterinarian. Put fresh tissue in the tray, extra sheets this time, and the cat will more readily pass its faeces. This sample should be put in another glass jar or a small polythene bag for transportation.

Other tests Other methods of diagnosing disease or

Taking the cat's pulse by counting the beats at the site of the femoral artery.

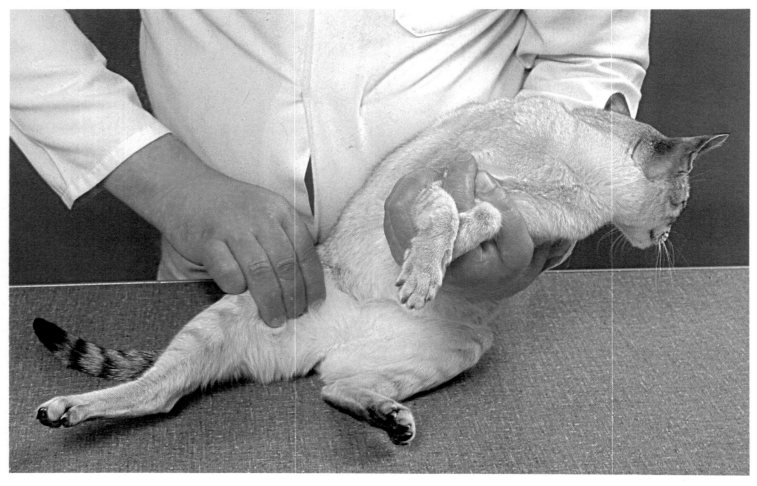

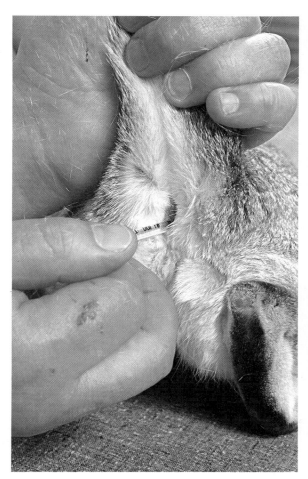

injury may be used by the veterinary surgeon. X-rays of bones and organs are generally taken while the cat is immobilized under a general anaesthetic. Leukaemia and other illnesses may be detected by a blood test, a small sample being taken from a vein in the cat's foreleg and sent for laboratory analysis. Other diseases may be identified by examination of swabs taken from various parts of the cat's body.

EXTERNAL PARASITES

Fleas Perhaps the most common of its external parasites is the cat flea (*Ctenocephalides felis*), which thrives and multiplies rapidly in warm, dry conditions. The adult flea feeds by biting the host and sucking its blood. Flea bites produce irritating reddish patches, which the cat may scratch quite vigorously, and around the bite may be found reddish grits, which are the flea's excreta. Some cats develop an allergy to the flea's saliva, and a serious and very common skin disease called flea eczema or flea allergy dermatitis may result from bites. In this condition, a wide band of skin along the cat's spine from the tail root to a point about halfway along the body is seen to be covered with numerous crusty pimples.

To treat a cat for fleas, a suitable proprietary brand of pesticide should be used exactly according to the instructions on the pack. The cat's coat should be groomed thoroughly to remove all dead fleas and excreta, and the debris burned. The cat's bedding and furnishings in the home should be sprayed with another preparation made specially for the purpose, which destroys the flea eggs and larvae. The cat should be removed while this is done to avoid a reaction to the toxic product. Special collars are sold for use on cats which are expressly designed to destroy fleas.

Above left: The most convenient and accurate way of taking the cat's temperature is by gently inserting the thermometer into the cat's rectum.

Above: The veterinary surgeon prepares to take an X-ray.

Mange mites Eight-legged and microscopic, mange mites provoke a wide range of skin conditions in the cat, from a simple flaking of the skin resembling dandruff to a full-scale condition with large scaly patches, all collectively referred to as mange. Mange is extremely contagious and is transmitted by direct contact between cats or through grooming equipment. Some mange mites live in the coat, some on the skin surface and some within the skin. To treat the mange mite it must first be identified, and this is usually done by a microscopic examination of a portion of the affected skin. Each species of mite is treated with a specific pesticide and this, together with a knowledge of the mite's life cycle and strict attention to hygiene, generally results in its complete eradication.

The fur mite is found on dogs and rabbits as well as on cats. However, it is readily contracted by humans, and it appears as itchy areas on the hands, wrists and inside the forearms, and sometimes on the chest. If you develop such itchy areas, regular washing with soap and water kills the mites. You should comb the cat and check the combings with a powerful magnifying glass to see whether there are tiny moving mites. The cat should be shampooed once a week for three or four weeks using a selenium sulphide shampoo, rinsing thoroughly and drying completely before allowing the cat to self-groom. All bedding and furnishings should be cleaned, and dichlorvos fly strips hung in the rooms inhabited by the affected cat.

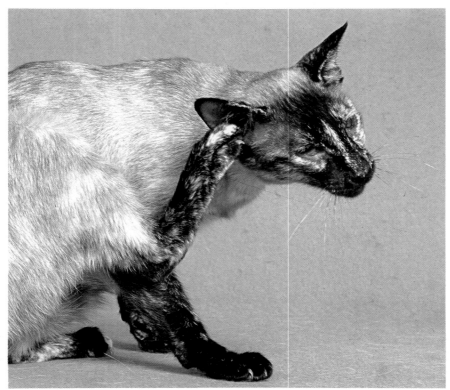

Harvest mites, *Trombicula*, live in decaying vegetable matter during their adult lives. As larvae, however, they are parasitic and appear as orange-red or yellow specks on the lightly furred regions of the cat's body, such as its ears, mouth and between the toes. The mite feeds by injecting saliva into the skin and then sucking the pre-digested blood. If left untreated, the cat may develop raw, bleeding patches and sores. This seasonal problem may be treated by washing the affected areas, drying thoroughly and then rubbing in a safe insecticidal powder.

Skin mites can be particularly troublesome, and the most common is probably the ear mange mite, *Otodectes cynotis*. It is thought that two out of every three cats harbour these ubiquitous parasites, which may live in small colonies within the ears causing very little trouble. However, under certain conditions they multiply rapidly, and the skin inside the ear reacts to the irritation of the mites' leg and body spines, producing a thick brown wax. As the mites breed inside the ear, dry, crusty material accumulates and, if neglected, may block the ear canal and cause other serious problems.

All cats should have regular weekly ear checks. A cottonwool bud wiped just inside the ear, never poked into the canal, will lift any wax and matter. If you suspect the presence of ear mites, have this verified by the veterinarian, who can look into the ear canal with an auriscope. If mites are present, a special preparation will be prescribed which must be used exactly as directed. Let the required number of drops into the ear from a dropper or syringe, while the cat is gently restrained with its pinna turned back. Rub the base of the ear just level with the cheek bone to disperse the lotion right into the depths of the ear canal. The cat will immediately try to shake its head to relieve the increased irritation as the liquid flows into the ear canal, but should be comforted and held for as long as possible to enable the lotion to do its work.

The head mange mite, *Notoedres*, causes notoedric mange, or feline scabies, a highly contagious and very debilitating disease, which sometimes affects whole litters of kittens as well as their mother. The mites are only spread by direct contact between cats, because they are fragile and unable to live off the host for more than a day or so. The minute female mange mite burrows into the cat's skin, making tunnels into which she lays her eggs. This action causes irritation, and wounds develop as the cat scratches and rubs the affected areas, generally the ears and the forehead over the eyes. Patches of hair fall out and the skin becomes scabby, thick and wrinkled into furrows. Bacterial infection can enter the opened skin and the cat may become seriously ill from blood-poisoning. In severe cases, the entire body is infected and the cat gives off a strange, mousy odour. The cat, and all other cats with which it may have been in contact, should be treated without delay under strict veterinary supervision.

Lice Just as mange mites rarely attack cats in tiptop health, so the small wingless insects called lice are more commonly found on sickly cats. Only cat lice affect cats and there is no cross-infection between species. The parasite's entire life cycle is spent on the cat, and it is spread only by direct contact or infected equipment. The biting cat louse feeds on hair and skin debris, while the sucking louse feeds on blood. An infected cat is restless and scratches a great deal. It may sleep badly, lose its appetite and become increasingly agitated and depressed if left untreated. While the adult lice are fairly easy to kill, the eggs, known as nits, are individually cemented to the hairs and are resistant to sprays and powders. If possible, the cat should be bathed every ten days, and when it is thoroughly dry, a suitable insecticidal powder should be massaged into the coat and brushed through. A 'Derbac' comb, sold for use in treating human lice, is an effective way of removing some of the eggs, but in long-coated cats it may be necessary to clip away some of the fur and burn it to destroy the nits.

Opposite top: Head mange in the cat is distressing and very debilitating. However, it responds to careful treatment.

Opposite bottom: When a cat scratches at its ear an examination should be made to determine whether or not the cat has ear mites.

Below: Ear mites are treated by the installation of a suitable veterinary lotion into the ear canal at prescribed intervals of time.

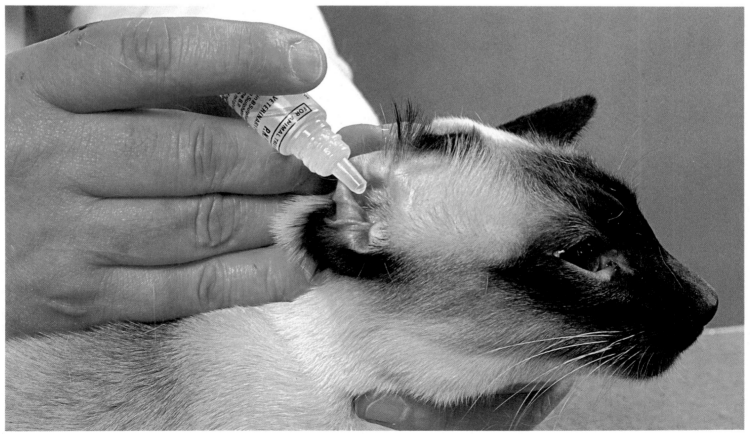

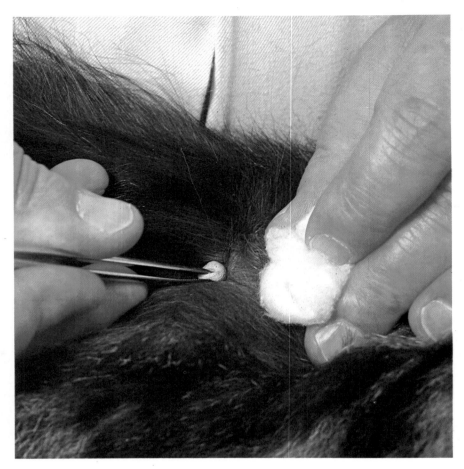

ers. If the tick is merely pulled off the cat's skin, the mouthparts will be left behind to fester and produce an abscess.

NON-PARASITIC SKIN DISEASES

Ringworm Though few non-parasitic skin diseases strike cats, and those they do contract are rarely contagious, ringworm, perhaps the most serious of all their skin diseases, comes into this category. Despite its name this disease is not caused by a worm at all, but by a fungus, *Microsporum canis*. Highly contagious and quite difficult to eradicate, ringworm affects dogs and humans, especially young children, and so is a zoonosis. The fungus grows on the surface of the skin, in the keratin of the hairs and around the claws. Toxins pass into the surface layers of the skin and may produce itching and inflammation, hairs break off at the base of the shaft, and in classic cases circular lesions appear, most commonly on the head and ears or on the inside of the forepaws.

Ringworm is treated by applying an anti-fungus lotion to the areas over and around the lesions, and the affected cat is isolated and nursed on disposable bedding and with disposable litter trays and dishes. Everything from the cat's environment must be burned after use, and combings from the coat are also burned, with strict hygiene measures being followed at all times. Alternatively, the disease may be treated internally with the antibiotic griseofulvin, which is given in tablet form over a four- to six-week period. Though usually safe, the antibiotic must not be given to pregnant queens.

Dermatitis The cat is subject to several sorts of dermatitis or eczema, in which the irritated skin may become dry and scaly or wet and weeping. Contact dermatitis is caused by substances such as detergents, cleaning materials, disinfectants and insecticides; allergic dermatitis is caused by the sensitivity to certain foods, or substances breathed in (such as fly sprays), or bites from parasites; while solar dermatitis is a reaction to the sun, most often encountered in white cats.

In all cases of dermatitis, the skin should be kept as clean and cool as possible, and every effort must be made to avoid the onset of extreme irritation, when the cat will scratch and inflict wounds that will become septic. The cat must be kept well fed and as fit as possible while the dermatitis is treated. Various creams can be applied to the skin or antibiotics, steroids and vitamins are available for internal treatment.

Stud tail This condition affects entire males and females as well as neutered males. It occurs when the pores which secrete the products of the sebacous glands become blocked. It can be avoided

Once the mouthparts of a tick have been relaxed by the application of surgical spirit, the engorged bodyparts may be lifted away with tweezers.

Opposite top: All cats need light, fresh air and sunshine. If a cat has been very ill, a glimpse of the garden may be just the tonic it needs to help it on the road to recovery.

Opposite bottom: Protection against upper respiratory diseases may be given by the veterinarian through a vaccine administered intranasally, rather than by injection.

Maggots Myiasis is a condition caused by fly larvae developing on or in the cat's skin. It most commonly occurs when for some reason, such as a debilitating disease, a cat has a heavily soiled anal region. Some flies may lay their eggs in the soiled and matted fur, while others lay eggs on organic matter on the ground, and when the cat lies on this, the larvae hatch and migrate into the animal's skin. To treat the cat, it is first necessary to clip away any matted or soiled fur, wash the area with soap and warm water and then remove the maggots one by one with blunt tweezers. After removing the maggots, apply a suitable antiseptic cream and leave the wounds to heal in the open air.

Ticks Occasionally picked up by free-ranging cats, ticks are usually found on the ears, neck or between the toes, where they resemble blue-grey or brown warts. Sucking the cat's blood with their mouthparts embedded in its skin, they rapidly swell from the size of a pinhead to about 1 centimetre (½ inch) in length. The fully engorged tick will then drop off the host. Free-ranging cats in a tick area should be regularly dusted with pyrethrum powder to keep these parasites at bay. To remove a tick it is necessary to first relax the mouthparts with a drop of surgical spirit before lifting it away with tweez-

by washing regularly around the greasy area at the base of the tail, using good-quality unscented soap. Afterwards, rinse and dry with talc.

Feline acne This is found on the lips and chin, and very occasionally over the eyes of some cats. It is a similar condition to stud tail and should be treated in exactly the same way. Antibiotic treatment is occasionally required when a cat already debilitated by some other disease develops acne.

Hormonal eczema Alopecia, or balding, occurs in some cats, notably neuters. The hair on the lower back and abdomen falls away leaving denuded areas or skin very thinly covered with fine and broken hairs. The cat rarely seems discomfited by the condition and there is no irritation. Synthetic sex hormones occasionally cause a regrowth of hair, and in some cases a change of diet with increased levels of vitamins in the B group has proved effective.

INTERNAL PARASITES

Most of the cat's internal parasites are worms, including the long, cylindrical roundworms, the flat, ribbon-like tapeworms and the little leaf-like flukes.

Toxacara and *Toxacaris* species are thick, white roundworms up to 10 centimetres (4 inches) in length, and may be seen in the cat's faeces or vomited bile. The adult worms feed on digested food in the cat's intestine, and lay eggs which are passed in the cat's faeces. Larvae may be passed to kittens through their mother's milk, and the young creatures may become ill rapidly as the larvae migrate through the lungs to the intestine. An affected kitten may cough or develop pneumonia, but more commonly looks undernourished with a staring coat and a swollen belly. It has diarrhoea and may vomit up worms. Control measures are essential in breeding queens – dosing regularly before mating and then keeping the pregnant cat away from any possible source of re-infestation. Infected kittens can be treated under strict veterinary supervision from the age of three weeks.

Hookworms cause problems in hot, humid regions, and are small, hook-headed roundworms, which suck blood from the small arteries in the cat's intestinal walls, causing anaemia and weakness. Infestation can be controlled by carefully administered drugs, and re-infection is prevented by keeping the cat inside, with clean, dry bedding and litter.

Whipworm (*Trichuris*) and threadworm (*Strongyloides*) are present in the cat in some regions of the world. Their eggs are ingested from contact with contaminated faeces. The tiny worms live in the large intestine and may cause anaemia, diarrhoea and subsequent weight loss. Laboratory analysis of faecal samples can identify the worms, which are then easily eliminated by suitable medication.

The common cat tapeworm (*Dipylidium caninum*) may be taken in with ingested fleas and lice, and *Taenia taeniaeformis* with ingested intermediate hosts such as rats and mice. Both inhabit the cat's intestine, and live segments resembling animated, flattened grains of rice may be seen around the cat's anus and in its bedding. Heavily infested cats may be very restless or shows some signs of gastritis. Drugs to eliminate tapeworms are very strong, and should be given under veterinary supervision.

Flukes are rarely found in cats, and are generally the result of eating raw, infected meat or fish.

Heartworms (*Dirofilaria immitis*) are slender roundworms found in cats as well as in their normal hosts, dogs, in many parts of the world. The microscopic larva is transmitted by the mosquito, being taken in with blood from one host and then

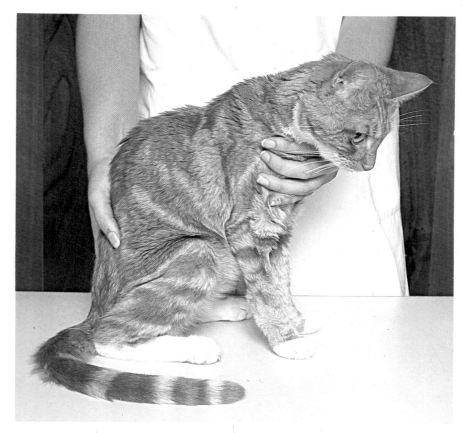

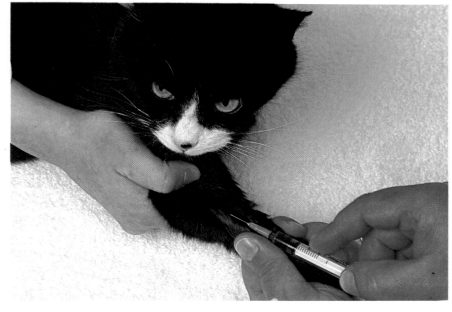

undergoing some changes in the insect before being passed to another animal in the mosquito's bite.

Cats infected with heartworm appear relatively unaffected until the parasite has matured, when symptoms include breathing problems, fluid retention in various tissues and breathlessness after exertion. Treatment of the adult worms is very difficult.

VIRAL DISEASES

Feline panleukopenia (FPL) or feline infectious enteritis (FIE) This highly contagious disease, with an incubation period of only two to nine days, is characterized by its sudden onset and quick succession to death. The disease primarily affects young cats. The affected cat appears depressed, refuses food and may vomit white froth or yellow bile. The temperature may rise to 40.5°C (105°F) at first and then rapidly descend until it is subnormal. The cat visibly dehydrates, sitting hunched and wretched, with its eyes glazed and its coat erect and staring. It may crouch over its water bowl but will not drink. If touched, the cat cries in pain, and the body feels rigid and cold. Death is normally rapid, but if the cat does survive for more than a few days, the condition shows itself with blood-stained diarrhoea is passed.

Early diagnosis and treatment are the cat's only hope of survival. Antibiotics to counteract secondary infections and warm fluids given intravenously by the veterinarian may stem the course of the disease, and constant and careful nursing is vital. During nursing, the cat must be meticulously confined to prevent any spread of the disease. All wastes must be burned and all equipment kept sterile. The usual period of quarantine for this serious condition is six calendar months from recovery date.

FPL or FIE is transmitted by airborne particles, on hands or clothes, or by fleas. Formaldehyde (formalin) is the only disinfectant known to kill the virus, and should be used with care. Vaccination is the only effective measure for the control of the disease.

Feline leukaemia virus (FeLV) The virus is contagious, being transmitted by saliva, urine and faeces, but it cannot live for long outside the cat and, therefore, is easily killed by suitable disinfectants. It is not as contagious as other feline viruses, and is spread mainly by close contact over a period of time. It may also be passed from a pregnant queen to her kittens.

Symptoms associated with the virus are varied, and include anaemia, diarrhoea, vomiting, fever and laboured breathing. A blood test will confirm the presence of FeLV, but there is no cure, although temporary remissions have been experienced in some cases. In a confirmed case, it is usual to perform euthanasia.

Opposite: Weanling kittens playing in the garden may ingest the eggs or larvae of parasites as they test new surfaces and objects by tasting, licking, rubbing and patting with inquisitive paws.

Top: This pet cat is in the terminal stages of its illness. Thin, with wasted muscles and anaemia, he is suffering from the disease caused by the Feline Leukaemia virus (FeLV) against which there is no effective vaccine or cure.

Above: Blood samples are taken to diagnose diseases such as Feline leukaemia virus. Many owners are now having this painless process carried out twice yearly, as part of a routine care programme.

Feline infectious peritonitis (FIP) Peritonitis is inflammation of the peritoneum, or lining of the abdomen, and is a serious condition that can result from toxins and bacteria spread from wounds or ruptured organs. It can also result from a particular virus, which attacks several parts of the cat's body. It appears that many cats develop a natural immunity to FIP, and the virus is so fragile that it cannot live for long outside the cat and is easily destroyed by disinfectants. In large cat colonies it spreads rapidly, infected cats and symptomless cats carrying the disease, and kittens and cats under three years of age are most vulnerable.

Any sudden stress in a cat developing immunity to FIP may cause a sudden full and fatal peritonitis. The incubation period can be very long, possibly months, and the symptoms are loss of appetite, weight loss and a swollen abdomen. There may also be diarrhoea, vomiting, jaundice and anaemia. FIP does not always attack the abdomen, and may affect other parts of the body, including the central nervous system. In some cases the chest fills with the straw-coloured fluid indicative of this disease. Though measures to combat dehydration and inflammation ease the cat's discomfort, there is little chance of a cure, and most cats that contract the disease are put to sleep painlessly to avoid unnecessary and prolonged suffering.

Feline viral rhinotracheitis (FVR) and feline calicivirus (FCV) Although a number of different viruses may be involved in the disease commonly termed cat 'flu, the most important are the FVR virus, which is of a similar form to that which causes sore throats in humans, and the FCV. In the United States, an organism midway between a virus and a bacterium, known as *Chlamydia psittaci*, gives a 'flu referred to as pneumonitis, and this can be partially controlled by certain antibiotics.

FVR and FCV are relatively short-lived away from the cat, and their transmission is by direct contact or by airborne droplets sneezed or coughed out by an infected animal. Stress plays an important role in the spread of FVR, for cats which have recovered are often carriers, and stress stimulates the shedding of viruses in droplets. Stress may be induced by strange surroundings, for example a move to a new home, a visit to a boarding cattery, or a queen's visit to a stud. Some carriers, on the other hand, continuously shed virus.

Toys for cats and kittens must be non-toxic, and must not have any components that can be chewed off and swallowed. The toys must be interesting and exciting to provide prey substitution for the cat.

FVR is the most common and severe of the cat's respiratory diseases, and is highly infectious, with an incubation period of two to ten days. The first symptoms include loss of appetite, general listlessness and sneezing. The temperature rises, the nostrils discharge, long ropes of saliva may hang from the lips and secondary infections may occur, producing conjunctivitis and broncho-pneumonia.

There are several strains of FCV, and a wide range of symptoms may be experienced, from a mild infection to a full and severe upper respiratory infection similar to FVR. Mouth ulceration is a typical symptom of FCV, and in some cases is the only symptom.

Antibiotics are administered to counteract the secondary effects of both FVR and FCV, and vitamins are given to counteract depression and stimulate the appetite. Affected cats should be isolated and carefully nursed. Very effective vaccines are available against FVR and FCV and may be combined with a kitten's vaccinations against FIE once weaning is completed, and then boosted by extra doses administered by the vertrinary surgeon at prescribed intervals.

DISEASES OF THE DIGESTIVE SYSTEM

The mouth The mouth may become ulcerated during an upper respiratory infection, and this condition is also seen when the cat has nephritis. The ulcers appear as blisters, spots or circles on the tongue, lips, gums and palate, and streams of saliva hang from the cat's mouth. The first symptom is loss of appetite, when the soreness of the mouth prevents the cat from eating. A veterinarian should be consulted to cure this ailment. Regular checking of the mouth is an essential part of cat care, and can prevent the build-up of tartar and the development of periodontal diseases. Gingivitis is an unpleasant condition in which the junction of the teeth and gums becomes inflamed and it should never be neglected. It may be associated with FCV, or it may be caused by injury, incorrect feeding or kidney disease. In severe cases, the teeth may have to be extracted and the mouth cleaned up. Antibiotics help to treat secondary infections, and multi-vitamins help to stimulate new cell growth. It may take a considerable time to cure, and even then the cat may have the characteristic thin red line along the gums.

Grooming equipment must be chosen for the individual cat. Each coat type needs different brushes, combs and care. The longer the coat the coarser the comb needed. A rubber brush is used for taking dead hair out of a very short coat.

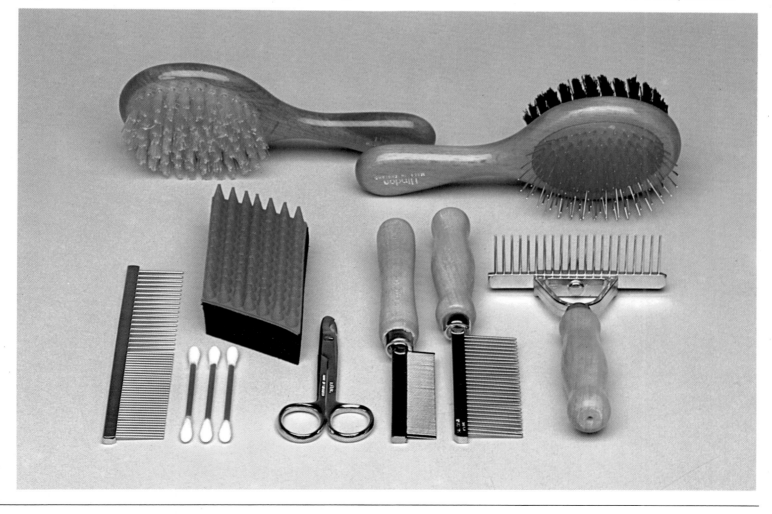

181

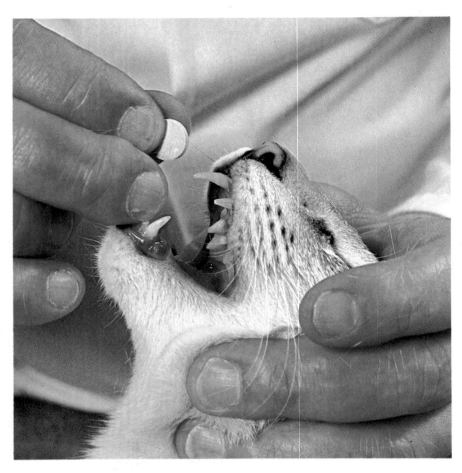

The free-ranging cat may need regular treatment for intestinal worms. This is usually given in tablet form, and it is important to see that the cat receives the full dose, by popping the pill into the cat's mouth at the back of the tongue, then gently rubbing the throat until the pill is safely swallowed.

Enteritis is inflammation of the intestines, and cats are prone to various forms of non-specific enteritis, which although not as serious as the fatal viral disease FIE (see page 000), should nevertheless be treated with concern. The first signs of enteritis are a staring, open coat and diarrhoea, often yellow in colour and very liquid and offensive. Sometimes the stools may be dark brown and blood-stained. Giving plenty of liquids and keeping the cat as warm and quiet as possible may bring it back to normal the next day when the toxic agent has passed through the system. In some cases, however, vomiting begins and this is a signal to consult the veterinarian. In severe cases of enteritis the temperature drops, the cat dehydrates, the region around the anus becomes scaled and blistered by the liquid stools and secondary infections may set in. Such cats need dedicated nursing to restore them to full health, and for a small kitten, a severe non-specific enteritis may be very serious indeed.

Enteritis caused by salmonella bacteria occurs in cats fed raw poultry meat from unreliable sources. Heavy infestations of intestinal worms can cause enteritis in the young cat, and some kittens develop severe enteritis at weaning. Such kittens must be taken from their mother and fed carefully on hydrolyzed meat extracts and jellies, with special electrolytic solutions being syringe-fed to rebalance the body's fluids. When the appetite returns, binding foods such as hard-boiled egg white and steamed white fish should be offered for the first few days.

Cats should be fed a proportion of crunchy food from kittenhood to prevent the onset of tooth and gum diseases.

The stomach Gastritis may be caused by a faulty diet or by the ingestion of toxic substances. Frothy white, yellow or blood-stained vomit heralds the onset of gastritis, and is soon followed by offensive diarrhoea. The cat must be kept very warm and quiet, and warm, boiled water may be given to counteract the often rapid dehydration until veterinary help is at hand. The cat may not eat for several days, but once the vomiting ceases, liquid foods may be given by syringe and vitamins by injection.

Colitis, or inflammation of the colon, is characterized by blood- and mucus-stained diarrhoea, and the cat must be confined in a warm bed until veterinary treatment is at hand.

Some cats become ill due to the presence of a hairball – a solid clump of hair formed from individual hairs swallowed by the cat during self-grooming. If the hairball cannot be passed in the normal way it will be vomited up, and may weaken the cat for a few days. Hairballs may be avoided by combing regularly to remove dead hair and giving the cat a mild laxative during moulting.

DISEASES OF THE UROGENITAL SYSTEM

The kidneys Poisoning, especially by phenols found in some disinfectants, causes acute nephritis in the cat, indicated by such symptoms as depression, loss of appetite, increased thirst, some vomiting, and the passing of very small amounts of highly concentrated urine. The cat sits hunched and cries when handled.

Chronic nephritis is encountered in old cats with malfunctioning kidneys. Such cats drink excessively, especially green or stagnant water, whenever possible. Large amounts of pale urine are passed, and the cat's breath is very offensive. Veterinary treatment can help nephritic cats, and special canned diets are available to aid the function of the kidneys.

The bladder Bacterial infection may produce cystitis in cats, but most cases are due to the formation of tiny stones or calculi, within the bladder, which block the urethra. A cat with cystitis goes frequently to its toilet tray and strains but does not empty its bladder. This symptom must never be ignored, and urgent veterinary treatment is required to prevent rupture of the bladder.

The urethra Urolithias means 'stones in the urinary tract', and the cat affected by this disease cries as he strains to pass water, and then licks persistently at the penis and prepuce. Veterinary treatment can remove the blockage, and the recovered cat is fed very carefully and encouraged to drink large quantities of fluid each day to prevent recurrence.

The ovaries Queens may develop cystic ovaries, when they appear to be constantly in oestrus, though if mated never conceive. Such cats lose condition rapidly and are constantly under stress, and so should be spayed.

The uterus Puerperal metritis can occur after kittening due to the retention of a dead kitten or a placenta. The affected cat will attempt to wash her genital region and then stop, turn away and give a plaintive cry. An offensive discharge will be seen on examination. Urgent veterinary treatment is required, for otherwise the milk supply will dramatically diminish, the kittens' navels may become infected, and the queen will become increasingly ill, vomit, dehydrate and possibly die.

In older queens, the condition known as pyometra may be encountered, in which pus forms in the uterus and the abdomen distends. The cat's temperature elevates, she is depressed and refuses to eat and she may vomit and will show excessive thirst. An emergency operation called an ovarohysterectomy is required to save the queen.

In queens held back from mating and allowed regular, persistent 'calls', endometritis, or inflammation of the uterine lining, may occur. The cat is listless with a raised temperature and spends a lot of time cleaning the gential area.

Many of the items in a comprehensive first-aid kit are shown below left, with a full checklist below. Keep the kit in a convenient cupboard or drawer, remembering to replace items as they become used up or exceed their storage life.

FELINE FIRST-AID KIT
This should be reserved solely for the use of your cat(s) and be kept in a convenient cupboard or drawer. On the lid of the box or door of the cupboard attach a label with the telephone numbers of your veterinarian, the police and the local feline charity/ rescue services.
Antiseptic, as recommended by your veterinarian
Cotton bandages of various widths
Elastic bandage
Absorbent cotton balls and roll
Cottonwool buds
Pack of small sterile dressings
Elastic adhesive tape
Curved scissors with round ends
Short-bladed pointed scissors
Square-tipped tweezers
Nail clippers
Metal fine-toothed comb
Eye dropper
Plastic disposable syringe
Rectal thermometer
Petroleum jelly
Medicinal mineral oil
Hydrogen peroxide
Light kaolin anti-diarrhoea preparation, as recommended by your veterinarian
Antihistamine cream
Pest spray made expressly for use on cats

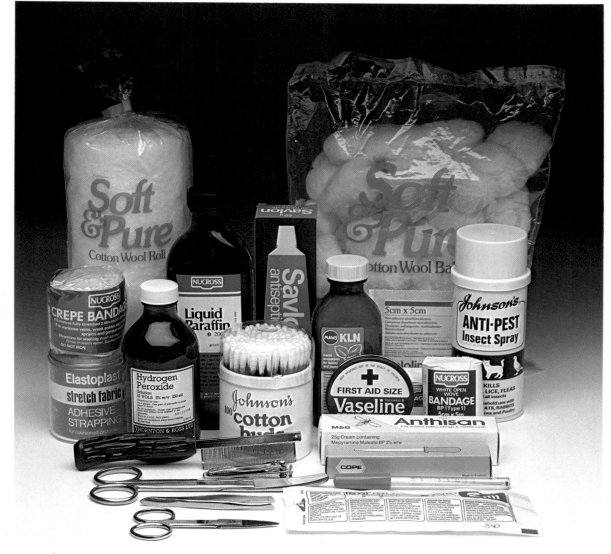

Right: An infra-red lamp of the type used to direct gentle heat on to a sick cat in a pen. Other suitable types can be suspended from the ceiling. The cat must not be so close that it becomes burned by the lamp.

Right: A wide range of equipment is available for the cat.
1. Climbing tree
2. Heated bedbox
3. Plastic travelling carrier
4. Automatic feeder
5. Scratching post
6. Dry shampoo
7. Towel
8. Litter scoop
9. Cat nip
10, 11, 12, 14. Cat food and drink bowls
13. Pill giver
15. Autofeeder
16. Wicker carrier
17. Covered toilet tray

CARING FOR THE SICK CAT

Disinfectants for use with cats Many disinfectants are extremely poisonous to cats, and so great care must be taken to select a safe one. The most dangerous of all disinfectants are those containing coal-tar or wood-tar or the chemicals derived from them, such as phenol (carbolic acid, found in many disinfectants for human use, like TCP), cresols (found in Jeyes Fluid and many 'pine' disinfectants, all of which are perfectly safe for dogs and people) and chloroxylenols (found in Dettol and similar products, quite safe for human babies). Few disinfectants are fully labelled with their components, so never use anything until you have had it thoroughly checked and approved.

Products marketed under the names Shield and Roccal, the hospital disinfectant Savlon, and the cattery owners' favourite Tego are safe for cats if diluted correctly and used in accordance with the instructions given on the pack. After serious infection, complete cleaning of the cat's accommodation with formaldehyde is often recommended. Formaldehyde is unpleasant to use, and great care is needed in its application. It is, however, very effective, especially in dealing with ringworm and other resistant diseases. Formalin is dilute formaldehyde, and 26 to 60 millilitres (1 to 2 fluid ounces) of commercial formalin, containing 40 per cent formaldehyde, should be added to 5 litres (1 gallon) of warm water. The formalin may be obtained from any large commercial chemist, or through your veterinarian. Sodium hypochlorite is much easier to obtain, more pleasant to use and is very effective indeed against feline disease. Commonly used for the sterilization of human babies' feeding bottles, and in commercial kitchens and dairies for cleansing equipment used in food preparation, sodium

hypochlorite or 'bleach' is marketed under names such as Milton, Domestos, Chloros, Delsanex, and so on. Directions for its use are printed on the containers. The strongest solutions must be used with care on bedding, carpeting and any absorbent surfaces, but can safely be applied to washable paintwork and floors covered with impervious materials such as vinyl sheeting or tiles. The strength advised for sterilizing feeding bottles is perfect for dealing with the cat's dishes and bowls. There is no need to rinse off the residual disinfectant before using equipment so treated.

Before using any disinfectant on a surface thoroughly remove all dirt and grease. If detergent

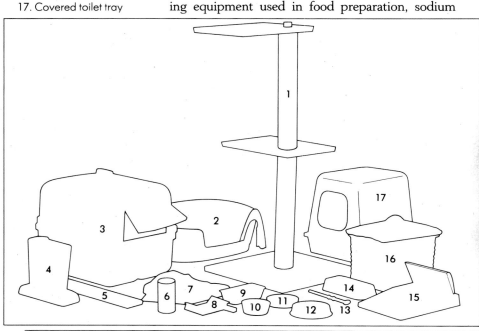

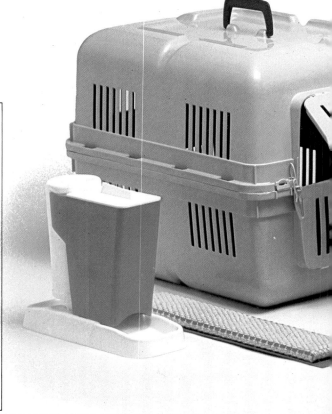

is used for this purpose, it must be rinsed away before the disinfectant is used, as some disinfectants are neutralized by soap or detergent.

Nursing Though expert veterinary treatment is an essential part of the sick cat's recovery, it is the quality of the home nursing that determines just how effective that recovery proves to be. The three essentials in successfuly nursing a cat are:

maintaining its will to live;
providing adequate liquids and foods;
keeping the patient warm and clean.

Though each feline illness has its own needs and characteristics, nursing follows the same general pattern. The sick cat must be closely confined within a quiet environment that is easy to heat and clean. A spot-heater suspended over the bed can be adjusted to give the exact degree of warmth required, and the infra-red variety also provides a comforting glow, appreciated by most cats. The area must be covered with some easily cleaned material, and all the equipment should be suitable for sterilization by strong disinfectants or by heat. Disposable equipment should be used whenever possible. The nurse should have a supply of disposable pinafores just outside the sick room, a pair of slip-on shoes to don before entering, and a shallow footbath of disinfectant, changed daily.

There should also be a holder containing a sack in which to place all materials to be removed from the sick room, including soiled equipment and pinafore. If no other cats are kept, or the patient is merely recovering from a severe accident or operation, then the above techniques of barrier nursing are not necessary. When other cats are kept and the illness is the result of a viral infection, barrier nursing is essential.

Nursing cats recovering from severe cat 'flu is time-consuming and often demoralizing. The patient may be so severely depressed that it seems quite ready to die. It may resent handling and fight against its food and drink. In severe cases ulceration of the mouth may cause pain whenever eating is attempted. The nostrils, eyelids and lips may be ulcerated and bleed when bathed, and diarrhoea and concentrated urine may scald the genital areas, which may also bleed when washed.

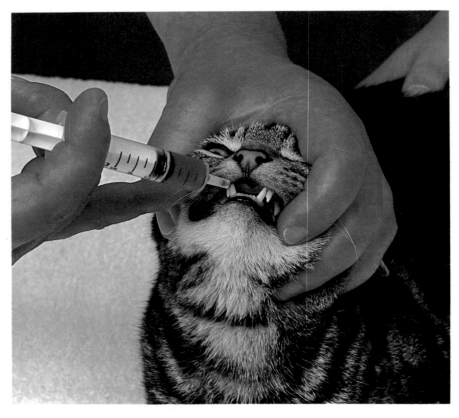

Below: It is important to ensure that the nose and mouth of a sick cat are kept clean. Apart from aiding breathing, this makes the cat feel better and prevents the formation of sores.

Right: Syringe feeding a cat. This is used to nourish a cat which is too sick to take food or is refusing to eat. The syringe is filled with a high-protein liquid food and inserted into the mouth.

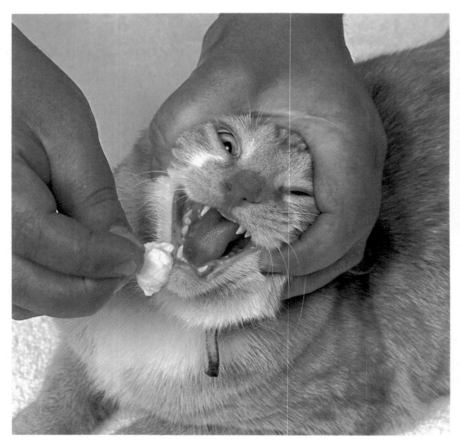

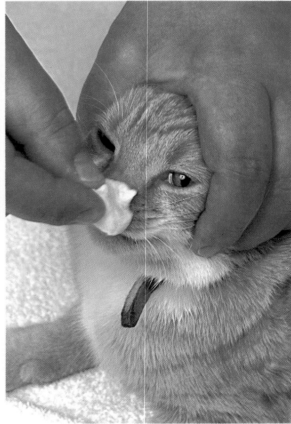

The cat must receive nourishment to live, as well as the antibiotics and vitamin injections administered by the veterinarian, and so if your pet will not eat, concentrated liquid foods must be gently syringed into its closed mouth. The tip of the plastic syringe is passed between the lips and side teeth, the cat's head is lifted slightly and the liquid is allowed to drip down the throat. Take care to prevent choking, and allow the cat to take a breath from time to time as its nostrils are probably blocked. Water with special added electrolytes must be given at intervals, too.

After feeding, the cat must be cleaned. First bathe the eyes, lips and nostrils using separate swabs dipped in warm saline solution, containing 1 teaspoon of salt dissolved in 0.6 litre (1 pint) of water. Dry each area as it is cleaned, and apply a smear of petroleum jelly to the skin. Next lift the cat and place it gently on its toilet tray, stroking the back and sides encouragingly. Even very sick cats prefer to use their trays whenever possible. The genital areas must be washed with a little soft soap if very soiled, and then rinsed, dried and smeared with petroleum jelly. If the cat is constipated or the anus is very sore, a little of the jelly should be placed inside with the aid of a cottonwool bud. Soiled areas of the coat should be cleaned with talcum powder and gently brushed into place. Soiled hair should be clipped away and, unless the cat is very emaciated, the body gently massaged with a pad of warm cottonwool to stimulate the circulation and tone the muscles.

Incontinent cats should be nursed with disposable pads made from napkins or diapers, torn into shape and tucked around the hindquarters. Choose the type which allows only a one-way flow of liquid to prevent soreness developing, and change frequently. Massaging the paws and legs often soothes and relaxes the sick cat. If it is unable to stand, place it on a different side each time it is attended to prevent pressure sores. As well as giving general care, tempt the cat with some strong-smelling food each day; potted herring, crab and lobster pastes are excellent for this purpose, and a tiny dab placed on the tongue often rekindles the cat's appetite. As its condition improves, move the cat's bed to the window, to stimulate its interest especially in the summer when the climate is warm.

Below: Massaging a sick cat helps to stimulate the body and maintain the circulation. Apart from toning the muscles it may also relax the cat.

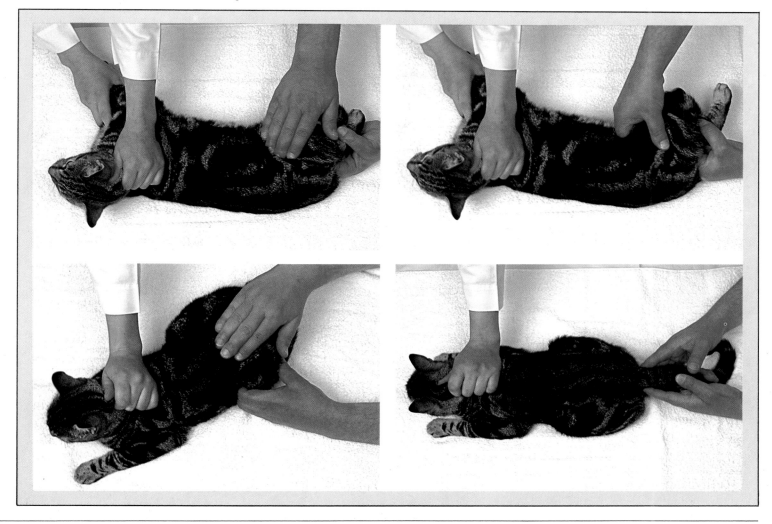

Right: Hot bran is rubbed into the cat, and then worked well into the skin. Then, having absorbed all the dirt and dust, the bran is brushed out (below right). The two photographs at the bottom of the page show the stages in bathing a cat. On the left, a specially formulated cat shampoo is used. On the right, a hand-held hair dryer is used to dry the coat. NB These two cleaning methods are alternatives; they should not be used together.

Opposite: Administering eye drops (top), and bathing a cat's eye with a damp cotton wool swab (bottom), as described in the text.

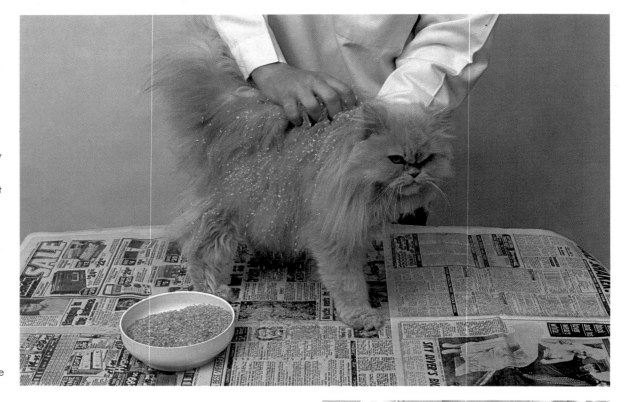

Inhalation treatment Inhalations help to clear the blocked nasal passages of the cat. First smear the animal's eyelids and nostrils with petroleum jelly and then place it in a mesh container. Make up the inhalant, according to the directions, in a small bowl, and put this in a larger washing-up bowl placed on the floor. The mesh carrier containing the cat should be balanced neatly on the edges of the washing-up bowl, and a plastic sheet spread over the carrier. After ten minutes, the vapours breathed by the cat will have released streams of

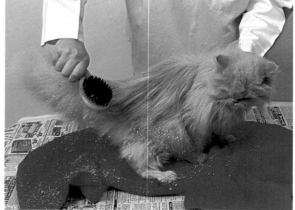

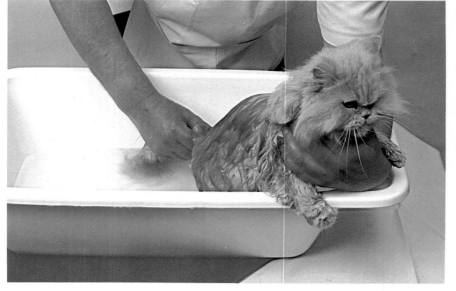

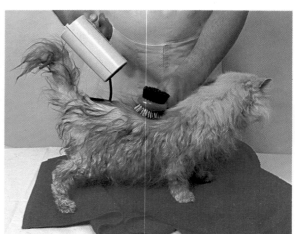

mucus from the nostrils which must be wiped away. Repeat this treatment as often as possible during the recovery period.

Bathing a cat Cats may be bathed if particularly soiled, or in preparation for a show. A double sink is ideal for the purpose, or use two large washing-up bowls. First carefully groom out the coat, removing all loose hairs, knots and tangles. Use water that is comfortably warm (test it with your bare elbow) to quarter fill one sink or bowl and half fill the other. Stand the cat in the shallow water and ladle over the warm water, thoroughly wetting the coat to the skin. If the cat is difficult you may need an assistant, but some cats accept bathing without making a fuss.

Once the cat is wet through, apply shampoo made expressly for use on cats, and massage this into the coat. Pay particular attention to the cat's underside, throat and tail, and between the toes and pads. Lift the cat while the water is tipped away, then ladle over fresh water to rinse away the foam. Make sure that every trace of shampoo is rinsed off, and then squeeze the excess water from the coat with the hand. Wrap the cat in a thick, hot towel and rub it as dry as possible. Some cats allow the use of a hair dryer, but if yours will not, sit it in a mesh container near a source of heat and dry it as fast as possible. When the coat is thoroughly dry, it should be carefully brushed and combed into place.

Giving a bran bath It is possible to clean a cat without making it wet by using bran, either the sort used for dietary purposes or broad bran sold for feeding to horses. Heat a double handful of bran in a baking tin in the oven until it feels comfortably hot and does not burn fingers sunk into it. Stand the cat on a spread newspaper, and quickly work handfuls of the hot bran into the coat, starting at the tail and working forwards. Then use both hands in a shampooing action to massage the bran right into the roots. When all the bran has been used, wrap the cat in a thick, hot towel, and pet it for about ten minutes. Remove the towel and methodically brush out the bran, again starting at the tail and working forward. This treatment will remove an astonishing amount of dust, dirt and debris. On the following day, groom the cat's coat thoroughly, and it will be fresh, smooth and shining.

Bathing the cat's eyes Use saline solution made by dissolving 1 teaspoon of salt in 0.6 litre (1 pint) of boiled water. Take separate swabs and bathe each eye from the outer corner to the inner. If necessary, flood the eye with saline and then blot dry with tissue. Eye ointment, when required, is applied to the lower lid and the eye is allowed to close, spreading the ointment across the orb. Gently wipe away the surplus with a clean tissue, not cottonwool, which may leave irritating fibres in the eye.

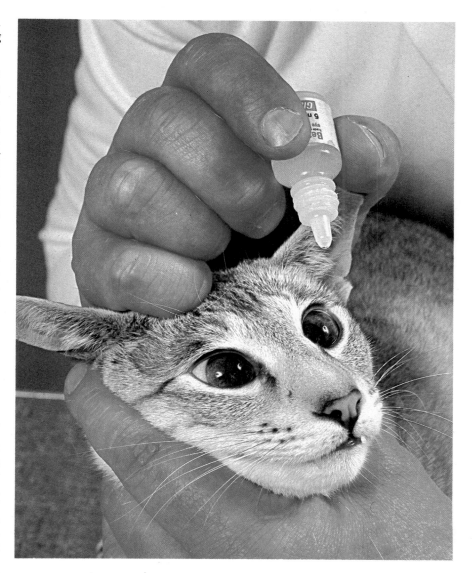

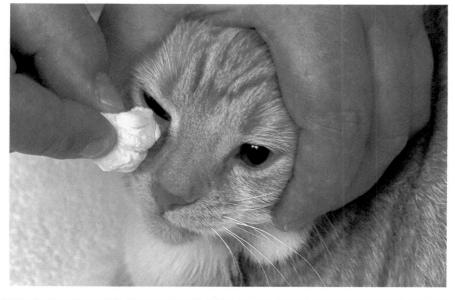

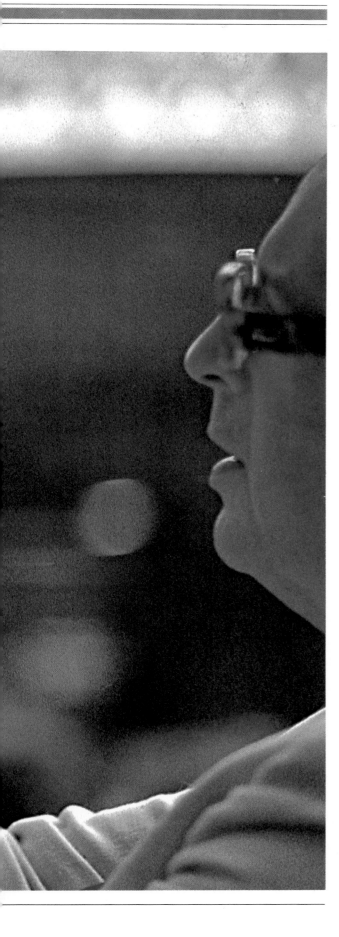

SHOWING

People who breed or show cats are called cat fanciers, and come from all walks of life. At any cat show you may see two cats penned side by side, one owned by a princess, perhaps, and one by a postman or a policeman! The owners have a common bond and consuming interest – the love of beautiful cats, bred to exacting standards of perfection and produced in sparkling condition. Though most cats themselves show total indifference to cat shows, the exhibitors gain tremendous personal satisfaction from competing successfully in their chosen classes. There is little personal gain, as entry fees are high and prize money is often non-existent; nevertheless, the winners' rosettes are eagerly sought and proudly displayed. Even so, exhibitors regard cat shows more as social occasions to be enjoyed by the whole family surrounded by their favourite animals – cats. Cat lovers all the world over plan their calendars around published show dates, and go without luxuries in order to buy show equipment, pay for entry fees and cover travel expenses. Exhibitors of cats are the backbone of the world's cat fancy. Without them there would be no new breeds, few pedigree breeds and, indeed, no cat shows.

The judge holds a cat aloft during a show.

The first cat show ever recorded was at St Giles Fair, Winchester, England, in the year 1598, but this bore no resemblance whatsoever to the cat shows of today. Benched shows, with cats exhibited in individual cages, began with a splendid affair organized by Mr Harrison Weir at London's Crystal Palace in 1871, while the first properly benched American cat show was held in New York's Madison Square Gardens in 1895. The idea of showing cats and competing for prizes spread slowly around the world, and today, the cat lover has hundreds of shows in many different countries at which to see, enjoy and admire fabulous cats. Each country with an active cat fancy has one or more controlling bodies, which accept cats on to their registers, promote the running of cat shows and usually produce a stud book.

In North America, fanciers have the choice of nine registering bodies:

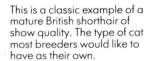

This is a classic example of a mature British shorthair of show quality. The type of cat most breeders would like to have as their own.

American Cat Association (ACA) America's oldest registry for cats, which has been active since 1899. It is a fairly small association, with shows in the south-east and south-west of the United States.

American Cat Council (ACC) A small association centred in the south-west, which holds modified 'English-style' shows, in which exhibitors are barred during judging.

American Cat Fanciers' Association (ACFA) One of three international associations with affiliated clubs in the United States, Canada and Japan. A very democratically run organization, ACFA produces a monthly news bulletin, and grants club charters and individual memberships.

Canadian Cat Association (CCA) The only all-Canadian body, its activities are centred mainly in eastern Canada, and its quarterly newsletter is published in both English and French.

Cat Fanciers' Association (CFA) America's largest registry, incorporated and run by a board of directors. There is a CFA show somewhere in the USA almost every weekend, and the association has affiliates in Canada and Japan. CFA produces an impressively large annual yearbook, packed with information, advertisements and photographs, many in full colour.

Cat Fanciers' Federation (CFF) A medium-sized association with its activities centred in the north-east region of the United States.

Crown Cat Fanciers' Federation (CCFF) One of the smaller associations, nevertheless CCFF has many shows each year in the north-east and south-east of the United States and in western Canada.

The International Cat Association (TICA) This is the youngest of the associations in the United States, but it is growing rapidly with affiliates in Canada and Japan. TICA produces the newsletter *Trend* six times each year and a hardback yearbook.

United Cat Federation (UCA) A medium-sized association centred in the south-west of the United States.

In Europe, many countries have at least two registering bodies, of which one is generally found to be affiliated to the Federation Internationale Feline (FIFe). This enormous and well-organized incorporated and chartered body also has affiliates in many other countries of the world. It is managed by an executive board of experts, each elected to serve for a term of three years. The FIFe has three commissions – the judges' commission is responsible for the study of new breeds and their standards, the modification of existing standards for recognized breeds, and the regulation of the stud book; the show commission is responsible for efficient show management, and the application of show rules and regulations; and the disciplinary commission hears complaints and problems from member countries, and arbitrates in disputes.

Fully established in 1949, today the FIFe is the largest cat body in the world, uniting more than

150,000 breeders and exhibitors in one cause – the love of the cat.

In Britain, registrations were originally taken care of by the National Cat Club, which was specially formed in 1887 and officiated in this capacity until 1910, publishing the first official stud book in 1895. Various clubs formed all around the British Isles, and most agreed to run shows under the rules of the National Cat Club. In 1898 another body, The Cat Club, was formed, and the cat fancy split its loyalties until 8 March 1910, when a special meeting of nineteen delegates from various clubs met in Westminster, London, and decided to form a new body called the Governing Council of the Cat Fancy (GCCF). This body is run by an executive committee, and affiliated clubs send delegates to council meetings to represent their members' wishes. The GCCF consists of representatives of more than sixty clubs, and until recently was the sole body responsible for registering cats and holding shows in Britain. Then in 1983, a group of breeders, judges and show organizers met in Oxford on 20 February and decided to form an alternative body called the Cat Association of Britain (CA). This was registered as a Company Limited by Guarantee so that it would be run entirely by its members, and keeps a register of all cats, pedigree, half-pedigree and non-pedigree, and holds all-breed championship shows in every region of Britain.

The Cat Association organizes a series of training schemes for judges, ring marshalls, clerks and stewards, all of whom may work towards certification in their various skills. Its shows offer Championship awards for non-pedigree cats as well as their purebred cousins, and winners may progress to Grand Champion and Supreme Champion status.

This longhair is a Cameo Persian, again a show quality cat, beautifully turned out.

CAT SHOWS

Around the world these are held either by individual clubs, under licence from their respective governing bodies, or by the bodies themselves. The various countries may have different rules and regulations, and different methods of setting out and judging their shows, but all have one thing in common – a cat show provides an opportunity for owners of cats to put their pets in direct competition with others to see which, in the opinion of the judge, is the best example of its breed. Cat shows also serve toi educate the public, teaching them about the various breeds, types and colours of cats, and helping them to achieve a greater awareness of the needs of and the best care for their own pets.

In Britain shows are normally one-day events, but in Europe and the United States of America two-day shows are common. American shows and those of the CA in Britain consist of several 'rings', each of which is a small show within a show. This allows exhibitors to get the very best value for their money by enabling the cats to be judged in open-breed competition for championships, without the need to go to several shows on different days and at different venues.

Shows may be all-breed affairs, or specialist shows for Longhairs, Shorthairs or specific breeds. Some smaller shows are really only social affairs, with no meaningful awards, such as championship certificates, ribbons or points, being awarded. A few shows are designed for the assessment and authentication of new breeds or colour varieties of existing breeds. Many shows allow non-pedigree cats to take part.

The largest cat show in the world is run under GCCF rules and takes place in London each year. It is organized by the National Cat Club, the same club which started it all in 1887. Over 2,000 cats take part and each is judged in one open or breed class, plus a range of miscellaneous classes and some offered by specialist breed clubs. Despite the size of this show, there is no climax to the proceedings, such as a best in show or Supreme award, and the judging is carried on in the body of the show hall, each cat sitting anonymously in a numbered pen and allowed only a white blanket, white litter tray and water bowl. This procedure is common to all GCCF shows held in Britain. The GCCF hold a Supreme show each year which is unlike any other cat show in the world, as entrants must qualify by winning open breed classes at previous shows. The cats are judged in rings in a fashion fairly similar to that employed in some American shows, and special awards are offered to winners. The cats are exhibited in decorated pens in the main body of the hall while awaiting judgement in the ring, and the climax of the day comes with the awarding of the supreme rosettes to the best cat, kitten and neuter of the pedigree exhibits, and to the best non-pedigree kitten and neuter.

In the United States of America, most shows are conducted on the open-ring system, and this method has been adapted by the Cat Association of

Opposite top: The qualified judge takes a pride in her careful assessment of the cats in her programme, matching the appearance of each against its official standard.

Opposite bottom: At open-ring shows cats wait comfortably in their decorated and lined cages between calls to the ring.

Below: Official standards of points are laid down by the various governing bodies for each of the recognized breeds. These refer to certain characteristics of the exhibition cat. The example below shows some of the points of a fine Cornish Rex.

Coat Short and plush without guard hairs. Curled, waved or rippled over back and tail.

Tail Long and in proportion to body length; fine and tapered without any kink.

Legs Long and straight, cat appears to stand tall; hindlegs longer than forelegs.

Head Length one-third greater than maximum width. Skull flat; straight side profile.

Body Hard and muscular and of medium size; straight back and tight abdomen.

Paws Small, neat and oval in shape. Five toes on the forepaws and four toes behind.

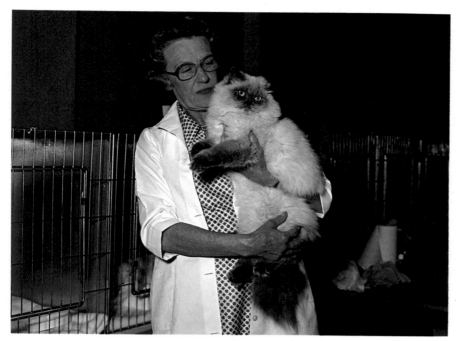

Britain. Open-ring judging is exciting for all participants. Exhibitors are able to dress their show cages, making them comfortable for the cats and colourful and interesting for the general public. They can add prizes won at previous shows and all sorts of information about their breed. The judges do not enter the body of the show hall and so there is no danger that the judges will be influenced by a cat's previous awards or the identity of the owners. In American open-ring shows, the owners bring the cats to correspondingly numbered cages in the judging ring. The judge officiates by taking each cat in turn, assessing it to the enthralled audience, and then awarding the placings. In British and Scandinavian open-ring shows, stewards carry the cats to the judging rings, while the anonymous and excited owners sit in the audience. In most European countries, ring judging is common, but the rings are isolated from the show hall and the judges work in private, being brought the exhibits by highly trained, very skilful stewards, who carry the animals displayed along one forearm and gently restrain them with the opposite hand.

In most open-ring shows, cats may accrue either points or certificates to earn titles on one day. This cuts down the number of shows necessary for each potential championship and grand championship, and also reduces stress and risk of infection for the cats. In closed-ring shows, cats are normally judged only once, and will need at least three winning shows in order to gain important titles.

In on-floor judging, the judge accompanied by a steward goes from cage to cage, taking out and assessing the exhibits before placing them in order and sending official prize slips to an administration table for processing. The prize slips are then posted on an awards board, and the administrative team allocates prize cards and, at some shows, corres-

ponding ribbons or rosettes, which are then placed on the show cages by a team of helpers. In closed-ring shows, the judges usually write a critique for each cat and allocate the placings, marking these on the critique forms. The forms are collected by an official, and the corresponding certificates, ribbons and rosettes are allocated and distributed by the show team. In open-ring judging, depending upon the rules of the association, the judge will write a points-score form, give only a verbal critique, or write a full critique for each cat. In most open-ring shows, all but the very top awards are presented at the time of judging, to be taken by the owner or steward back to the cat's own show cage for display.

Whatever the mode of judging, the criteria are

A European show layout. Exhibitors may remain with their cats except when these are taken to the rings for judging.

the same. Every judge must be an expert in the breed or breeds that he or she is to judge. Judges must follow rigorous training programmes and sit demanding examinations in order to qualify in many associations, such as the American bodies CFA, ACFA and TICA, the worldwide FIFe, many independent associations around the world and the Cat Association of Britain. GCCF judges do not have to qualify in any academic way, but breeders of long standing who have stewarded for existing judges, and who are approved by their breed clubs, may be nominated as potential judges. If approved by delegates at a Council meeting, these start as probationer judges, assessing kittens, and then progress to full judge status. Several GCCF judges

are highly respected by other bodies and receive regular engagements to act as judges at cat shows held overseas.

It is normally necessary to have your cat registered with the appropriate body before you can enter a show run under its rules. Most associations allow non-pedigree cats to be shown in household pet classes without being registered, though such cats may not win particularly special awards. A few associations, notably TICA in the United States and the CA in Britain, have special facilities for the non-pedigrees to be registered and entered on to a computer, and to compete for titles such as Master and Grand Master, CA Champion Pet, CA Grand Pet and CA Supreme Pet, all national awards.

Overleaf: The Champions relax with their awards at the end of a successful day at the show.

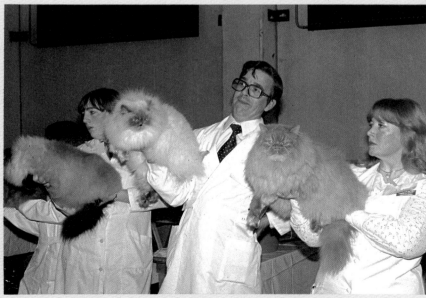

At British shows run under GCCF rules, judges and their stewards go to each pen in turn, extract the cat and assess it as it stands on a portable judging table. To help check eyecolour and the cat's profile, the judge may hold the exhibit up at eye-level, which also enables an accurate assessment of its body weight and muscular development. It is important for cats to handle well. GCCF judges and stewards wear white coat coveralls and wash their hands and judging tables between handling each exhibit. The cats stay in anonymous shows cages throughout the day identified only by numbered cards, and the only items allowed in the cages are a white blanket, drinking bowl and litter tray.

painlessly freeze-tattooed on the inner thigh.)

Cat shows are advertised in the cat press, and lists of forthcoming events may be obtained by writing to the relevant body for an official show list, show rules and registration information (see page 205). It is not always necessary to belong to a club or association in order to enter your cat in its shows, but you may find that you are not eligible for top awards or particular prizes unless you are a member in good standing. There are often other benefits to be gained from memberships of associations, too – reduced entry fees, free vouchers for catalogues and show admission, and the opportunity to attend informative meetings and social events. Membership can be passive, or you may be the sort of person who enjoys participation in such things as show administration and organization, in which case your cat can introduce you to a whole new absorbing and often very stimulating hobby.

Having received a show list, write to the show director or manager for a schedule or flyer of the show in which you are interested. Bear in mind that show entries may close well before the show date – some small associations will close about three weeks before the show, while larger shows, such as those run under the rules of GCCF in Britain, may close up to two months prior to show date! Make a close study of the show rules for they vary considerably, and if you have any doubts, ask an experienced exhibitor or telephone the show manager for help in filling out the forms. You will need accurate details of your cat in order to complete the forms, and you should use its registration form for reference. Send the form with the correct fees to the show office, and enclose a stamped addressed envelope if you need an acknowledgement of entry, or a reply to any queries.

You should spend the time from sending in your entry until show day in getting your cat ready for the show. Your pet should be up to date with all vaccinations and you should have a certificate to that effect, in case this is required for admission to the show hall. Your cat must be easy to handle and be trained to allow examination of all parts of its head and body without showing resentment. You must feed a well-balanced diet, and institute a regular, sensible grooming routine aimed to produce the perfect pelage on show day. Some breeds may need bathing two or three days before the show, and some associations require the tips of the claws to be trimmed.

You will normally be mailed a set of show documents prior to show day, and you need to take these with you to the show. Many shows require the exhibits to pass a veterinary inspection just inside the entrance. The veterinarian will look for general signs of disease, fungus infection and parasites, and the object of the examination is to prevent infectious animals entering the show and posing a health threat to others.

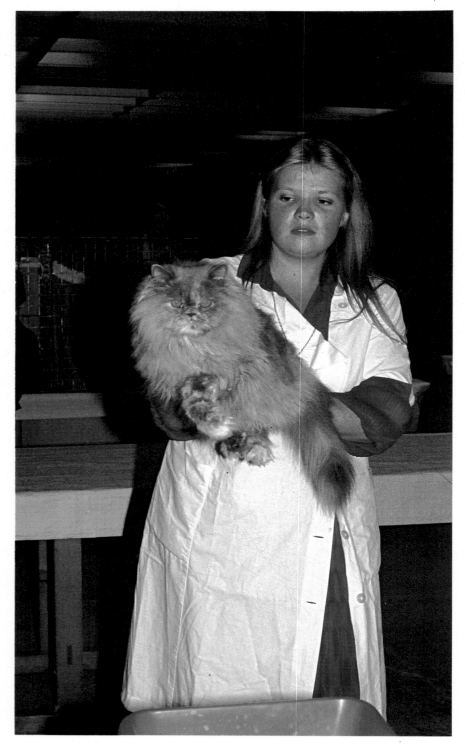

In European cat shows, each cat is taken in turn to the judging area, carried by a highly trained steward, well versed in the art of transporting and presenting a cat safely and securely, without distress.

(Associations providing registration facilities for non-pedigree cats also provide a very useful identification service for pets which may be lost, stolen or stray from home. The full description of each cat can be readily retrieved from the computer system, and individual cats may wear their registration number on a collar disc or tag, or may have it

Left: The world's largest cat show is the one held in London's Olympia Exhibition Hall each year by the National Cat Club.

Top: For the Best in Show line-up at a Dutch show, stewards hold their designated cat ready for final assessment.

Above: For acclimatization to the stress of showing, first train a potential champion to accept the confines of a small wire cage.

A show-quality White Persian.

unaccustomed collar and try frantically to remove it. Use very narrow tape, ribbon, or the elastic sold for shirring or millinery work to keep the label in place.

Take your cat to the show in a safe carrier, preferably one which opens at the top so that the animal can be removed and replaced easily at vetting-in and at the show cage without disarranging its coat. Arrange to arrive early so that neither you nor your cat are stressed by having to hurry through any of the pre-show procedures. Once past the veterinary examination, take your cat and belongings into the show hall and locate your show cage by its number. Disinfect it if you wish, and arrange your cat's equipment inside. Put just a little litter in the tray at first and pop your cat in the cage. If you have had a long journey, it will almost certainly want to use the litter tray, and you can then empty it and refill it with fresh litter for the rest of the day. After the cat has used the tray, you may want to spend time grooming and settling it before the commencement of judging is announced.

In ring shows, you may be required to take your cat to the ring as your number is announced, so you must be alert and ready, having checked the estimated times of your breed's assessment in each ring. You should not speak to any judge until the end of the competition, but then you will find that most judges are friendly and very willing to discuss your cat's good and bad features, and give you tips for better presentation. Prizes are generally given out during the show, and some shows also have Best of Breed awards or Best in Show judging and awards, and in ring shows, each judge may be required to produce a set of Finals winners and a Supreme exhibit. In this way, some shows, especially the open-ring variety, are exciting right through the day, and the tension mounts as winners progressively compete until the day's top cats emerge.

Win or lose, most exhibitors thoroughly enjoy cat shows, and pack up their belongings, cat, rosettes and ribbons at the close of the show, happy in the knowledge that they have taken an active part in an entertainment for hundreds of cat lovers, who are enchanted by an exhibition of cats of all shapes, sorts and sizes. After the journey home you should allow the cat to rest for two or three days and watch carefully for any signs of infection picked up at the show or induced by the stress of unaccustomed activity and exposure. If your cat does show any symptoms, you should seek veterinary advice and inform the show organizer without delay. Luckily, due to the veterinary inspection beforehand, very few cats contract any illnesses at shows.

In some countries, reports of cat shows are published in the cat press, and in some associations each judge is required to submit for publication a full critique on each winning and placed cat assessed during the show. Other cat magazines

The type of equipment needed for the show will depend upon the association running the event and its rules. In an open-ring show it is usual to dress your cat's pen. Most show cages are standard within an association, and details can be obtained in advance from the management. Curtains or drapes of washable material in a colour to complement your cat's coat or eyes can be made gathered or pleated into curtain tape, and hooked or tied to the top rails of the cage. A piece of washable fur, bathroom carpet or covered foam makes an ideal base, and matching toilet tray and accessories complete a comfortable and attractive environment for your cat during the show's duration. In an on-floor judged show you will need all white equipment, and must not put any written matter, or any distinguishing material or objects on or in the cage.

Be sure to take along your cat's favourite snacks, and some water for the drinking bowl; a cat's strong sense of taste may cause it to refuse water from a strange source. If the weather is cold, it is advisable to take along a hot-water bottle, and fill this with hot water at the show and conceal it among the cat's bedding for comfort. Be sure to take along your cat's usual litter for its tray, and a plastic bag for disposing of soiled litter and other rubbish. If the association's rules call for the cat to wear a numbered label or disc, be sure your cat is used to wearing such an item around its neck well before the show, for it may be distressed by an

The end of a perfect day —
this non-pedigree kitten
rests after judging, having
won a grand array of prizes.

print lists of top winners, breed class winners and winners of championships, trophies and special awards. When a cat achieves a title such as Champion, it may be necessary to write to the association to claim this win, or the award may be given automatically. It may be commemorated by a medal or a specially inscribed certificate. The procedure should be outlined in the show rules of the association concerned.

Most cats enjoy an outing to a cat show, behave well, and never show any after-effects. If, however, you find that your cat hates every moment of the proceedings, do not subject it to any more traumatic days. Instead, buy a kitten to train for the show bench, or go to shows in another capacity — learn to steward or to act as administrator, or, if you are a good organizer, work towards becoming a member of the all-important show team. Cat shows can add another dimension to the lives of all who truly enjoy everything to do with cats.

USEFUL INFORMATION

QUARANTINE REGULATIONS

Regulations change frequently, and should be checked at the embassy of the country to which you are travelling or exporting.

AUSTRALIA
Quarantine – three months for cats travelling by air, direct from country of origin in a sealed, noseproof, pawproof and tongueproof kennel. (If seal is broken en route, cat will be returned to country of origin.) Import permit required. The completed import permit is forwarded to

Assistant General,
Animal Quarantine Branch,
Commonwealth Dept. of Health,
PO Box 100 Wooden A.C.T.2606,
Australia.

The cat must be accompanied by a certificate of vaccination against feline enteritis, feline calicivirus and feline rhinotracheitis – administered at least 30 days, and not more than twelve months before departure – and various official declarations. The cat must be examined and certified as healthy, free from clinical signs of disease and parasites, and fit to travel by an approved veterinarian at the airport, before being officially sealed into its air kennel.

AUSTRIA
Quarantine – none; bilingual health certificate required; rabies vaccination necessary.

BELGIUM
Quarantine – none; rabies vaccination necessary.

CANADA
Quarantine – none; health certificate and export certificate necessary.

CHINA
Quarantine – none; import permit, health certificate and rabies vaccination necessary.

DENMARK
Quarantine – none; entry restricted for unaccompanied animals.

FINLAND
Quarantine – none; import permit and special health certificate necessary.

FRANCE
Quarantine – none; import permit generally required; cats under one year require feline enteritis vaccination at least 30 days prior to travel, and either export certificate or rabies vaccination at least 30 days prior to travel.

WEST GERMANY
Quarantine – none; import permit may be required; bilingual vaccination certificate against rabies required – vaccine to be administered at least 30 days prior to travel.

GIBRALTAR
Quarantine – none; import permit, rabies vaccination, health certificate and ministry certificate necessary.

GREECE
Quarantine – none; health certificate and rabies vaccination necessary.

HOLLAND
Quarantine – none; authenticated rabies vaccination necessary.

HONG KONG
Quarantine – may be enforced except for cats travelling direct by air from UK; import permit and ministry certificate of health necessary.

ITALY
Quarantine – none; import permit required for unaccompanied cats; rabies vaccination necessary.

JAPAN
Quarantine – none; export and health certificates necessary.

MALTA
Quarantine – variable period; import permit and rabies vaccination necessary.

NEW ZEALAND
Quarantine – none; import permit application form when completed should be sent to

Animal Health Division,
Ministry of Agriculture and Fisheries,
Private Bag,
Wellington,
New Zealand.

Other documents include a health certificate, rabies vaccination certificate and various certified declarations. The cat must be certified free from clinical signs of disease and parasites, and fit to travel by an approved veterinarian at the airport before being officially sealed into its approved design air kennel.

NORWAY
Quarantine – none; import permit contains health certificate.

PORTUGAL
Quarantine – none; export certificate and authenticated health certificate necessary.

SOUTH AFRICA
Quarantine – none; import permit obtained directly from

The Director of Veterinary Services,
Private Bag X138,
Pretoria,
Transvaal, SA.

Import permit includes health certificate and export certificate; various other declarations also required.

SPAIN
Quarantine – 20 days unless rabies vaccinations in order; export certificate and health certificate must be authenticated and a visa granted immediately prior to departure.

SWITZERLAND
Quarantine – none; regulations variable, but health certificate and vaccination against rabies generally necessary.

UNITED KINGDOM
Quarantine – six months; import permit from Ministry of Agriculture, Fisheries and Food. Cat must travel in noseproof, pawproof and tongueproof container, and on arrival will be transferred by licenced carrier to the quarantine kennel previously booked; examined by veterinarian on arrival and vaccinated against rabies (second injection given 28 days later).

UNITED STATES OF AMERICA
Quarantine – none; health certificate required by airline.

PERIODICALS AND MAGAZINES

Throughout the world there are many publications concerned with cats. Here is a selection of the most popular and wide-ranging of these.

All Cats (Monthly)
Pacific Palisades, California, USA.
Stories and articles of general interest to all cat lovers.

Cats (Weekly)
5 Leigh Street, Manchester, England.
Show results of British cat shows, and some articles.

Cats Annual (Yearly)
5 Leigh Street, Manchester, England.
Some articles of interest to breeders/exhibitors; lots of cattery and product advertising.

Cats Magazine (Monthly)
PO Box 37, Port Orange, Florida, USA.
News of the North American Cat Fancy, plenty of cat care articles and contributions from cat lovers and breeders.

Cat World (Monthly)
Scan House, Southwick Street, Southwick, Brighton BN4 4TE, England.
Lively articles, features and contributions of interest to cat fanciers and cat lovers alike. British show and diary dates.

Cat World International (Bi-monthly)
PO Box 35635, Phoenix, Arizona, USA.
North American show features, news on worldwide winners, and many serious articles aimed primarily at the breeder/exhibitor.

Cat Fanciers Association Yearbook (Yearly)
1309 Allaire Avenue, Ocean NJ 07712, USA.
Superb annual in hardback, packed with excellent photographs of American top-cats in colour and black-and white. Good articles and overseas reports, along with all CFA news.

International Cat Association Yearbook (Yearly)
211 East Olive (Suite 208) Burbank, California, USA.
De-luxe hardback edition, packed with TICA news, glossy photography, and interesting, well-illustrated avertisements.

PROTECTION AND CARE SOCIETIES

Many organizations exist to promote the rights of cats and other animals, and for the administration of care to sick animals. The following are among the foremost of such bodies.

American Humane Society
5351 S. Roslyn Street, Englewood, Colorado 80111, USA.

American Society for the Prevention of Cruelty to Animals
441 East 92nd Street, New York, NY 10028, USA.

Cat Action Trust
The Crippetts, Jordens, Beaconsfield, Bucks, England.

Cats Protection League
20 North Street, Horsham, Sussex, England.
(subscribers receive bi-monthly magazine *The Cat*)

Cat Survival Trust (for endangered species of wild cats)
Marlind Centre, Codicote Road, Welwyn, Hertfordshire AL6 9TU, England.

Feline Advisory Bureau
350 Upper Richmond Road, Putney, London SW15 6TL, England.
(subscribers receive quarterly bulletin free of charge)

Petcare Information and Advisory Service
254 George Street, Sydney, NSW, Australia.

Pet Health Council
418–422 The Strand, London WC2R 0PL, England.

Petwatch (missing pets bureau)
PO Box 16, Brighouse, West Yorkshire HD6 1DS, England.

Royal Society for the Prevention of Cruelty to Animals
The Manor House, Horsham, Sussex RH12 1HG, England.

Society for the Prevention of Cruelty to Animals
Wellington, New Zealand.

CAT REGISTERING BODIES

American Cat Association (ACA)
Contact: Secretary, ACA, 10065 Foothill Boulevard, Lake View Terrace, California 91342, USA.

American Cat Council (ACC)
Contact: PO Box 662, Pasadena, California 91102, USA.

American Cat Fanciers' Association (ACFA)
Contact: General Manager, ACFA, PO Box 203, Point Lookout, Missouri 65726, USA.

Canadian Cat Association (CCA)
Contact: CCA General Office, 14 Nelson Street West, Suite 5, Brampton, Ontario, Canada. L6X 1B7

Cat Fanciers' Association (CFA)
Contact: Executive Manager, CFA, 1309 Allaire Avenue, Ocean, New Jersey 07712, USA.

Cat Fanciers' Federation (CFF)
Contact: CFF Recorder, 9509 Montgomery Road, Cincinnati, Ohio 45242, USA.

Crown Cat Fanciers' Federation (CCFF)
Contact: CCFF Recorder, PO Box 34, Nazareth, Kentucky 40048, USA

The International Cat Association (TICA)
Contact: TICA, 211 East Oliver, Suite 208, Burbank, California 91502, USA.

United Cat Federation (UCA)
Contact: Secretary, UCA, 6621 Thornwood Street, San Diego, California 92111, USA.

Federation Internationale Feline (FIFe)
Contact: General Secretary, 33 Rue Duquesnoy, B1000, Brussels, Belgium.

The Governing Council of the Cat Fancy (GCCF)
Contact: GCCF, 4–6 Penel Orlieu, Bridgwater, Somerset, TA6 3PG.

The Cat Association of Great Britain (CA)
Contact: CA National Information Office, Hunting Grove, Lowfield Heath, Crawley, West Sussex RH11 0PY.

INDEX

GENERAL INDEX

Acknowledgements

The publishers wish to thank the following individuals and organizations for their kind permission to reproduce the photographs in this book:

Animals Graphics/Solitaire 11, 12, 22, 25, 26 left, 27 below, 30 left, 31 below, 36–37, 39 left, 42, 43, 45, 48 left, 50–51, 60 below, 63, 66 above left, 66–67, 68, 70 below, 71 above and below left, 72–73, 73 above right, 74 left, 76, 77 right, 78 above left, 78–79, 82–83, 84 below, 85, 86–87, 86 below, 87, 89, 90–91, 93 below left, above and below right, 99 below, 100 above, 101 above, 102, 103 above, 104, 105 below, 108 left, 108–109, 110 below, 111, 112 above, 113, 114, 116 below, 117, 118 right, 120, 124 above right, 132, 133, 135, 138, 139, 141, 145, 146, 150, 151 left and above right, 153 below left, 158–159, 158 below left, 169 above and below, 160–161, 166–167, 170–171, 171 below, 174, 179, 190–191, 193, 194, 195 above, 196, 197 above and below left, 200, 201 below right, 203; Mrs P Brownsell 91 right; Bruce Coleman Ltd (Hans Reinhard) 88 above and below, 101 below, 114 above, 123 right; Robert Estall 57; Spectrum Colour Library Half Title, 13 below, 27 above, 31 top and centre, 34, 35, 36, 41, 47, 48 right, 49, 54 above, 83, 100 below, 151 below right, 159, 160, 166,178 below; Zefa Picture Library (M Wegler) 8–9, 19, 23, 30 right, 38–39, (Schneider) 39 right, 44.

We also wish to thank the following owners for kindly allowing their Cats and Kittens to be photographed by Robert Estall, Peter Loughran, John Moss and Ron Sutherland:

Mrs P Annuskans (Zils Scorne) 110 above; Mrs J Baker (Tigger) 37 below and 130, (Tilly) 38 right; Mrs A Beadle (Sharamka Ka-Sita) 56 and 81, (Jalien Thor) 64–65 and 80, (Abbotsbrook Tanya) 121, 158 below left; Mrs E Berry (Aljora Cream Cromwell) 14–15 and 26 right and 97 below right and 152–153, 38 left, (Kavida Red Pepper and Kavida Flaming June) 60 above, (Champion Kavida Prizeguy) 94 right and 192, (Ashmere Elbereth) 96–97 and 146–147, (Beeble-brox Plum Crazy) 154 inset, 157 below; Miss V Berry (Kavida Kuan Yin) 58 and 128–129 and 142, (Champion Jesbar Bandit) 123 above and below left; Miss S Bolston (Premier Patrystar Nicolas Nye) 71 below right, (Champion Patrystar Andante Jennysue) 78 above right; Mrs P Brice (Smuggie) 70 above, (Myvana Abbey) 112 below; Mrs P Brownsell (Patriarca Percy Filv) 118 left, (Patriarca Parkin) 153 below right; Mrs E Constable (Annika Snow Maiden) 94 above left; Mrs V Daglish (Champion Gangaili Schwarzer Teufel) 32–33, (Gungaili Blue Berry and Gungaili Black Magic) 114 below; Ms L Driegert, USA (Cestee Patrick O'Shay) 97 above right; Miss M Forster (Samoto Allsorts) 66 below left, (Samoto Makrel May) 74 right, (Samoto Tam Tam) 77 above

left, (Jonquil Jeremy) 77 below left, (Kinkletons Kandice) 79 above left, 153 above; Mrs A Freisinger (Champion Calliope Allround Wizard) 99 above; Mr and Mrs Elmer Goldman, USA (Grand Champion Temeks Teje) 126 above and centre, 126 below; Mrs U Graves (Champion and Premier Cassiobury Silver Argent) 60–61 and 95 below right; Mrs P Hoare (Bloduedd Red Reynard) 95 above, (Victensian Tequila) 96 above, (Victensian Carryon Girl) 137, (Victensian Red Sunset) 144; Mrs M Howes (Honeymist White Snowcandy) 69 and 148–149; Mrs M Ireland (Champion Shirar Montgomery) 73 below right, 156; Ms J M Kapetanakis, USA (Champion Mera's Theodosius) 98 above; Mrs B Lambert (Grand Champion Nomis So-Lareta) 171 above; Mrs G Lee above, (Gleeway Arctic Starlight) 202; Mr and Mrs MacKenzie, USA (Grand Champion Cherie of Luvsweet) 55 below and 75 below; Mrs J S McAllister 58–59, (Champion Shamari Rasputin) 122 above, (Macnovitch Checkoff) 124–125; Mrs D A Miller (Patrystar Victoria) 164 above, (Patrystar Bagheera) 177 above; Mrs Murphy (Foxicat Faro) 84 above, (Champion Salentu Stryn) 116 above; Mrs E Norman (Kaiwon Pricilla) 75 above; Mrs J Potts 103 below, 105 above; Mrs P Proctor (Chestnut Chocolate Dandy) 119 right; Mrs A P Rawthorn (Merrymew Lilac Cascade) 29; (Champion Pussinboots Petroushka) 118–119, (Merrymew Davida) 125 inset; Mrs J Reed (Grand Champion Horchata Nieto Decarlos) 106; Ms M Schmalz (Gangaili Lilac Lion) 2 and 53 and 107; Ms J Thomas, USA (Grand Champion Patchet's Patriot of Gyzndolz) 92, (Grand Champion Miribu's Ring Around The Rosy) 93 above left; Miss J Toogood (Champion Tilovet Touchstone) 95 below left, 131; Mrs P Turner (Chermat Kris) 125 above left; Mrs C Vials (Champion Paripassu Dusky Lama) 4 and 94 below left; Mrs R Warren-Hurlock (Champion Premier Kayserling Khazan) 62, 154–155, (Litter of Linlinkye Princess Zarina) 178 above; Mrs P Watson (Sonata Rhapsody) 79 above right; Mrs A Wright (Coerulea Cupperan) 40, 157 above; Baroness Miranda Von Kirchberg (Astahazy Ivander) 122 below

Additional special photography: Robert Estall 98 below, 197 right, 201 below left; Peter Loughran 6; John Moss 46, 52 above and below, 54 below, 164 below, 165, 171 below, 172, 173, 175; Ron Sutherland Title Page, 168, 176, 177 below, 180, 181, 182, 184–185, 189 above, 195 below, 198–199, 201 above; George Taylor 20 below, 21 left and right, 169 centre, 179 below, 183, 186, 187, 188